THE EGYPTIANS

THE EGYPTIANS

An Introduction to Egyptian Archaeology

JOHN RUFFLE

Cornell University Press

ITHACA, NEW YORK

Frontispiece. The heart of New Kingdom Egypt, the west bank of the Nile at Luxor, showing the temple of Hatshepsut at Deir el-Bahri. Many of the major kings were buried in the hills behind.

Amicis et praeceptoribus
  D. M. MEACOCK
  J. L. ARCHER
  J. A. THOMPSON
  L. T. WEAVER
Qui me in antiquitati studendo
ducentes benigne foverunt

First published 1977 by Cornell University Press

Published in Great Britain and the British Commonwealth under the title *Heritage of the Pharaohs*

International Standard Book Number 0–8014–1003–7
Library of Congress Catalog Card Number LC 75–39567

Printed in Great Britain by
Cox & Wyman Ltd, London, Fakenham and Reading

Contents

Preface

The culture of Ancient Egypt survived as a recognizable entity for some 3000 years and it is salutary to remember that the pyramids of the Old Kingdom are separated from the great temples of the Greek Period by a greater interval than that which separates those same temples from our own day. Obviously the material remains of such a long–lived civilization are many and various and to describe them thoroughly would require a much larger volume than this. I hope to be forgiven by those who look for detailed information and discussion of many unresolved questions.

It is a pleasure to record the invaluable help of many colleagues, outstanding amongst whom has been Dr K. A. Kitchen, whose friendly criticism and helpful advice has never failed. Others who have given much assistance include Mr Cyril Aldred (Royal Scottish Museum, Edinburgh), Mr T. G. H. James (British Museum), Miss Janine Bourrieau (Fitzwilliam Museum, Cambridge), Dr P. R. S. Moorey (Ashmolean Museum, Oxford) and Professors H. W. Fairman and A. F. Shore (University of Liverpool). Thanks are also due to our Museum Photographer, Mr W. G. Belsher, Mr Martin Davies who took many of the photographs, Mrs Dorothy Partridge who typed from a manuscript worse than any hieratic papyrus, and Mark Ritchie and Freda Harmer of the Phaidon Press for their toleration.

In addition to the four school-teachers to whom this is dedicated, I should also thank the members of several evening classes and Nile cruises who have shown what sort of questions a book like this should try to answer. Mr John Aitken of the University of Birmingham, whose patient organization of two study tours to Egypt enabled me to check many points at first-hand, and Mr John Ray, who shared the conduct of the classes and study tours and still somehow remains a valued friend, both deserve a special mention.

To my family, for their encouragement and forbearance, I owe the greatest debt.

Stourbridge, West Midlands, 1976   JOHN RUFFLE

How these curiosities would be quite forgott, did not such idle fellowes as I am putt them downe.

John Aubrey, *Brief Lives I* ('Life of Venetia Digby')

I

Introduction

Few peoples can have been so consistently misunderstood as the Ancient Egyptians. They are too often dismissed as oppressive taskmasters, cruelly lashing gangs of slaves into building useless and uninspired monuments to their own megalomania, or as a nation of undertakers, preoccupied with preparation for death and burial, worshipping a bizarre collection of gods and beasts, writing mumbo-jumbo in a hopelessly complex and quite unintelligible script, striding sideways into eternity with a permanent crick in the neck.

Dazzled by the riches of Tutankhamun's treasure, awed by the huge mass of the pyramids and fascinated by exotic gods and esoteric scripts, it is easy for us to overlook their real and worthwhile achievements in the arts and sciences, in technology and politics, religion and philosophy. For 3,000 years they practised these skills, forming a heritage of fine sculpture, painting, literature, scientific observation, religious speculation and moral philosophy, while at the same time they reached a high level of achievement in the practical arts and a position of influence in the world politics of the day. It is the purpose of this book to present the material remains of this legacy, together with sufficient background information to explain its purpose and idiosyncrasies.

HISTORY OF EGYPTOLOGY

Up to the end of the seventeenth century AD, knowledge of Egypt in Western Europe was based primarily on incidental references in the Old Testament and classical writers. In the fifth century BC, the Greek traveller Herodotus journeyed through Egypt as far as Aswan, hearing all, seeing all, and recording all, despite being slightly sceptical of the more outrageous of the dragomans' tales. He was followed by a line of distinguished writers, amongst whom were Strabo in 25 BC, who claimed to have entered the Great Pyramid, and, in the first century AD, Pliny the Elder, who speculated on the possibility that the pyramids were not tombs but treasure-houses. There was considerable Roman interest in things Egyptian; the complex hieroglyphs and outlandish deities no doubt had a strange appeal to the formal Romans, who carved pseudo-hieroglyphic inscriptions of their own and carried away no less than twelve obelisks to decorate their own city—where they formed the basis of intellectual speculation about the Egyptian script throughout the Middle Ages.

Some of the medieval Arab rulers tried to blast their way into the pyramids or to deface the commandment-breaking image of the sphinx by gunfire. A few hardy European travellers also made their way to Egypt: Bellonius in 1553 and George Sandys in 1610 both entered the Great Pyramid and, as a fake ushabti (see p. 208) presented in 1635 to the Ashmolean Museum by Archbishop Laud bears witness, the possibilities of the tourist trade were already recognized.

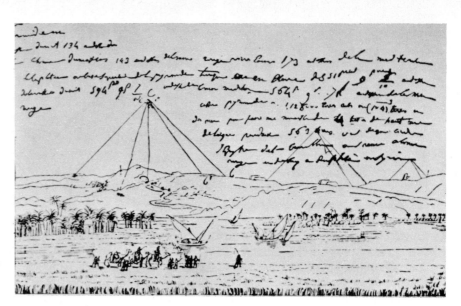

1. Sketch of the pyramids at Giza, annotated by Napoleon.

The first scientific approach to Egyptology was made in 1638 by John Greaves, who made accurate measurements and drawings of the Giza Pyramid group. In the eighteenth century, Richard Pococke carried the investigations further by studying the Dahshur and Sakkara groups. The principal step forward, however, was taken during Napoleon's campaign in 1798–9 which, whatever it did for his own reputation, saw the foundation of Egyptology as we know it. His army was accompanied by a team of savants, which included Dominique-Vivant Denon, a nobleman impoverished by the Revolution whose other claim to fame is the authorship of one of the classic works of pornography, *Oeuvre Priapique*. Denon accompanied Napoleon's general Desaix on his campaign in Upper Egypt and was completely captivated by the sights he saw. The minutely detailed, accurate drawings which he made formed the first illustrated book on Egyptology, the *Déscription de l'Egypte*, published by Jomard in 1809–13. This work opened up an unknown world to a society brought up on the antiquities of Greece and Rome. The sudden revelation of a strange and exotic civilization older than any so far known aroused immense public interest. The fascination was the greater because the historical records of Egypt were in a script that baffled decipherment [1].

In fact, the clue to the script was provided by the same campaign of Napoleon, for one of his engineers discovered the Rosetta Stone and recognized its value. After Napoleon's withdrawal from Egypt, the Stone became the property of the British as one of the spoils of war and was removed to the British Museum, but not before casts had been made, from which Champollion was able to decipher the script. His discovery in 1822 led to a new burst of interest in Egypt, and he himself led an expedition for eighteen months in 1828–9, on which he eagerly harvested inscriptions. Other scholars joined the search [3]. With funds from King Friedrich Wilhelm IV of Prussia, Richard Lepsius made a great survey of the monuments (published in a mammoth twelve-volume work) and collected many objects, which formed the basis of the great Berlin collection. The increasing scholarly interest highlighted the need for orderly and controlled excavation. Auguste Mariette, who was sent by the Louvre to collect antiquities in Egypt, realized this. With the support of the Khedive he founded the Egyptian Museum and Antiquities Service and became

2. View of the Great Pyramid by Lane, made in 1827, showing the north-east corner of the pyramid and the entrance in the north face.

its first director, often pushing through his scientific policies in the teeth of opposition from other European Egyptologists.

Mariette's concern was matched by the painstaking methodology preached by William Matthew Flinders Petrie, grandson of the explorer of Australia and the first person to hold a chair of Egyptology in this country—at University College, London. This chair had been founded by Amelia Edwards whose unintentional Nile cruise—she had gone there when a sketching holiday in France was rained off—had filled her with an enthusiasm for Egypt that led her to found not only Petrie's chair but also the Egypt Exploration Fund. Other learned societies were also formed—notably the Deutsche Orient Gesellschaft in 1888, and the Mission Archéologique Française in 1880, later the Institut Français d'Archéologie Orientale.

3. This view of the temple of Horus at Edfu, drawn by David Roberts in 1838, shows the court piled high with accumulated debris, and a small town on the roofs of the main building. There is a similar accumulation outside the temple.

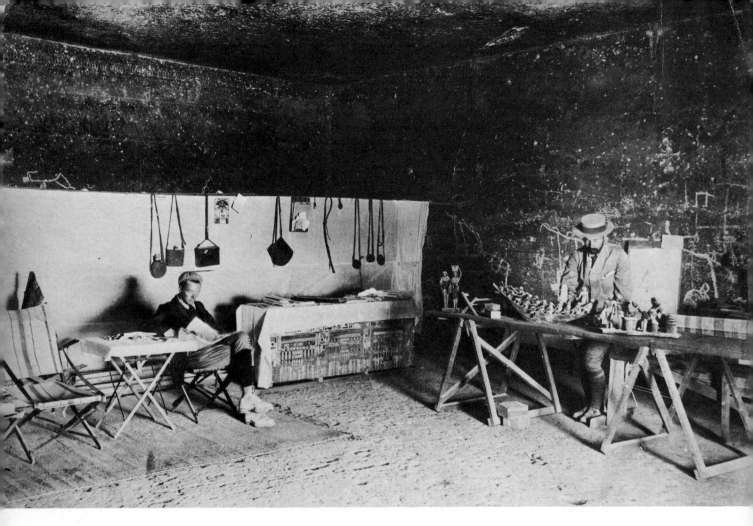

4. One of the large Middle Kingdom tomb chapels at Beni Hasan being used as the head-quarters of the University of Liverpool Institute of Archaeology excavation, 1902–4; Professor John Garstang, director, standing, Harold Jones, artist, seated.

Petrie set high standards which he himself did not always maintain, for he was continuously moving from site to site in an attempt to forestall illegal digging or to establish his own claims to a site. His methodology, however, was followed by the excavators who came after him, and extensive and careful studies were made; for instance, by George Reisner in Nubia and at Giza. The years before the Second World War were in many ways the heyday of excavation in Egypt [4]. Many important sites were dug, sometimes for the second time, as the excavators laboriously sifted the debris of their predecessors in order to complete a thorough survey. H. E. Winlock worked from 1911 to 1931 at Deir el-Bahri on the Middle and New Kingdom tombs and temples. Bernard Bruyère meticulously sifted his way through the village of Deir el-Medina. J. D. S. Pendlebury dug the city of Akhenaten at Amarna, and Howard Carter methodically cleared the Valley of the Kings at Thebes, to be rewarded for his painstaking work by the spectacular discovery of Tutankhamun's intact tomb.

At the same time, methodical recording of the inscriptions and reliefs that stood exposed was under way. In 1919, with the backing of John D. Rockefeller Jr., James Henry Breasted founded the Oriental Institute, whose architectural and epigraphic survey of the temple of Medinet Habu set the highest standards. Other surveys were undertaken at Abydos by the Egypt Exploration Society, and by Theodore M. Davis and Norman and Nina de Garis Davies in the Theban tombs.

Work on the many important sites south of Aswan was not undertaken on any large scale until the decision to build a dam at Aswan in 1898. The flooding this caused to the temple of Philae aroused much concern, and a survey of Nubian monuments was conducted by Arthur Weigall. This was followed by four seasons of excavation by Reisner after the dam was heightened in 1907, and a second survey was made from 1929 to 1934, when the dam was heightened again. When the High Dam was proposed at Aswan in 1960 a much larger area had to be surveyed, and several countries co-operated in the enormous task of identifying, excavating and, in some cases, removing the many monuments threatened by the waters of Lake Nasser [79]. The mammoth problem of salvaging the rock-cut temples of Ramesses II at Abu Simbel provided a focal point of popular interest, but work on the less spectacular sites revealed much of interest and importance. The full results of these excavations have still to be published and evaluated.

In recent years, much of the burden has fallen upon the Egyptians themselves, who now provide all the staff for the Antiquities Service. The latter is responsible for the great Cairo Museum and all the monuments; it conducts its own excavations and provides inspectors to work alongside foreign colleagues.

GEOGRAPHY OF EGYPT

The basis of Egypt's wealth is the Nile—as almost every writer since Herodotus has been quick to point out. The Nile is the only river to flow northwards across the Sahara, and only along its banks could an agricultural community survive the absence of rainfall. The Ancient Egyptians called their land 'Kemet', the Black Land, because of the black silt which used to be deposited on the soil by the annual flood, caused by the rising waters of the Blue Nile when the river is swollen by the rainfall in Ethiopia. This silt is rich and fertile, and with careful irrigation enabled the Egyptians to produce two crops per year in some areas. Although occasional failure of the inundation brought disastrous famine, Egypt's food-producing ability was famous throughout antiquity.

The climate differed little from that of today: consistently warm, dry, and clear, with about 20 cm. of rain per year in the Delta, and 2·5 cm. in ten years in Upper Egypt—although that rainfall could occur in one tremendous cloudburst. This may be why the Egyptians regarded rainfall as a curse and as an inferior method of irrigation sent by the gods to less-favoured lands.

The land could be cultivated only up to the point to which water could be brought. Here, the Black Land gives way to the Red Land of the low desert, which stretches to the foot of the cliffs. The latter sometimes come within a few yards of the river, hemming in the cultivation. At other places, they may be up to 15 km. away, but they are always present, forming a frontier past which only a few hardy souls would normally venture. The high desert beyond the cliffs was the country's best defence, for on the west it was an impenetrable barrier, and the only routes through the eastern desert from the Red Sea were along the Wadi Hammamat to Coptos and along the Wadi Tumilat in the north.

The river highway was effectively sealed at the southern end by the series of six cataracts from Aswan to Khartum, through which passage was easily controlled. In the north, the maze of river channels and irrigation canals of the Delta were a trap for any invader. In fact, the weakest link in this range of defences lay through the Wadi Tumilat and across the Isthmus of Suez towards the dense populations of west Asia, and this was Egypt's major point of contact with the outside world.

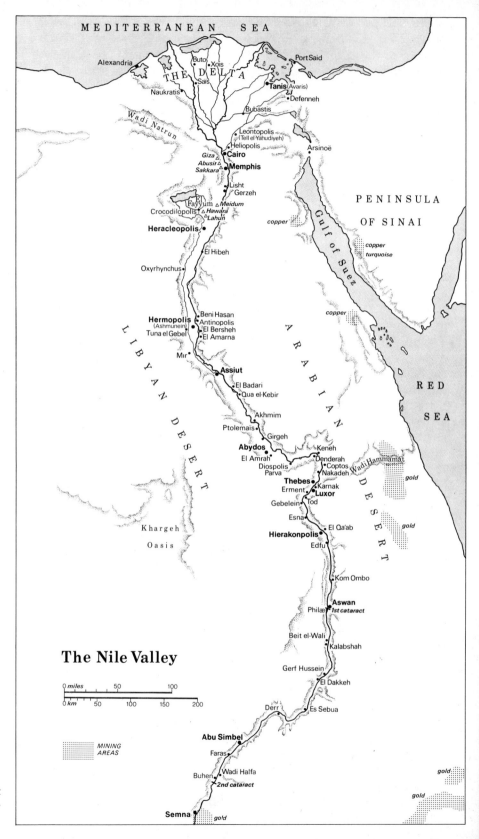

The Nile Valley

MINING
AREAS

5. Map of the Nile valley below the First
Cataract, showing the principal sites mentioned in the text.

Internally, the country falls naturally into two major divisions: Lower Egypt, the Delta region northwards from Memphis, and Upper Egypt, the long narrow valley to Aswan [5]. In fact, Middle Egypt, though usually administered with the southern area, sometimes allied itself with the north when political differences made it necessary to take sides. Memphis was the most convenient centre from which to administer these two disparate and not always friendly regions. The southern religious capital of Thebes, and cities like Aswan and Abydos, had their counterparts in the north in Tanis, Sais, Buto and other centres now mostly submerged below the high water-table.

Just to the west of the Nile valley, between Hawara and Lisht, lies the largely dried-up lake bed of the Fayyum. It was linked with the Nile by a natural channel, which was occasionally blocked for long periods; and the height of the lake surface varied enormously before it was artificially regulated in the Middle Kingdom. Intensive drainage and cultivation in the Greek period contributed to the importance of the area in Ptolemaic times.

CHRONOLOGY

The Egyptians themselves recorded what they considered to be the important facts of history: the names of rulers, and the length and order of their reigns, and occasional events such as campaigns or expeditions, yet they seldom give evidence of viewing their history as a continuous developing sequence of related events. They make no overt comment or evaluation of various rulers and their achievements. They were more concerned with the underlying concept of *Ma'at*, which may be described as the endurance of the accepted order or arrangement of society, government, religious affairs and even physical and natural occurrences, such as the recurrence of the inundation.

This emphasis on continuity may partly explain why the Egyptians never selected an event, even one so fundamental as the union of the Two Kingdoms, as a basis for era dating. Instead they relied principally on a system of dating by counting the years of a king's reign. This would have presented no problem for us if we had a complete list of kings in their correct order and knew how long each reigned. Since this is not the case, a number of problems arise in the chronology of Egypt, generating not a few scholarly feuds.

For the predynastic period there are two major approaches; the first is Petrie's system of sequence dating, and the other is the newer, scientifically based techniques, such as radiocarbon (C14) and thermoluminescent dating.

In his excavations of the predynastic cultures Petrie found few settlement sites but many cemeteries. Unfortunately the cemeteries lacked overall stratification, and there was nothing to pin the discernible cultures firmly in sequence. Petrie therefore worked out his own sequence and then attempted to establish some kind of chronology for it. He did this by building up a corpus of pots from his excavations at Naqada and Diospolis Parva, and arranged them into a typological sequence based on what appeared to him to be the order of development and degeneration of a particular ceramic style. It was then possible, according to the type of pots found in a particular tomb, to place it at a point in this sequence.

Other objects in the tomb, stone vessels and tools, amulets, slate palettes, etc. could then be dated by association and eventually a line of development worked out for them, too. The vast amount of information acquired eventually provided a series of cross-checks and enabled Petrie to narrow the margin for each tomb group.

Once the sequence was established, he divided the range into fifty arbitrary sections numbered from thirty to eighty. A gap was left at the beginning in case new material from earlier cultures was subsequently discovered, and at the other end the series terminated with pots that appeared to be contemporary with the Ist dynasty. Petrie could then refer to a tomb group as coming between Sequence Dates (SD) 38–40, for example. There was, of course, no indication of how long such a period actually covered, but the system made a convenient framework for Egyptian prehistory.

It is a different story when we attempt to fit this relative system into an absolute framework. There has been little work on predynastic sites since the development of the radiocarbon method of dating: the predynastic specimens first used for C14 dating were those collected long ago, and are consequently subject to varying degrees of contamination. The method itself is not without its deficiencies. These were first suggested when early dynastic samples dated by the C14 process were found to be seriously at variance with the dates suggested for them by documentary means. Recent new determinations, using revised calibrations and samples collected under properly controlled conditions, have produced results compatible with the documentary evidence, but much more work is needed and a concerted project using all the new scientifically based methods might well cause us to revise our impression of Egyptian prehistory.

One of the major documentary sources of information for the dynastic period is the Greek history of Manetho, an Egyptian priest from Sebennytos who lived c. 323–245 BC. His work is now lost, but extracts were quoted by Josephus, and abridgements were made by Africanus in the third century AD and Eusebius in the fourth century. His permanent contribution to Egyptology is his arrangement of the kings into thirty dynasties which, although it has faults, is still useful.

Of the earlier annals kept by the Egyptian government scribes only one survives and that in fragments only, the major fragment being in the Palermo Museum. The Palermo Stone is a black basalt slab, originally about 2 m. × 0·75 m., containing a record compiled in the Vth dynasty of every preceding king, the number of years he reigned and the principal events in his reign. It even records some of the kings of the two separate kingdoms before unification. Unfortunately it is so fragmentary and so large a proportion of it is missing, that reconstruction is difficult and its use is limited.

King-lists also provide further information. In his temple at Abydos, Seti I is shown making an offering to seventy-six of his predecessors; a similar king-list, now in the Louvre, was set up at Karnak in the time of Tuthmosis III, and two others were compiled in the reign of Ramesses III. One is now in the British Museum, the other is in a tomb at Sakkara. Apart from the Abydos list, they have all suffered damage and have been edited according to principles that are not immediately obvious to us, but nevertheless they do make some contribution to the chronology of Egyptian history.

The final document of this type is a papyrus of Ramesside date that begins with a list of gods who reigned for fabulous lengths of time. It then documents the reign of King Menes and succeeding rulers, noting their length of rule and occasionally the total of years for several reigns. However, it does not always coincide with Manetho's dynastic divisions. This document (now in Turin) was allegedly complete when purchased by Drovetti but, stuffed into his waistcoat pocket (or in a jar tied to his belt—the story varies), it was fragmented by the jolting of his donkey. The surviving fragments were skilfully re-arranged by Sir Alan Gardiner and Hugo Ibscher in 1938, but again we are frustrated by the loss of many vital pieces.

These texts form the basis of our present knowledge of Egyptian history but they can be cross-checked and augmented in several ways.

A few dates can be fixed by astronomical data. The most useful of these are those which date a particular year of a king's reign, recording the number of days that elapsed between the heliacal rising of Sothis and the first day of the civil year (see p. 116). From this it is possible to calculate how many years have passed since the beginning of the Sothic cycle, and since these are known to have begun in AD 139, 1317 BC, 2773 BC, etc. *ad infinitum*, it only remains necessary to know which cycle is in question to date a king's reign absolutely, although a slight margin of error has to be allowed for technicalities such as the exact site of the observations.

Two dates are fixed in this way: the seventh year of Sesostris II can be shown to be 1870 BC $\pm$ 6, which provides the peg on which all the Middle Kingdom chronology hangs. The other date is for the ninth year of Amenophis I, *c.* 1541 BC if the sighting was made at Heliopolis, or *c.* 1522 BC if sighted at Thebes. A third Sothic observation is recorded in the reign of Tuthmosis III, but the year of his reign is not specified.

Other dating checks are provided by the biographies on tomb inscriptions, for a man may well record the names of the kings under whom he served, thus confirming their order and indicating a limit to the length of time their reigns might span. Links with other cultures that can be dated independently also help to narrow the field. The close stylistic comparisons between Archaic period art and that of the Jemdet Nasr period in Iraq help to confirm a third millennium date for the beginning of dynastic Egypt. The New Kingdom rulers corresponded with their counterparts in Syria, Palestine and Anatolia, and provide an intricate web of cross-references, but unfortunately neither side of the correspondence can be dated with absolute precision.

OUTLINE OF EGYPTIAN HISTORY

The history of ancient Egypt is confusing when studied for the first time, for Egyptologists still find it convenient to follow the division into the dynasties devised by Manetho. Some of these cover long periods of time and include several important kings, others are short and insignificant. Their principal value lies in the fact that they provide a convenient way of marking phases in the political development of Egypt. Cultural development is a slower process and fits into a framework of larger divisions.

The earliest traces of human occupation in Egypt are the palaeolithic and mesolithic settlements on the extreme borders of the Nile valley; they are followed by the neolithic settlers, whose villages are known from sites in the western Delta, the Fayyum and later within the Nile valley itself [5].

Elsewhere in the Near East, and notably in Sumer, neolithic communities established a city-dwelling way of life and made considerable technological advances, the influences of which were felt in Egypt. The individual settlements in Egypt gradually coalesced into larger regional units until there were only the two divisions of Upper and Lower Egypt. These regions were apparently united by the military conquest of the Nile Delta by Upper Egypt *c.* 3000 BC. This more or less coincided with the introduction of a system of writing: thus simultaneously with the first historical documents, the period of dynastic Egypt began.

The thirty dynasties that followed are grouped into three major periods, when stable and unified government provided the opportunity to practise the arts of civilization. These periods are usually termed the Old, Middle and New Kingdoms, and they are interrupted by two major intervals (the so-called Intermediate Periods) of social and political upheaval, seen by the Egyptians themselves as Dark Ages, when government was weak or in the hands of foreigners. All these periods fall into what is archaeologically termed the Bronze Age, and the upheavals in Egypt correspond to similar, and usually even more violent, contemporary events elsewhere in the Near East.

THE PREDYNASTIC CULTURES

	Southern Egypt	Northern Egypt	Sequence Date
Before 5,000 BC	Palaeolithic cultures		
4,500	Badarian	Fayyum Neolithic Merimde?	
4,000	Early Naqada (Petrie, Amratian) Kaiser I–IIa	Similar cultures are found in the northern part	30–39
3,500	Late Naqada (Petrie, Gerzean) Kaiser IIb–IIIb	of the Nile valley after a time lapse to allow for penetration	40–65
3,100	Union of the Two Lands		c. 65–80

Petrie further distinguished the Semainean culture, which probably overlapped the end of the predynastic and beginning of the dynastic period. A new study by W. Kaiser now suggests four basic divisions, shown here related to the older terminology and to Petrie's sequence-dating, together with a suggestion of the absolute dating. For the purpose of this book the Naqada period has been divided into two phases, corresponding to Petrie's Naqada I and II, but described as Early and Late to avoid confusion with other schemes with different numbering.

The Predynastic Cultures

A few years ago it was generally assumed that Egypt and Mesopotamia were the main areas where the phenomenon described as the birth or dawn of civilization took place. Man's early attempts at writing, cultivation of crops, domestication of animals and settlement in communities, it was thought, began here. This picture was drastically altered in the 1950s, when Dame Kathleen Kenyon at Jericho and James Mellaart at Haçilar and Çatal Hüyük found evidence that the 'Neolithic Revolution' took place in those areas as early as 8000 BC. More recently, discoveries in northern Greece and Cyprus and elsewhere have added to our knowledge of the spread of civilization, and Egypt appears to be something of a cultural backwater. It remains to be seen whether future work on the predynastic cultures, which in recent times have been neglected by archaeologists, will confirm this picture.

In the Pliocene period the Nile valley was submerged below a gulf which stretched as far south as Kom Ombo, but a drop in the sea level in the Pleistocene period led to the withdrawal northwards of these waters and the erosion of the river bed. This was not continuous; there were gaps in the process that resulted in the formation of gravel terraces, the most obvious of which are 98 and 78 m. above the present river along the western bank from the Delta to Mallawi. The gravel terraces were formed when the fall in the sea level was halted during pluvial periods, which corresponded with the onset of the glacial periods in Europe.

The earliest (highest) terraces bear no trace of human occupation, but stone implements have been found on the 30 m. terrace formed in the middle of the Pleistocene period. They are made of brown chert and belong to the bifacial tradition of tool-making, in which the core of the flint is used in preference to the flakes. In the Near East generally, this bifacial tradition is more frequently found near rivers and lakes and seems to be associated with a hunting economy.

Later implements found on the 15 m. terrace and on the 9 m. level included both bifacial and flake tools. Examination of developments in the lower terraces is not easy in the Lower Nile valley, since erosion continued below the present level and they are now covered by later deposits of silt. In Upper Egypt, however, the flake industry continues on the 3–4 m. terraces.

The Late Paleolithic period saw the end of the cultural uniformity which had hitherto prevailed in the Near East. In Egypt, the Sebilian culture, distinguished by small flake tools, developed around Kom Ombo. Their camps are close to the river and their middens show a diet of molluscs, fish, auroch and buffalo; they had bone and ivory tools but no pottery. They presumably collected grain, for querns are also found. Poorer cultures existed in Lower Egypt and the Fayyum; at Helwan, near Cairo, implements similar to the

Natufian types from Palestine have been found, and in the Khargeh oasis there was a culture with connections with north-west Africa and the Sahara.

Our present understanding of Near-Eastern sites suggests that the next stage might be the emergence of settled neolithic communities practising some degree of crop-raising and domestication of animals, but without pottery. In fact this stage has not been found in Egypt—or at any rate not recognized—and we move straight on to some isolated pottery-using neolithic cultures. These probably date to the fifth millennium BC, but there is still controversy over whether they are truly early neolithic or simply poorer later cultures.

The best known is the Fayyum Neolithic, which was a group of farming communities practising crop-raising but which do not appear to have had domesticated animals. The sites in the Fayyum were excavated in the early 1930s by Dr Gertrude Caton-Thompson, who examined several sites on the northern shore of Lake Moeris. Bone harpoons and points show that fishing and hunting formed a large part of the economy, but types of emmer wheat and barley were also found, which show rapid mutations as if they had been recently introduced. The grain-types are known from western Asia and probably indicate the arrival in Egypt of the new concept of crop-rearing. The grain was stored in underground silos lined with well made basket-work. Flax was also used in quantity—perhaps cultivated—and woven into linen. The pottery was hand-made in coarse clay with some variety of forms. There is no incised or painted ware, but some pieces have a red slip and are well burnished. Flintwork shows great skill; lance-heads and long knives appear for the first time in this period and arrowheads, tips, sickles and scrapers are very delicately worked.

A few personal ornaments were made from sea-shells from the Mediterranean and Red Sea, and their beads of amazon-stone probably came from Tibesti in the middle of the Sahara. Tibesti was also the source for the amazon-stone beads found at Shaheinab, a neolithic site near Khartum which has other features in common with the Fayyum culture, such as the burnishing of pottery and the absence of any on-site cemetery.

Much less can be said about the other possibly neolithic culture, which was based on Merimde on the western edge of the Delta. A number of mud huts with beaten earth floors have been identified. Burials within the huts suggest a link with the much later beliefs that regarded the tomb as a house for the departed spirit or with the funeral practices of early neolithic Jericho. However, it seems more likely that, where house and burial are superimposed, they are not contemporary but coincidental, due to the gradual spread of the village over its earlier burial ground. The site was also occupied in late predynastic times but the stratigraphy was not recognized and many of the artefacts cannot be assigned with certainty to any particular period. The earliest pottery was a fine hard ware, polished in contrasting areas of red and brown and incised with parallel lines made with a fish bone. A variety of flint implements was found, several of late predynastic date or even later still. The confusion that exists in the evidence is disastrous, for this is potentially a key site in our understanding of the early stages of Egyptian civilization.

There is no direct link between the Fayyum Neolithic or the Merimde Neolithic and the cultures which follow. Nowhere has anyone exposed a stratified sequence which proves beyond doubt that the neolithic cultures found in the Nile valley proper are later than those of the Fayyum or the Delta, but this is usually assumed to be the case, because even the earliest of the Upper Egyptian groups possessed some copper tools and sufficient food surplus to allow them respite from unremitting toil and opportunity to create works of art.

The first farming cultures so far found in the Nile valley are on the east bank, between Assiut and Akhmin, and are named after a group of cemeteries around Badari. The Badarians are best known from their cemeteries. Guy Brunton described some objects, such as cooking pots, baskets, and bone and flint tools that came from their settlements, but recorded no details. At Matmar he found basket-lined granaries associated with querns and cooking pots, still in layers of ash, but no clue to the nature of their houses or the size of the settlements, although the two larger cemeteries, at Badari and Mostagedda, each contained over 300 graves.

The Badarians were buried singly in roughly circular graves, about 1·5 m. across and 1 m. deep. One or two pots were tucked into a niche, and a covering of matting and sticks was placed over the body, which was often wrapped in wickerwork or matting (occasionally in goat- or gazelle-skins) and buried with a number of possessions.

Their dress was made from linen or skins, sewn with bone needles—some of which survive still with the thread in place. The garments were kilts and shirts and perhaps a turban, for linen was often found near the skull. One piece of cloth was fringed but a more common ornament was a belt of several strings of blue-glazed steatite cylindrical beads, with the odd one of genuine turquoise. Studs of black pottery were found, perhaps worn in the ear lobe or nostril. Bracelets of ivory, bone and horn, some with a sharp ridge round the circumference, others with knobs or a chevron pattern of inlaid blue beads, were worn on the forearm, and in the hair were ivory or bone combs, carved with animal or bird shapes.

The body was also decorated with green malachite, powdered and mixed to a paste, probably with castor oil. The malachite was ground on a rectangular slate palette with a concave curve or notch on the short sides to enable it to be firmly held when in use. Later palettes have a pointed oval shape.

The flint tools of the Badarians were rather poor and probably were not made by professional craftsmen. They ignored the nearby flint outcrops and used surface nodules to make push-planes with steep ends for dressing skins, and sickle blades with bifacial serrated edges. Copper tools have not survived, apart from one solitary pin, although other pieces may well have been melted down and re-used. A few copper beads were also found. Other tools were ivory or shell fish-hooks, flint arrowheads and curved flat wooden sticks, variously interpreted as boomerangs or castanets. Weapons are not recorded.

Their pottery consisted of fine, thin-walled bowls with a central keel or ridge finished in black, red or brown, with a black top and a burnished slip or rippled pattern, as well as more common coarser brown ware. Sometimes the fine ware has a burnished design inside.

There are some cylindrical vases in ivory, which are also used for intricately decorated spoons and combs. Ivory was also used for statuettes of women, intended to serve as companions for the dead men in whose tombs they were buried along with crude clay and pottery figures. Other evidence for their religious beliefs may be found in the hippopotamus and antelope amulets which were probably hunting charms. They also buried animals—dogs or jackals, cows and sheep—in the same cemeteries as humans and in similar graves, wrapped in matting or linen but without any tomb furniture.

The Badarians had a simple economy of agriculture and stock-breeding, augmented by a considerable amount of hunting and fishing. Even so, they

6. Baked clay vase in the shape of a model hippopotamus. Late Naqada Period. From Hu. Now in the Ashmolean Museum, Oxford. Height 16·5 cm.

7. Left: flint knife with the handle covered with a thin sheet of gold, inscribed with the name of King Djer. 1st-dynasty. Now in the Royal Ontario Museum, Toronto. Length 37 cm. Right: flint knife with ivory handle decorated on both sides with finely carved rows of animals and birds. The boss is pierced to take a cord by which the knife was secured to the belt or waist of the owner. From Abu Zeidan, near Edfu. Late Predynastic Period, *c.* 3200 BC. Now in the Brooklyn Museum, New York. Length 23·2 cm.

must have had a food surplus to barter for imported goods, or to support expeditions to Sinai for copper and to the Red Sea for shell. The type of grain and of domesticated sheep and goats point to Asiatic connections and may indicate their original homeland.

A neat picture is often projected of the Badarian culture developing into a second stage—still essentially a native tradition and limited to Upper Egypt—which was challenged and finally overcome by a new culture, Naqada, with Asiatic connections introduced in the north via the Delta. It is perhaps almost too neat. The Badarian and Early Naqada cultures (so-called after the main site at Naqada; Early and Late Naqada are sometimes called Amratian and Gerzean after the other sites, El-'Amrah and Gerzeh) overlap peaceably but some characteristics of Early Naqada persist well into its later stages, suggesting a continued gradual development rather than a confrontation.

Moreover the Late Naqada is stronger in Upper Egypt than one would expect if it were a northern implant, and it could well be that the strong Asiatic influence reached Egypt via the Wadi Hammamat and the Red Sea. The picture is further clouded by the fact that the cessation of Upper Egyptian influence in the north at Assiut, which used to be thought of as a cultural gap, can be shown to be possibly an accident of excavation since there may well be sites in the Assiut to Fayyum stretch of the valley below the present areas of cultivation.

The Early Naqada Period is generally agreed to cover SD (Sequence Date) 30–40/5. It was first distinguished by Petrie in 1895 and reaches from Matmar and Mostagedda in the north to Hierakonpolis in the south, with outlying sites around the First Cataract.

The most abundant artefacts of the period are the pots. A fine burnished red ware was introduced, sometimes painted in white with animal and plant shapes, or geometric patterns. A variety of forms was used, including some based on animals and birds. Black burnished vases standing on a small splayed foot were also made. Copper tools are rare, but the stone tools of the Early Naqada Period are particularly fine, perhaps because a professional class of flint workers was growing up who used mined flint rather than surface nodules. Double-edged blades show careful pressure-flaking, but the most striking implements are the so-called 'fish-tailed' knives or lances. They were hafted into a wood or bone handle and the cutting edge is, in fact, a saw, with tiny teeth less than 1 mm. across [7].

So-called mace-heads are made of a variety of hard stones. They are low cones with concave sides and a narrow perforation that suggests they may have been hafted on a leather thong rather than a wooden handle, which would have broken under any severe impact.

There are interesting figurines in pottery [8], ivory and bone. Ivory human figures are very long and slender; often the tusk is plain except for a bearded head carved at the tip. The beards and tubular penis sheaths that some of them wear are thought to show a link with their western neighbours, but similar examples also come from the chalcolithic culture of Beersheba in Palestine of about 3500 BC. A quite different type is the crude pottery female figurine, with stumpy arms, a stylized head, a white-painted lower half, perhaps representing a skirt, and tattoo marks on the arms and body. Animal figurines or amulets [9] are more naturalistic and a variety of beasts decorate the long-toothed ivory combs and pins. Animal-shaped slate palettes replace the earlier plain lozenges.

The evidence for settlements at this period is very thin. Little has been positively dated except for some huts at Hemamieh *c.* SD 35. They are circular, between 1 and 2 m. in diameter, with walls about 30 cm. thick of rough lime-stone and mud. These were probably the bases for walls of reed bundles, impressions of which were found on the outer face; the inner face was smoothed mud curving into the beaten mud floor. There is a suggestion, based on a small fragment of a model from Diospolis Parva, that some of the settlements were fortified with a mud-brick or *pisé* wall.

The cemeteries are not much more informative. The bodies usually lay in a contracted posture, facing west, with their heads to the south [10]. Some of the tombs contained up to seven bodies in quite large oval graves of a type that continued unchanged through to SD 40/45.

The transition to the later phase of the Naqada Period is a gradual one, although it used to be regarded as coming after a complete break following an Asiatic invasion. Many cultural traits alter only gradually, such as the change from lozenge to animal palettes and from disc- to pear-shaped mace-heads, while others continue with only small modifications, such as the fish-tailed lances and other flint types. The white cross-lined pottery and black-topped red ware both continue in Petrie's Gerzean period, only later giving way to the new decorated ware.

This later phase is found in more widely distributed sites, ranging from a group near the Fayyum almost to the Second Cataract. The absence of sites farther north may be attributed to the encroaching alluvium, or perhaps the culture was centred in the Theban area and did not penetrate the Delta. Certainly the number of cemeteries suggests an enlarged population, no doubt the result of the increasingly high standard of living as agricultural and stock-breeding skills continued to develop, and as copper-working became better understood. Even so, the number of identifiable settlements is very small and information on the culture is still largely obtained from the study of grave furniture.

The best clue to Naqada is a pottery model-house from El-'Amrah [11], *c.* SD 44–64. Rectangular in plan, it has high walls and a single door leading to a courtyard half-open to the sky, the half farthest from the doorway being roofed over with a clay slab. No wall divides the room from the courtyard, but this may be artistic licence for the modeller does show two windows in the rear wall, which would not have been necessary if the opposite side were entirely open. The plan of a mud-brick house at Badari shows such a rectangular plan divided by a cross wall about two-thirds of the way along its length.

Although the poorer graves were still round in plan, the more elaborate ones were rectangular like the houses. Some of these were also lined with the newly introduced rectangular sun-dried mud-brick, others with matting or wooden planks.

The distinctive wares of the period are the decorated and wavy-handled types. The first is a buff or a pale grey ware painted with elaborate designs in red. There are scenes showing boats with cabins, standards later associated with some of the gods, dancing women, men hunting in the desert, trees, rows of hills, antelopes, ostriches and other animals. Others are shaped and painted to imitate mottled stone vessels. Initially, the wavy-handled type has close parallels in Palestine, but its development, from a well-rounded profile with big ledge handles to a cylindrical jar with a wavy line as the only trace of the original handles, is confined to Egypt.

The excellent craftsmanship in flint is maintained but copper is now introduced on a fairly wide scale and several tools and weapons are found in

8. Painted pottery figurine of a woman with the head of a bird, from Hierakonpolis. Early Predynastic Period, *c.* 4000 BC. Now in the Brooklyn Museum, New York. Height 29·3 cm.

9. Group of amulets of ivory, bone and stone: they are based on stylized forms of animals or parts of animals. Late Predynastic. Now in the City Museum and Art Gallery, Birmingham.

10. Late Predynastic burial from Hierakonpolis. The body lies in a flexed position with simple funerary equipment in a shallow rectangular grave.

that metal. A spiral ring of gold wire, cylindrical beads and a foil pendant are some of the earliest gold ornaments, and there are also silver beads of various shapes. Silver was used for two daggers found at El-'Amrah, which have triangular blades with midribs and a semi-circular plate for hafting. A few beads of iron made from meteorite fragments are recorded.

As well as metal beads we now have the first faience examples [12], where the glaze is applied to a composition base instead of stone as in the Badarian pieces. Both the material and the Egyptian word for it seem to have come from the western Delta area. Other beads are of hard stones like chalcedony, agate, turquoise, carnelian and haematite, lapis lazuli imported from Afghanistan and obsidian from an as yet unidentified source.

11. Clay model-house, from a tomb at El-'Amrah, *c.* 3250 BC. Now in the British Museum. Length 45 cm.

Towards the end of the predynastic period the pressure of foreign influence seems to have increased and there is more and more evidence of western Asiatic contacts. The events that led up to the union of the Two Lands probably happened in a very short space of time and may have been the result of this strong contact. Certain motifs used on the big ceremonial palettes from Hierakonpolis are closely reminiscent of Mesopotamian art and actual artefacts such as a cylinder seal of the Jemdet Nasr type and pottery suggest a trading contact.

Writing was introduced into Egypt at this point. There is no slow process of development such as one can trace in Mesopotamia, rather it arrives fully armed with a complete range of signs of all types suggesting that the idea had been thoroughly worked out elsewhere, but the signs are entirely Egyptian in form and late predynastic in date. The Egyptians soon showed themselves masters of this new art and their subsequent history is illuminated by documentation in varying degrees.

12. Glazed frit figures of animals; the pig and scorpion are from a large deposit that predates the Archaic Period temple at Hierakonpolis, the hippopotamus head and jerboa are from a XIIth-dynasty tomb at Heliopolis, as is probably the frog; the hedgehog is from a XIIth-dynasty tomb at Beni Hasan. All now in the Fitzwilliam Museum, Cambridge.

The Archaic Period

THE ARCHAIC PERIOD

Ist dynasty 3100–2890

Scorpion ⎫
Narmer ⎬ = Menes?
Aha ⎭
Djer (Zer)
Queen Merneith (Meryet-nit)
Wadji (Djet)
Udimu
Anedjib (Enezib)
Semerkhet
Ka'a

IInd dynasty c. 2890–2686

Hotepsekhemwy
Ra-neb
Ninetjer (Neteren)
Peribsen (Sekhemib)
Sendji
Neterka
Neferkara
Khasekhem (= Khasekhemwy?)

NOTE: In this and subsequent tables kings are listed by the common form of their names, usually the Greek form. Alternative forms are sometimes indicated but there are often several variant spellings.

The introduction of writing fortunately occurs in time to provide some documentary evidence for the next major step in the history of Egypt, the creation of the united kingdom of Upper and Lower Egypt. This coincidence of the beginning of documented history with the setting up of the first stable union is fortuitous. Although the records are ambiguous, it is possible to give names to most of the personalities and generally to fill in some of the historical background to the archaeological record.

Upper Egypt was probably united under the rule of a king at Hierakonpolis [5]. This large town and its immediate subsidiary villages supported a population of up to 10,000, and a late predynastic tomb with painted walls discovered here is possibly the grave of one of the early rulers. Certainly, several of the documents associated with the union of the Two Lands were discovered here by Quibell in 1894. These documents are, for the most part, inscribed mace-heads and palettes which seem to record significant events and to have fulfilled ceremonial rather than practical purposes. They are best explained as part of the regalia, and their presence at Hierakonpolis may indicate that this was the seat of government.

In Lower Egypt, the picture is less clear. The evidence seems to suggest that it was sufficiently well organized to pose a positive opposition to the south, and that its conquest was a recognizable event and not a gradual absorption of an amorphous group of independent cities. It seems to have been united behind its own king, who wore a distinctive crown and whose capital was probably at Buto (Tell Fara'in).

Around 3100 BC, the archaeological evidence shows the late Naqada culture of Upper Egypt making sudden inroads into the Delta in concentrations which suggest a military conquest by the south. This is supported by several additional pieces of evidence, chiefly from palettes which show groups of prisoners or defeated cities, sometimes bearing symbols indicating their northern origin. Traditionally, unification was achieved by a ruler called Menes, but he is principally known from the king-lists and later traditions. The name does not occur on any contemporary documents and may be a second name or epithet of kings Scorpion, Narmer or Aha, each of whom has left a claim to conquest of the northern kingdom. The union certainly seems to have been stable enough for King Aha to have established his capital at Memphis and he may have taken the credit for temporary conquests by his predecessors, kings Scorpion and Narmer [13].

It is possible that Aha bore an epithet derived from the Egyptian word *mn*, meaning 'To be firm'—an appropriate description for the founder of a state, and a possible origin for the name Menes.

The history of the remainder of the period after the unification is quickly told because of the paucity of the records. Apart from isolated jottings on a few ivory labels found in the royal tombs, the events recorded on the Palermo Stone, and apart from the occasional graffito, there is very little historical material.

The Ist dynasty began in an atmosphere of economic and cultural expansion which continued strongly for about two centuries. The Palermo Stone (see p. 14) and various graffiti record expeditions in Nubia and on the eastern border. Less is known about the IInd dynasty and even the order in which the kings reigned is disputed. During the reign of Peribsen there appears to have been a considerable political upheaval, perhaps resulting in the breakdown of the Union, which was ultimately restored by Khasekhem, who may have changed his name to Khasekhemwy ('The Appearance of the Two Powers') in celebration of this event. However, Egypt seems to have remained basically strong and the cultural development continued without interruption [14].

MONUMENTS

Apart from these few historical records we can also learn something of the various rulers from the size of their respective tombs. Ist–dynasty kings, in fact,

13. Ceremonial palette of Narmer from Hierakonpolis. Obverse: in the upper register, the King Narmer, wearing the Red Crown of Lower Egypt and accompanied by his officials, inspects the decapitated corpses of his enemies. In the centre the entwined necks of two animals form the central hollow of the palette. The stylized representation of the animals suggests Mesopotamian influence. Reverse: the king, now wearing the White Crown of Upper Egypt, prepares to execute an enemy. The same story is told symbolically by the figure of the falcon, the Horus bird representing the king, which leads a captive man whose body is shown as a papyrus clump representing the people of the Delta. At the top of the palette between the figure of Hathor is shown a *serekh* containing the king's name. Beginning of 1st dynasty. Now in the Cairo Museum.

14. Limestone stele of King Wadji, from his tomb at Abydos. The representation of the palace facade (*serekh*) is extended in typical Egyptian manner to suggest the plan of the building behind the facade, wherein the King Wadji is shown by the hieroglyph for his name. The *serekh* is surmounted by the Horus falcon of Upper Egypt. 1st-dynasty. Now in the Louvre, Paris. Height 2 m.

provide a double ration of such evidence for each seems to have had two tombs, one in the south at Abydos and another at Sakkara in the north. The Abydos royal cemeteries lay in the Umm el-Qa'ab, the Mother of Pots, a promontory in front of the western cliffs. Abydos was a sacred burial city and, at first, there was every reason to suppose that the tombs discovered there by Amélineau and Petrie were the burial places of the rulers whose names were inscribed on the objects found in them. However, in 1938, W. B. Emery began to excavate the early dynastic cemetery at Sakkara, and, by their contents, several of the tombs there were also attributed to 1st-dynasty rulers. The Sakkara cemetery is obviously associated with the capital city of Memphis, and the other with the traditional burying ground of Abydos. Perhaps also, the dual nature of the kingship is reflected by one burial in Upper Egypt and one in the north. Whatever the reason for two graves it is plain that one man could not occupy both, but since none was excavated intact it is not possible to say for certain which actually contained the corpse and which was merely a cenotaph. Good arguments can be advanced for both sites but there is no conclusive evidence.

At a later period of Egypt's history, one of the tombs at Abydos was thought to be the tomb of Osiris and a large granite sarcophagus inscribed with a figure of the god was installed in it. It became the centre of pilgrimage for the great festival celebrating his victory over evil and the large numbers of pots containing offerings left by pilgrims gave rise to the modern name for the site. In 1897, when the labels and sealings from the tomb were studied by Sethe, the 'tomb of Osiris' was discovered to belong to Djer, and other tombs to his fellow monarchs of the 1st dynasty.

The earliest royal tombs at both Abydos and Sakkara have similar substructures [15]. They consist of a large pit, about 3–4 m. deep, containing a number of rooms, the largest in the centre being the burial chamber. They are roofed over with beams and planks covered with rubble. Above this, at ground level, the Sakkara tombs have a large mass of brickwork with a hollow interior divided on a grid into a series of compartments, which have an elaborately panelled exterior painted in gaily coloured patterns to imitate the façade of the dead man's house. The proportions suggested to the modern Egyptians the shape of the much smaller benches in their villages which are called *mastabas*, and this term is now generally applied to these tombs. The superstructures of the Abydos tombs were almost all destroyed, but the tomb of Wadji preserves a mound of sand and gravel within a plain oblong retaining wall. There was probably a skin of brickwork over the top.

The body was buried with a large amount of equipment for use in the Afterworld. The bulkier goods were stored in the upper rooms and the more valuable objects, including the body, were placed in the subterranean chambers before the superstructure was finished. The body was not mummified but carefully wrapped in linen and placed in a wooden sarcophagus, with a funeral meal laid out alongside and boxes of garments, jewellery, furniture and weapons in the rooms nearby [16]. The quality of the provisions improved as the dynasty proceeded: more and more food and drink was supplied, and grain was left for the occupier to grind his own flour when the bread supply ran out; similarly, nodules of flint enabled him to replace any tools he might lose or damage.

Some of the occupant's servants were buried in rows of subsidiary graves to see to his comfort in the next world. Sometimes considerable numbers were involved. Queen Merneith was buried with groups of retainers, numbering forty-one and seventy-seven respectively, at Abydos, and Wadji had 335 servants

buried with him there. This practice is not known in the later periods in Egypt, but it has parallels in nearby areas of Africa, where there are comparatively recent eye-witness accounts, and roughly contemporary parallels in Mesopotamia—for example in the great death-pits of Early Dynastic Ur.

By the middle of the dynasty a stairway was introduced, providing direct access from outside to the burial chamber. This meant that the tomb could be completed before the death of its intended occupant. To prevent robbery, large stone slabs placed vertically in the ceiling of the stairway were dropped into place when the body had been laid to rest.

In a few tombs at Sakkara, a small mound was built over the burial shaft and completely covered by the superstructure of the mastaba. It has been suggested that this may well represent a fusion of the Abydos mound grave and the Sakkara house grave into one composite design. At the end of the dynasty, in the tomb of Anedjib, the mound was much larger and occupied almost all the space of the superstructure [17].

Some mastaba-type royal tombs of the IInd dynasty have been found at Sakkara near the pyramid of Unas [26], and kings Peribsen and Khasekhemwy have tombs at Abydos. They are free-standing burial chambers surrounded by rows of magazines, all built in a large openwork pit.

The nobles' tombs were smaller versions of the tombs of the royal family, with a solid superstructure instead of the store-rooms, and fewer rooms below ground. These also adopted the stairway to the burial chamber and were gradually cut deeper into the rock. Greater experience of stoneworking led to an increased use of stone for roofing, lining and paving slabs in the chambers, which themselves took on a more complicated layout in an attempt to reproduce the rooms of the dead man's house, arranged so that the body lay, as it were, in the bedroom.

The best examples of the tombs of the lower classes are those of the subsidiary burials around the royal tombs. Their graves are simple, brick-lined pits with a rectangular mound above. In later stages this was provided with a false

16. Ivory models of a lion and lioness, from a tomb at Abydos. Now in the Fitzwilliam Museum, Cambridge.

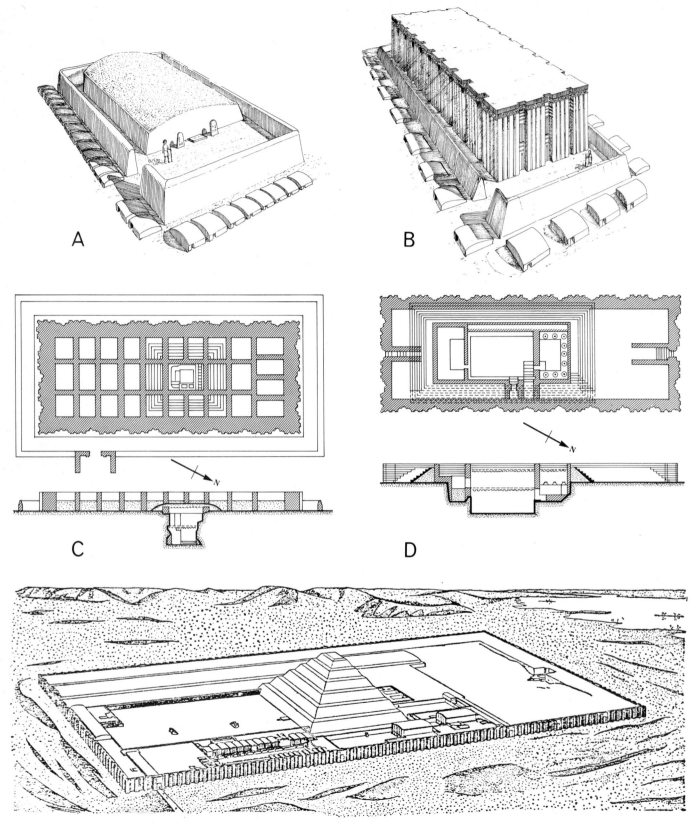

A

B

C

D

E

door like the bigger tombs. The body was wrapped in linen and placed in a small wooden coffin with food and drink and usually one or two of the tools of the owner's trade. At Abydos they were marked by small crudely worked stelai. Even poorer burials were in oval or oblong pits, the contracted body lying in a reed mat or wooden box, with a few vessels and tools by way of grave goods.

Of the homes that these people occupied during their lifetimes we know far less. The poorer people presumably lived in small simple mud-brick dwellings, sufficient to provide shelter at night but cramped and ill-lit as one might expect in a nation that spent most of its time out of doors. The nobles' tombs show a larger type of house with rooms set apart for different purposes and suitably equipped.

We know little about the homes of the poorer people, but the royal cemetery at Abydos does provide some evidence for the shape of the royal palaces. There is a series of mysterious buildings originally identified as 'forts', although clearly not sited for military purposes. They are large, rectangular structures up to 75 × 140 m., sometimes with double walls and narrow, towered gateways. The façade has the niched appearance of the early Sakkara tombs and within the walls are traces of other buildings. They are interpreted as funerary buildings because the early ones seem to be surrounded by subsidiary graves like the early tumulus tombs. These structures are perhaps based on the fortified palaces or castles used by the living rulers, but obviously they tell us little about the detailed layout of these buildings beyond the appearance of the façade [*Pl 2*].

It seems likely that each king had in his burial arrangements at Abydos a tumulus up on the old burial ground of the Umm el-Qa'ab, and a funerary castle down on the low plateau where there was more space. At Sakkara both buildings were incorporated in one structure, ranging from the small mound in a grid superstructure of the early Ist dynasty to the later massive mound within a solid mastaba.

The other big public buildings in Egypt were the cult temples. In later periods these are the principal monuments, but very little is known about such structures in the Archaic Period. A wooden label from the tomb of Aha seems to show a building, with a god's standard and two banners in a courtyard, which could be a primitive form of cult temple. There are traces of temples at Meda-mud and Hierakonpolis, but the only surviving recognizable example is the brick-built temple of Khentamenty at Abydos. Khentamenty, the original local god of Abydos, was later associated with Osiris (see p. 197), and had a small temple which is the earliest surviving building of the temple complex. It consists of three principal rooms, one behind the other with doorways offset to ensure the privacy of the rites. Against the end wall of the inner room are three smaller rooms, the centre of which would be the shrine, the flanking ones either subsidiary shrines or store-rooms. To the north-west is a slaughtering yard, where sacrifices might be prepared for the god and perhaps for the dead kings. It lies beside the processional way from the city to the royal cemetery, and funeral processions would no doubt stop at this point to worship the protective deity of the cemetery.

The palettes and mace-heads which are the basis for the early history of this period are also important in the art history of Egypt, for they represent the first examples of several motifs and formulae that are standard in later periods. The careful division of the field into horizontal registers, the combined full-face and profile view of the human body, differences in rank reflected as differences in size, the whole study of relationship, the use of space and the combination of

17. (A) Reconstruction of typical mound tomb of royalty from Abydos with solid super-structure and offering place between two stelai. Outside the wall are rows of tombs of servants. (B) Reconstruction of a house-type royal tomb from Sakkara. Its *serekh* facade resembled the palace of the ruler and the superstructure was subdivided into compartments representing rooms. (C) The section through the tomb of Her-neith at Sakkara, a house-type tomb in which the Abydos mound tomb is represented by a small mound over the mouth of the shaft. (D) Section through the tomb of Anedjib at Sakkara, a later version of (C) in which the mound, though still within the *serekh* facade, almost completely fills it. (E) Reconstruction of the Step Pyramid of Djoser at Sakkara, showing how the pyramid stands in relation to the *serekh* facade of the enclosure wall in similar relation-ship to the combined tomb types shown in (C) & (D).

hieroglyphs in the framework of the picture are all met here in their embryonic stage.

Works of sculpture on a large scale are rare. The principal royal pieces are the small statues of Khasekhemwy and of Ninetjer, which are important as early documents in the long tradition of monumental sculpture. The few private statues that there are, tend to have rather squat bodies and disproportionately large heads with a minimum of detailed modelling.

The Egyptians were, however, acquiring a facility in stoneworking, and a distinctive feature of this period is the variety of forms of slate dishes imitating hieroglyphs and vegetal forms with complete confidence. This skill was to be fully exploited in both the pyramid building and the works of art of the Old Kingdom which follows.

In the Archaic Period we see the Egyptians finding their feet as a nation. The dual nature of the kingship is formulated, the hieroglyphic script is developed, the principles of the art style are established, and in many other ways the style of Egyptian life for the next 3,000 years is fixed.

OLD KINGDOM AND FIRST INTERMEDIATE PERIOD

IIIrd dynasty c. 2686–2613

    Sanakht (= Nebka?)
    Djoser
    Sekhemkhet
    Khaba
    Huni

IVth dynasty c. 2613–2494

    Snofru (Sneferu)
    Cheops (Khufu)
    Redjedef (Djedefre')
    Chephren (Khafre')
    Mycerinus (Menkaure')
    Shepseskaf

Vth dynasty c. 2494–2345

    Userkaf (Weserkaf)
    Sahure'
    Neferirkare'
    Niuserre'
    Unas (Wenis)

VIth dynasty c. 2345–2181

    Pepi I (Phiops)
    Pepi II (Phiops)
    Queen Nitocris

VIIth dynasty c. 2181–2173

VIIIth dynasty c. 2173–2160

IXth dynasty c. 2160–2130

Xth dynasty c. 2130–2040 at Heracleopolis

XIth dynasty c. 2133–1991 at Thebes

4
The Old Kingdom

The four dynasties of the Old Kingdom see the working out of the Archaic Period achievement and, in the end, the failure of the administration to maintain the momentum with which the period began.

In terms of political history we know next to nothing about the IIIrd dynasty. Even the number of kings, let alone their order, is not firmly established and, apart from their funerary monuments, they are little more than mere names. Djoser, the king of whom we know most, has left inscriptions claiming control over copper and turquoise mines in Sinai, and a stele at Sehel on the First Cataract, cut in Ptolemaic times, claimed that he presented land to the priests of Khnum in Nubia when they ended a seven-year famine in his reign. Sekhem-khet and Sanakht also left graffiti in Sinai. The other rulers, Khaba, Nebka and Huni have not left that much: even the order and identity of some of them are in doubt.

Little more is known about the rulers of the IVth dynasty. The Palermo Stone annals record raids against Nubia and Libya and there is mention of the construction of several large boats in cedar-wood of Byblos origin. The size and arrangement of the monuments in the Giza cemetery suggests that the country's resources were well organized and fully exploited by a strong central government dominated by the king, just as his pyramid dominates the cemetery [18]. In contrast to Snofru's reputation as a beneficent ruler, Cheops and Chephren were known as cruel despots. This is largely due to a tradition preserved by Herodotus, but the austere nature of the monuments of their reigns may be some confirmation. Redjedef's pyramid at Abusir and Shepseskaf's singular tomb at Sakkara may be indications of divergencies of loyalty in the family [*Pl 1*].

There were certainly problems at the beginning of the Vth dynasty, when the monarch's power came up against the growing influence wielded by the priesthood of Re' of Heliopolis. In other respects, the history of the dynasty is much the same as before, with campaigns in Libya, Syria and Palestine, wood imported from Byblos and expeditions to Sinai and Punt, and these practices were continued in the VIth dynasty.

VIth-dynasty rulers continue to build pyramids, to join battle with the Asiatics and to send expeditions abroad to Nubia. Uni, a noble of Pepi I, led an army of Egyptians, Libyans and Nubians into Palestine as far as Mount Carmel. Harkhuf took expeditions deep into Nubia, and in Pepi II's reign Sabni and Hekaib made punitive expeditions to the south to retrieve the bodies of murdered explorers.

These men were apparently loyal supporters of the throne, but many other nobles were concerned to feather their own nests. Economic demands on the royal exchequer to maintain pyramid and temple endowments became ever

18, 19 Aerial view and plan of the pyramid field of Giza, dominated by the three great pyramids of Cheops (top), Chephren (centre) and Mycerinus (bottom). Each pyramid had a temple at its east face and a causeway leading to the valley temple, although little remains of those attached to Cheops's pyramid. Smaller pyramids were built nearby for close members of the royal family and near Cheops's pyramid were ranged the tombs of members of his court. East and south of Cheops's pyramid are the pits for funerary boats. West of Chephren's pyramid is a line of barrack-like rooms which served to accommodate the construction workers, and at the foot of the oblique causeway is the Sphinx. Recent excavations south of the line of Mycerinus's causeway have revealed the remains of a settlement where the priests and other necropolis workers may have lived.

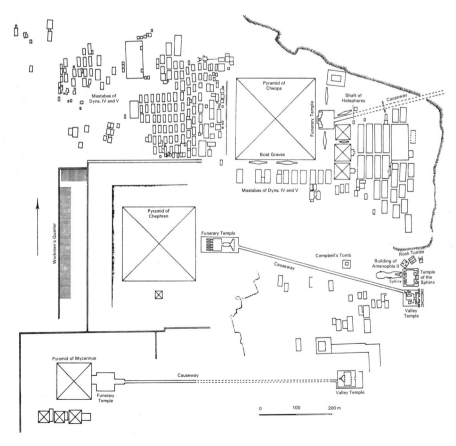

more urgent, and along with other factors weakened the monarchy, which could not hold out through the final years of the ninety-four-year reign of Pepi II. Although his pyramid was a magnificent monument, the power of the crown was exhausted and Egypt broke up into several smaller units.

FUNERAL MONUMENTS

The dominant monument of the IIIrd dynasty is the Step Pyramid, the tomb of King Djoser [20]. It is the culmination of the mastaba tomb and the beginning of the new tradition of pyramids, and as such it marks the change from the Archaic Period and sets the pattern of burial for the Old Kingdom and indeed for later periods as well.

It is a building of paradoxes: the building stones are dressed with great precision, the reliefs are carved only a few millimetres deep with an unerring sureness of touch, and there is a fine strength of design in the way in which the bundles of reeds forming pillars, the wooden stake fences and the roof beams are all rendered in stone. Yet at the same time there is a hesitancy and doubt

Pl 1. View across the Nile valley from the top of the cliffs behind Deir el-Bahri. This view shows the extreme narrowness of the occupied area of Egypt. At the edge of the vegetation lies the Ramesseum and the Colossi of Memnon can be seen beside the road leading to the river.

20. The mass of the Step Pyramid of Djoser, at Sakkara, now bare of its original casing of fine white limestone and revealing, in the damaged area of the base of the south face, the form of the original mastaba. In the foreground the remains of a small temple within the complex, showing the fine fluted columns, partially reconstructed.

21. Plan and sections of the Step Pyramid of Djoser at Sakkara. (1) Original mastaba; (2 & 3) extensions; (4) royal family tombs; (5 & 6) later extension; (7) entrance; (8) burial chamber; (9) funerary temple; (10) *serdab*.

about the new material. The pillars are not allowed to stand free but are attached to a wall or built in pairs, while in the mass of the pyramid itself there are baulks of timber, which might have stabilized a mud-brick mass, but which are structurally unimportant in a stone building. The plan of the building reveals a growing confidence. Through damage to the pyramid mass, it is possible to trace a series of changes from a plain mastaba to a three-stepped one, then the big change into a four-stage and finally a six-stage pyramid [21].

Around the pyramid the area was laid out like a small city, with many courts, shrines, altars and store-rooms. Some of the buildings are dummies, consisting simply of a mass of rubble behind a façade of Mokattam limestone, and a large area on the north and west sides appears to be unfinished. We are also uncertain about the function of some of the buildings because there are no texts or reliefs anywhere above ground, and the statues which took their place have largely disappeared. Even so, there is enough surviving to convey the achievement of Djoser and his architect Imhotep in the construction of the first stone building complex ever undertaken on this scale in Egypt.

Later kings of the dynasty appear to have been inspired by Djoser's pyramid, but were unable to carry out their plans. Sekhemkhet began a pyramid designed on very similar lines but, although the sarcophagus was found apparently sealed and intact in the burial chamber, it was disappointingly empty, and the actual structure did not rise far above ground level. Two other large but unexplored enclosures can be seen from the air near the Step Pyramid, but there is no indication for whom they were built.

At Zawiyet el-Aryan there are two more IIIrd-dynasty structures, one an unfinished pyramid consisting of a series of inward sloping layers, attributed to King Khaba because of the number of vessels found there inscribed with his name, and the other, little more than a vast open pit, thought to be the burial chamber of a projected pyramid for Nebka. Another layer pyramid at Meidum was probably begun by Huni and cased by Snofru, to whom it was attributed by later graffiti-scrawling visitors. Its primitive construction suggests the experimental stage of pyramid building but its plain finish is in IVth-dynasty style. At this point in the story there is somewhat of an *embarras de pyramides* and a shortage of possible occupants. There are two pyramids at Dahshur and only one king, Snofru, who can be associated with them. Snofru already probably had had a hand in the layer pyramid at Meidum. Quarrymarks on both the Dahshur monuments, however, confirm that he was the builder of both the Northern Pyramid and the Bent Pyramid, in which the angle was reduced when the structure was about half-finished [22].

These pyramids are the first to show what might be called the typical pyramid complex. This consists of the pyramid itself, with an entrance about half-way along the north face slightly above ground level, sloping down to a burial chamber which is usually cut into the rock just below ground level. Against the east face is a temple or shrine for the mortuary cult, connected by a long causeway with another temple on the edge of the cultivation. This is the valley temple to which the body of the king was brought by boat for mummification and burial. By the main pyramid there might be smaller ones for close members of the family, and some complexes incorporate one or more boats buried in pits, the ritual purpose of which is not yet fully understood.

The pyramids of Meidum and Dahshur seem almost to be a series of trial runs for the great pyramids of Giza slightly farther to the north, where one sees the form at its perfection. The plateau here is dominated by the Great Pyramid of Cheops and the almost equally large monument of Chephren rising high above the regular rows of nobles' mastabas laid out around them. There are changes of mind evident in the construction of Cheops' monument—the original underground burial chamber was abandoned for first one and then another chamber high up in the bulk of the pyramid, and the final plan involved the majestic corbel-vaulted Grand Gallery. The subsidiary buildings of Cheops' pyramid have mostly disappeared, apart from the three small pyramids of his queens at the south-east corner and five sealed boat pits, in two of which well-preserved cedar-wood boats were found. The valley temple is under the present village of Giza.

The Great Pyramid is striking for the absence of any blatant declaration of the name of its builder and occupier. His supreme self-confidence can well be judged by the utterly plain coffin and burial chamber in which, unsupported by any magical inscriptions or blazoned records of his mighty deeds, he calmly made the entry into eternity, assured of recognition and acceptance. Chephren's monument is similarly almost bare of inscription, but this was perhaps compensated by the large number of statues that were placed in the pyramid complex. Twenty-three great statues of Chephren carved in Nubian diorite stood in this valley temple, and there were more in the court of the funerary temple, now largely destroyed, where they were framed by vertical inscriptions giving his titles. The excavator, Reisner, calculated from extant fragments that between one hundred and two hundred statues might have been placed there, and a similar number probably stood in Cheops' complex. Even so, these buildings are comparatively unadorned and gain their strength from the huge red granite slabs with which the interiors are faced. Chephren could afford some modesty in his monuments [23]: he had, after all, constructed for himself what must have been for a long time the largest portrait in the world, when he caused a knoll of rock to be carved to form a giant sphinx and gave it his own features. It was probably intended as a protective figure for the whole cemetery area, but it was also certainly a good memorial for Chephren [24].

The construction of these huge monuments seems almost the dream of a megalomaniac. Although the core blocks were obtained locally, some of them

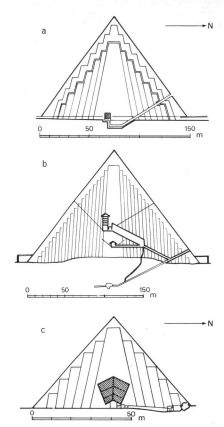

22. (a) Section through the pyramid of Snofru at Meidum which is composed of six layers of masonry held together by the angle of slope at which they were built. A casing of Tura limestone was added over the stepped layers, which were subsequently heightened by about 12 m. (b) Section through the pyramid of Cheops at Giza. This pyramid underwent alterations during the course of construction. First a chamber was cut in the bedrock, but after several courses of the superstructure were in place a new chamber was planned and a corridor cut from the original descending corridor, upwards through the masonry to this new level. Before this was completed the plan was altered and a new chamber planned, higher in the superstructure, approached by a corbelled gallery built as the construction progressed. Five small chambers were built above the chamber apparently to carry the weight of the masonry above. (c) Section through the pyramid of Sahure' at Abusir. This pyramid is of poorly dressed local limestone set in six battered walls, with a sand and rubble fill between each, and a fine limestone casing.

weigh over two hundred tons, and some of the granite facing-blocks, which were brought five hundred miles from Aswan by boat, exceed thirty tons. All these were put together with joints 1/50th of an inch thick and placed on an alignment with the cardinal compass points with a maximum error, in the case of the Great Pyramid, of just over five minutes. This indicates tremendous resources of manpower, technical ability and accurate measuring. Organization was no doubt the major problem. Manpower would be free during the inundation period, when the peasants could not work their fields and blocks could be delivered by boat to the desert edge. They were manhandled up ramps and dressed in position by a comparatively small permanent staff of skilled workmen —nothing like the 100,000 slaves that Herodotus speaks of [*Pl 3*].

In the Vth dynasty the monarch's tight control was relaxed and vast funeral constructions were no longer erected for him. Userkaf had a small pyramid near the Step Pyramid, with the funerary temple on the south face and only a small shrine against the east side. Sahure' moved to Abusir, and was followed there by Neferirkare' and Niuserre', while the later kings of the Vth and VIth dynasty moved back to Sakkara. The cult of Re', the sun god of Heliopolis, was now making its power felt and increasingly throughout the dynasty several of these later rulers felt obliged to build special temples for this deity.

Six of these Sun Temples are mentioned in Egyptian texts, but only Niuserre''s and Userkaf's are now known; Niuserre''s stone building is the

23. One aisle of the valley temple of Chephren, built of huge granite blocks from Aswan. The blocks of the end wall are not laid in level courses but trimmed to avoid unnecessary wastage. Height of the monolithic pillars is just over 4 m.

24. View of the southern part of the Giza pyramid field showing the pyramids of Chephren (right) and Mycerinus (centre). In the foreground at the bottom of the causeway lies the valley temple of Chephren and in front of the Sphinx is the ruined XVIIIth–dynasty temple.

better preserved. It stands on the desert edge at Abu Gurab and is in two parts [25]. There is an entrance porch, rather like a valley temple in conception, leading, by a covered causeway, to a built-up platform, on which is a plain courtyard with a huge centrally placed altar and, on the north side, store-rooms and an area for preparing the sacrifice. Behind the altar is a tall truncated pyramid, serving as a base for the squat obelisk that is the sun god's symbol. In a corridor on the east and south sides of the platform are reliefs showing the various seasons, and in the small chapel are representations of the temple-founding ritual and the Sed festival (see p. 111). Just south of the temple a brick boat was built, a symbol of Re''s daily journey across the sky.

The pyramids of these rulers, though less imposing than the early efforts, were none the less splendid buildings, but they have suffered from the depredations of later inhabitants in search of building stone, and many of their fine reliefs have been destroyed and taken away. The finest was probably Sahure''s, with basalt floors for the valley temple and main temple courtyard, a granite dado to the funerary temple and elegant, plant-shaped granite columns. Both buildings were elaborately carved in relief with scenes of the king hunting and his activities in Syria. The pyramid of Unas is a modest building with an important new feature; the burial chamber contains extensive hieroglyphic inscriptions known as the pyramid texts (see p. 197). They are seen as a sign of the waning power of the monarch, already challenged by the priests of Re' and now under increasing pressure from his nobles. The god-like calm confidence of the IVth-dynasty rulers is exchanged for a trust in the magical power of spells and incantations [26].

The VIth-dynasty pyramids at Sakkara show the pyramid complex in a highly developed form, with elaborate ranges of subsidiary buildings attached to the temple areas. Although still massive—Pepi II's was about 52 m. high on a base nearly 80 m. square—the central core was of small stones laid in Nile mud. This was faced with Tura limestone and, when the casing was removed later, the inadequacies of this method of construction were soon revealed as the pyramid collapsed into an ungainly heap. The basalt and alabaster pavements of the Vth dynasty were now followed by plainer limestone floors, and there was not the same amount of relief carving on the walls of the temples.

25. Calcite altar *in situ* in the ruined courtyard of the sun temple of Niuserre' at Abu Gurab.

26. The pyramid of Unas at Sakkara seen from the causeway. With its limestone outer casing removed, the pyramid is a sad eroded heap of rubble. The causeway walls, now preserved to two or three courses, originally stood more than two metres high and were decorated inside with fine relief carvings.

Pl 5. Painting of a man spearing fish from the much damaged tomb chapel of Ankhtifi at Moalla. XIth–dynasty.

The queens of these rulers were buried near their husbands. Some, like those of Cheops and Mycerinus, were honoured with mini-pyramids ranged alongside their lords; others had a separate burial, like Shepseskaf's queen, Khentikawes, who had a mastaba with mortuary chapel, causeway and valley building alongside the causeway of Mycerinus [19]. Near the Pyramid of Cheops, a deep vertical shaft with a plain burial chamber at the foot and the top plastered over and disguised, contained the burial equipment of Queen Hetepheres, wife of Snofru. The equipment included a portable pavilion with an interlocking wooden frame, a bed and a carrying-chair [Pl 23], all richly ornamented with gold and ebony inlay. However, the splendid alabaster sarcophagus was empty and it is thought that the original burial took place elsewhere but had been robbed and the body removed and stripped of its jewellery. The crime was discovered and the surviving tomb equipment reburied in secret for safety. Hetepheres's original burial is probably to be found with other, as yet unexcavated, tombs of the court of Snofru near his Bent Pyramid at Dahshur. Still more unexcavated cemeteries lie near the Meidum pyramid.

The mastaba form of the Archaic Period at first remained basically unchanged for members of the court. The simple burial chamber [27], about 15–30 m. below ground, was reached by a stair, or more commonly a vertical shaft, and sometimes a second shaft and chamber was provided for the deceased's wife. The

Pl 4. False door from the large chapel of the mastaba of the vizier Mereruka at Sakkara. In this particularly elaborate example [cf. 155] the tomb owner himself is shown realistically walking through the doorway from the Afterworld. Vth–dynasty.

27. The mastaba of Khnumhotep and Ny'an-khkhnum was demolished because it lay in the line of the causeway of the pyramid of Unas at Sakkara. This view of the mastaba, now reconstructed, shows the plain exterior, slightly battered walls, portico and central court of a typical tomb of a Vth–dynasty noble.

solid rectangular masonry mass of the superstructure was arranged with its long axis lying north–south, and the niched façade replaced by a smooth surface with a niche containing a stele at each end of the long east wall. The practice soon grew up of providing a small chapel in the enlarged southern niche where the mortuary offerings could be made. The stele now represented a niche containing a door through which the *Ka*, or spirit, could pass to and from the Afterworld [*Pl 4*]. A small room with a narrow slit-like entrance (called a *serdab* after the Arabic word for cellar) contained a statue of the tomb owner which his *Ka* could use as a base if his mummy were destroyed.

In the IVth dynasty, perhaps by royal prescript, the super-structures of the mastabas were plain solid blocks without *serdabs*, and only small chapels were built against the wall over the southern niche. The mastabas were arranged in orderly rows around the royal pyramid, with precedence given to the larger tombs of the more intimate members of the royal household. In the Vth and VIth dynasties this restriction was dropped and the superstructures became larger, some up to 30 m. long, with more and more complex interiors developed from the chapel until whole suites of chambers, representing rooms in the deceased's house, were provided [28].

As early as the reign of King Mycerinus, a few rock tombs were cut at Giza but they only became popular amongst the southern Egyptian nobles in the Vth and VIth dynasties. At first, an attempt was made to reproduce a mastaba façade in the rock-face, but later a colonnade was sometimes cut, behind which lay a pillared hall suitably decorated. Most impressive are the tombs of the princes of Elephantine—Mekha and Sabni—high above the river at Aswan with long stairway approaches [29].

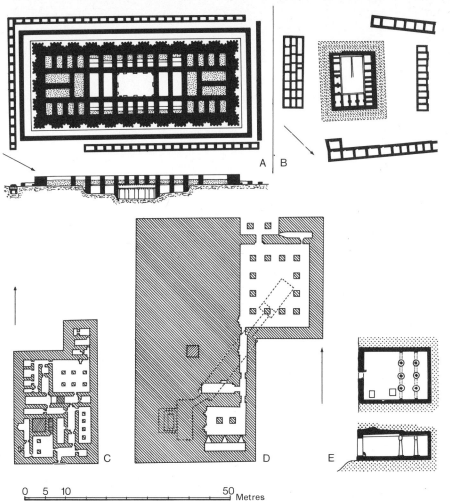

28. (A) Mastaba tomb of Wadji at Sakkara [cf. 15]. (B) Mound tomb of Wadji at Abydos. (C) The mastaba of Mereruka and his family at Sakkara, VIth–dynasty. Its superstructure is almost completely taken up by rooms and *serdabs*, most of them decorated with fine reliefs. The fake door [*Pl. 4*] stands on the north side of the six-pillared hall, almost opposite the doorway. (D) The mastaba of Tiye at Sakkara, Vth–dynasty, consists of an almost solid superstructure containing two chapels decorated with reliefs and equipped with offering tables and *serdabs*. The approach is through a fine pillared portico and colonnaded court, in which is a pit leading to the burial chamber below ground. (E) Plan and section of the rock-cut tomb chapel of Khnumhotep at Beni Hasan, XIIth–dynasty. The burials are in deep shafts cut in the slope in front of the chapels [cf. 45, 158].

0 5 10   50 Metres

29. Opposite the town of Aswan lies a range of rock tombs of nobles of the Old and Middle Kingdom. Two are approached by steep stairs leading up from the river edge, others are cut into the rock-face to the north.

Pl 6. Seated statue of Mentuhotep II dressed in the robes for the Sed festival or jubilee. Statues in granite and other hard stones are unlikely to have been decorated to the same extent as this piece, which is in sandstone. XIIth–dynasty. Now in the Cairo Museum.

44

STATUARY AND RELIEF

The surviving works of art from the Old Kingdom are almost all pieces of statuary or relief from the cemeteries associated with the royal court at Memphis. They were made by, or under the supervision of, the craftsmen attached to the great craft school associated with the temple of Ptah of Memphis, whose High Priest also bore the title of 'Chief of Craftsmen'. In this way an accumulation of skill and experience was built up and a craft tradition emerged that produced work of exceptionally high quality. It also led to the acceptance of certain proportions and arrangements developed during the Archaic Period as the standard formulae, but did not rigidly exclude all stylistic development or experimentation in technique.

Although a large number of the royal statues are damaged or lost, it is possible to see in the surviving pieces a line of development from the work of the Archaic Period. The hardest stones were worked with complete confidence and mastery and a truly monumental form evolved, which is seen at its best in the great diorite statues of Chephren [30]. Here, a completely balanced and restful pose is established and the majestic calm of the features, unperturbed by any suggestion of human frailty, make this an ideal expression of divine majesty that was a model for many succeeding generations of craftsmen. The precursors of this statue are the massive but mutilated statue of Djoser and several fragmentary statues of Redjedef austerely worked in red granite.

Pl 7. View northwards from the Theban peak looking down into the Valley of the Kings [cf. **50**]. The tomb entrances were at first carefully concealed and even in the later stages of its use they were comparatively unobtrusive. Most are situated near the road that runs along the valley bed.

30. Monumental diorite statue of King Cheph-ren from the valley temple of his pyramid complex at Giza. Height 1·67 m.

31, 32. Above: triad of King Mycerinus with the goddess Hathor (left) and the goddess of Diospolis Parva, who wears her nome symbol as a headdress. From the valley temple of Mycer-inus at Giza. Height 98 cm. Below: statue of the shipbuilder Bedjmes, in red granite, IIIrd-dynasty. Height 65 cm.

From the valley temple of Mycerinus comes a series of slate statues of the king with his queen and with a pair of goddesses who have her features [31]. The king is sculpted with the same air of majestic aloofness but the introduction of his queen brings in a gentler note. The use of alabaster for two royal heads from the end of the IVth dynasty also gives a slightly less severe impression, but from the early Vth dynasty we have a colossal red granite head of Userkaf, which shows that the feeling for monumentality was not lost.

There are various small statuettes from the VIth dynasty. One, in slate, shows Pepi I kneeling to offer libations, others in alabaster depict Pepi I in Sed festival costume and Pepi II on the lap of his mother, Queen Ankhes-mery-re'. In contrast, a large statue of Pepi I and a smaller one, perhaps of his son, from Hierakonpolis, of beaten sheet copper, now badly corroded and lack-ing the inlaid eyes and kilt, are still magnificently impressive as works of art and technical achievement. They lend credence to the existence, recorded on the Palermo Stone annals for the reign of Neferirkare', of an electrum statue of Ihy, son of the goddess Hathor, which is now lost; doubtless it was melted down for re-use.

Statues of private individuals are more difficult to date than the royal counterparts, since the person himself may be quite unknown apart from his statue, which, stylistically, may lag considerably behind the fashionable work-manship done for the king. This is well illustrated by a few pieces, the best examples of which are statues of Nedjem-ankh and Bedjmes [32], that are now dated to the IIIrd dynasty, but which closely resemble in scale and posture the statues of Khasekhemwy.

The colourful painted limestone figures of Rahotep and his wife Nofret are good examples of the private statuary of the IVth dynasty. They reflect the same quality of confidence found in the royal pieces and are sculpted in the same massive manner. With the simpler mastabas of the IVth dynasty there was no *serdab* for the *Ka* statue, which was replaced by a portrait head placed be-low ground in the antechamber to the burial room. These fine portrait heads were perhaps made in the royal workshops as a sign of royal esteem. They are all cut off cleanly at the neck and careful attention is paid to the features; the hair and ears and other details were added in plaster and are often damaged. They prob-ably have a similar function to the *Ka* statues and the grimly humorous technical name of 'reserve heads' has been given to them in modern times [33]. The *Ka* statues which reappear at the end of the IVth dynasty often seem to be convinc-ing portraits executed during the owner's lifetime and showing him at the peak of his career and manhood, sometimes with a subtle similarity to the reigning monarch. They are sculpted in wood or stone, usually limestone. The arms of the wooden ones are often made separately and joined to the body by a tenon, and both are made more realistic by careful painting and sometimes by having the eyes worked in stone inlay. Also at the end of the IVth dynasty, there are a number of sculptures of royal princes which portray the subject as a scribe. Perhaps they show a pride in newly acquired literacy, which was until then regarded as the proper domain of professional scribes.

In the Vth dynasty there is a trend towards group statues of the man and his wife [34], and sometimes a separate one of their children. Often several statues are found together; as many as eleven were discovered in the tomb of Mitry at Sakkara, for instance.

In the Vth dynasty, and especially the VIth dynasty, servant statuettes became increasingly popular. Sometimes in wood but more often in stone, they are fairly crudely sculpted but often have great vitality. The most popular subjects are women grinding corn [35] and men making beer, but a whole host of occupations are recorded: making pots, tending a fire, sieving, making bread, or cooking a goose, playing harps and drums, even feeding a dog and playing leap-frog. These are delightful genre figures, which supplement the relief scenes and are the precursors of the wooden models of the Middle Kingdom.

Carving in relief in the Old Kingdom reached a high degree of skill. The earliest known examples of relief carving of any size are a group of six panels from the Step Pyramid and some fragments from a shrine at Heliopolis, both groups showing Djoser taking part in the Sed festival [86]. These figures conform almost exactly to the canons of proportion finalized later in the Old Kingdom, but are slightly more slender than usual. The very shallow cutting of the relief and delicacy of the surface modelling indicate the skill of the stone workers at this early stage in the period.

33. Portrait head from the royal cemetery at Giza. Limestone. IVth–dynasty.

The inscriptions on the slabs set in the offering niches of early IIIrd-dynasty private mastabas are irregularly cut and carelessly arranged, and the relief figure of the dead man at a table is little more than an outline. Decoration was introduced into the private tombs about the beginning of the IIIrd dynasty and, since it was carried out by probably the same craftsmen employed on the royal tomb, it is of consistently good quality. Particularly interesting are the wooden panels from the tomb of Hesire', rare examples of work in this medium [36].

With the enlargement of the offering niche into a small chapel, a larger area was available to the artist, whose repertoire increased accordingly. The dead man was joined at his funeral repast by members of his family and a series of scenes from daily life were introduced. Scenes of hunting, fowling, driving cattle and boat-building were common, and liberally sprinkled with well observed minor incidents [37]. There are a few examples of painting from this period, executed on the mud-brick walls of the corridors, notably some exquisite work from the mastaba of Atet, and there is also some experimental work, in sunk relief filled with inlays of coloured paste, that was evidently not successful and was discontinued.

34. Group statue of the family of the dwarf Seneb, who was a priest in the funerary temples of the IVth–dynasty kings, Redjedef and Cheops. From Giza, VIth–dynasty. Height 33 cm.

It was until comparatively recently thought that the funerary temples and causeways of the IVth dynasty were left plain, but Herodotus speaks of the 'carvings of animals' that decorated the causeway of Cheops and it is almost certain that there was a limited amount of relief carving on the temple of the two large Giza pyramids. The queens' pyramids and the royal family's and nobles' mastabas were decorated with some of the finest reliefs ever executed. There is no single technique but a variety of styles, the shallow relief favoured by Djoser is found sometimes alongside the bold high relief of the later half of the IIIrd dynasty. A new sunk relief with the figure cut below the surface of the stone and the background left raised was also used.

The funerary temples of the Vth dynasty were certainly decorated, as befitted a royal tomb, with work of the highest standard. Notable are the reliefs of the temples of Userkaf and Sahure' and the Sun Temple of Niuserre'. The subjects are often developed in the private tombs with appropriate alterations: for instance, the line of offering-bearers representing the nomes of Egypt are altered to represent the deceased's estates. There are, however, some elements that are only linked with the monarchy, such as the king slaying his enemies or celebrating the Sed festival. Portrayals of the gods are common in the funerary temples, and there are scenes showing the succession of the seasons with the appropriate flora and fauna and seasonal activities.

35. Limestone statuette of a servant woman grinding corn. Vth–dynasty.

Pl 8. The painted quartzite sarcophagus of Tuthmosis III in the cartouche-shaped burial chamber of his tomb in the Valley of the Kings. The chamber walls are painted to represent a papyrus copy of one of the *Books of the Dead*.

Throughout the Vth and VIth dynasties, as the number of rooms in the superstructures of private tombs continued to grow, so the available area was taken up with more elaborate scenes and new motifs, but at Giza there was no diminution in the standard of workmanship in spite of the often poor quality of the stone surface. Some of the tombs of the nobles at Aswan are rather cruder than their Memphite counterparts—probably because they used less skilful local craftsmen, as one might expect in an area so far removed from the cultural centre. The practice, introduced by Unas, of decorating the funeral chamber with magical protective texts was copied in some private tombs, where the walls of the burial chamber were painted with a list of food and equipment, and sometimes included a portrait of the owner with the same magical intent.

THE FIRST INTERMEDIATE PERIOD

After the death of Pepi II and the end of the VIth dynasty a few local monarchs, notably those at Thinis, Dendera, Assiut and Koptos, remained loyal to the tradition of monarchy, which was maintained at Memphis for the next twenty years, and supported the fifteen or so rulers that constitute the VIIth and VIIIth dynasties. In return the rulers acknowledged the fact that the nomarchs were essentially independent by a series of special decrees. The period was described by later chroniclers as one of unmitigated disaster, and a number of texts written at the time or soon after give a graphic picture of political disintegration and social revolution. They are often very colourful pieces of writing but probably only reflect the state of affairs at the court at Memphis—life in other parts of the country no doubt went on without much change under the control of the local governors. We read elsewhere, for instance, of men still being appointed to serve the mortuary cults of some Old Kingdom rulers, suggesting that some degree of traditional order survived [38].

The VIIIth dynasty was eventually replaced by the nomarch of Heracleopolis, Achthoes, whose new dynasty received nominal acceptance throughout the Nile valley from Memphis to Aswan. However, it was probably not accepted in the Delta, where there is evidence of a large number of Asiatic immigrants—the result of the greatly increased population pressure in Palestine following the Amorite invasions there. After a peaceful transfer to the Xth dynasty these invaders were ejected and Egypt's border with Sinai strengthened by a fortified wall, 'The Wall of the Prince'. In the south, the nomarchs of Thebes led a coalition in revolt and, after initial reverses, succeeded in occupying the Thinite nome. Some years of peaceful coexistence ensued, but eventually the Thebans pressed on northward and successfully completed their rebellion.

Throughout this period the local nomarchs enjoyed a degree of independence. Some nomarchs, such as those of Assiut, actively supported the Heracleopolitan rulers. Others, such as Neheri of the Hare nome at Hermopolis, were less interested in national politics and more concerned with the well-being of their own people, maintaining a token resistance to the Thebans until their eventual success seemed obvious, and then openly supporting them.

The number of provincial governors now setting up more or less independent courts led to a demand for more sculptors and artists, and provincial schools were founded, at first under close supervision from Memphis, but soon developing their own distinctive styles. The level of professional skill is very low and the work is often uninspired. Blind repetition of forms and over-attention to minor details brought some very strange results. A willingness to experiment

36. Wooden relief panel, showing the noble Hesire' seated at an offering table: he carries his staves of office and has a writing set slung over his right shoulder. IIIrd–dynasty. Now in the Cairo Museum. Height 1·14 m.

37. Relief of a hippopotamus hunt, from the mastaba of the vizier Mereruka at Sakkara. Vth–dynasty.

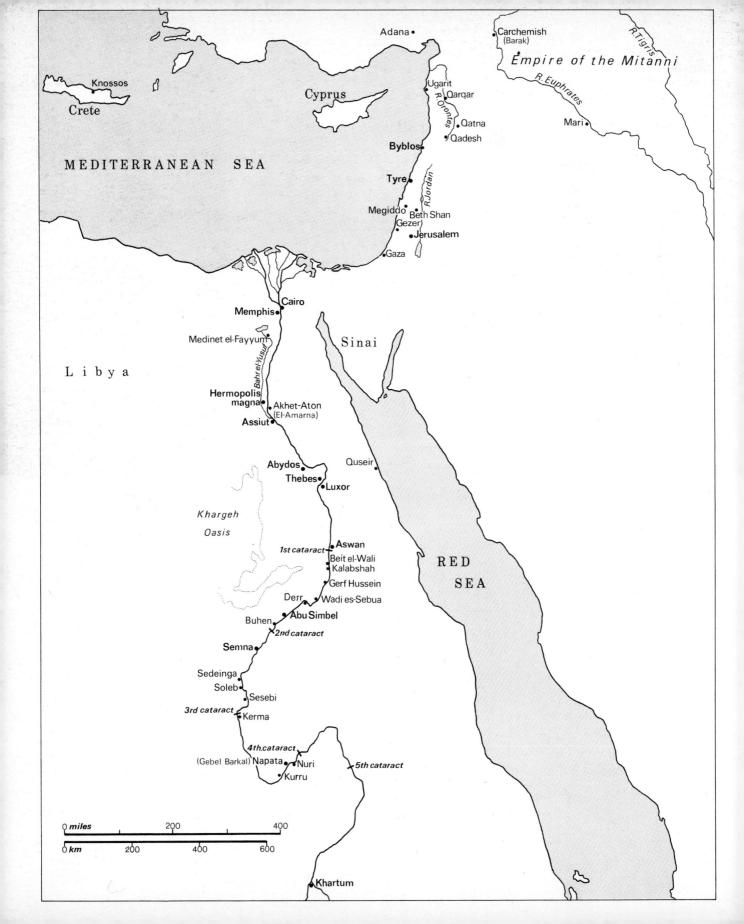

led to some bizarre colour schemes, such as the pink donkeys and yellow- and red-spotted cows in Ankhtifi's tomb at Moalla, but in the hands of more skilful artists it resulted in a sort of gawky liveliness [*Pl 5*]. The subject-matter remains much the same as in the Old Kingdom, except that scenes of animal hunting in the desert become popular and the uneasy political situation is reflected in some pictures of sieges and fighting. It is difficult to trace developments in the north during this period, but the ease with which the Memphite art tradition was taken up again once the Theban nomarchs assumed power suggests that it had been kept alive by the Memphite and Heracleopolitan rulers. This is confirmed by a few isolated pieces, such as the Xth–dynasty stele of King Merikare' from Sakkara in classic VIth-dynasty style and by the technical skill evident in work from Assiut in the Heracleopolitan period.

Monuments from this period are few. Although the despoliation of the pyramids reduced confidence in them as a 'castle of eternity', they continued to be built, but rarely sufficiently strongly to survive, except for the one erected by the VIIIth-dynasty king, Ibi, at Sakkara.

Political conditions also increased the popularity of the rock-cut tomb, which was more secure than a mastaba. The usual plan is a façade cut into the cliff-face in front of a decorated chamber or series of chambers from the floor of which a hidden shaft leads down to the burial vault. Often several generations of the family were buried in the same tomb. Not until the emergence of stable government in the Middle Kingdom could more elaborate monuments be undertaken [39].

39. Exterior of the rock-cut tomb of Harkhuf at Aswan. He is shown with his son on the panels beside the doorway together with the inscriptions recording his expedition into Nubia. VIth–dynasty.

38. Map of Egypt and neighbouring countries.

MIDDLE KINGDOM AND SECOND INTERMEDIATE PERIOD

Lower Egypt: Upper Egypt:
Xth dynasty c. *2130–2040*   *XIth dynasty* c. *2133–1991*

                                                   Mentuhotep I
                                                   Intef I (Inyotef)
                                                   Intef II
                                                   Intef III

Mentuhotep II 2060–2010
Mentuhotep III
Mentuhotep IV

XIIth dynasty 1991–1786

Ammenemes I 1991–1962
Sesostris I 1971–1928
Ammenemes II 1929–1865
Sesostris II 1897–1878
Sesostris III 1878–1843
Ammenemes III 1842–1797
Ammenemes IV 1798–1790
Sobekneferu 1789–1786

XIVth dynasty c. *1786–1603* (at Xois)   *XIIIth dynasty* c. *1786–1633*

XVth dynasty c. *1674–1567* ('*GreatHyksos*')
XVIth dynasty c. *1684–1567* (*Minor Hyksos Chiefs*)
←————————————*XVIIth dynasty* c. *1650–1552*

XVIIIth dynasty c. *1552–*

5

The Middle Kingdom

Sometime during the IXth dynasty the hitherto almost unknown city of Thebes emerged, first as the new capital of the Fourth Upper Egyptian nome under a line of nomarchs of the Intef family, and then as leader of the rebel coalition in southern Upper Egypt, the area called the Head of the South. A fierce struggle was fought for Abydos and eventually the Intefs apparently felt strong enough to claim the title of king, *c.* 2133 BC, and formed the XIth dynasty.

This new dynasty at first controlled only Upper Egypt: Wahankh Intef II captured the Thinite nome and under his successors the Heracleopolitans came to accept the situation and a trading relationship emerged. When Mentuhotep II came to the throne in 2060 BC, however, his youthfulness encouraged them to try to recover the city of Thinis, but the new king carried the battle into their territory and Heracleopolis eventually fell in about 2040 BC. A policy of restoration was put in hand at once. Some nomarch families changed allegiance and continued in office, and trusted Thebans were appointed to many state offices. Mediterranean trade was restored and contact with Nubia re-established.

The XIIth dynasty was founded by a usurper, the vizier Ammenemes, who under Mentuhotep IV had led an expedition of 10,000 men to the Wadi Hammamat to quarry stone for the royal sarcophagus. The changeover of power seems to have been smoothly effected and, as the central government increased its hold on the country, the capital was moved from Thebes to Ithet Tawy, near Memphis, a more convenient administrative centre from which to administer the re-unified kingdom [40].

The successors of Ammenemes I were vigorous rulers: Nubia was conquered under Sesostris I, and the relatively peaceful reigns of Ammenemes II and Sesostris II saw many cultural and mercantile contacts with Western Asia. Mining operations were re-opened in Sinai, in spite of Bedouin pressure on the border along the Isthmus of Suez. The period is also noteworthy for large-scale public works, such as the canal which Sesostris III built through the First Cataract, probably on the line of Merenre''s, and the barrage across the Hawara Channel to lower the water level in the Fayyum and reclaim some 6,800 hectares of land.

The trauma of the collapse of the monarchy in the VIth dynasty was still felt and appears to have bred, amongst other things, a practical concern for the welfare of the people. The king was regarded as the shepherd of his subjects, following the *Precepts for King Merikare'*, which warned him to rule justly, for after death comes judgement—even for kings. A degree of self-examination not found in the Old Kingdom is also seen in the monuments and literature: the realistic portraits of this period show the worries and preoccupations of human rulers, rather than the sublime self-confidence of the gods of the Old Kingdom. The rulers confirmed their control by undermining the power of the feudal

40. Right: limestone relief of Mentuhotep II
dispatching a fallen Libyan chieftain identified
by a feather in his hand, and a fish hanging
behind him. The relief, from Gebelein, is now in
the Cairo Museum. Below: King Ramesses III
about to slaughter a number of foreign captives
in the presence of Amun. Below the king are two
lines of ovals, each containing the name of a
foreign city which he had supposedly conquered, and surmounted by the figure of its
bound chieftain. From the front of the pylon of
the funerary temple of Ramesses III, Medinet
Habu, Thebes. These two reliefs each re-echo
the earliest occurrence of this motif on the
Narmer palette, interpreted in the contemporary
style [cf. 13, 113].

lords. Sons no longer automatically succeeded to their father's position, but
were appointed to different posts and, as the old principle of hereditary appointments was broken, a new class of civil servants was formed. Sirenput, the
nomarch of Aswan, a descendant of the Old Kingdom nomarch family of
Hekaib, exercised considerable power under Sesostris I and built an impressive
tomb but, like many others throughout Egypt, his family disappeared in the
reign of Sesostris III.

ARCHITECTURE

The XIth-dynasty rulers continued the burial customs of their nomarch ances-
tors and remained uninfluenced by the Memphite style. Their cemetery at
Thebes represented a departure from the traditional royal cemeteries near
Memphis and was the first use of what was to become the final resting-place of
some of Egypt's greatest rulers. At Dra Abu-el-Naga, on the level ground at the

eastern edge of the mouth of the Valley of the Kings, are a group of tombs of the *saff* type. To make height for a façade a sunken courtyard was sloped down until it was some 3–4 m. deep and a row (Arabic *saff*, hence the name) of openings was cut, leading through to a main chamber with subsidiary chambers for courtiers' burials on either side of the courtyard. Three tombs, with very large forecourts some 60–70 m. wide, and orientated towards Thebes, were identified as the tombs of Intef I and II and Mentuhotep I by their excavator, H. E. Winlock, on the basis of stelai either found in them or alleged to come from them. Above the portico of these tombs a small brick pyramid was raised on a platform, and there may have been a small temple in the courtyard.

Mentuhotep II moved to a new site slightly to the south, in the cliff-bay of Deir el-Bahri, where, hard against the cliff-face, he built a terraced temple, surmounted by a pyramid, and approached by a causeway and ramp passing through a grove of trees [*Pl 9*]. On a podium in the centre of this a pyramid probably stood, although this has recently been questioned, with an ambulatory and colonnade around it. Behind the podium is an open court with a cloister-like colonnade, and beyond that a densely pillared hall with a small shrine at the back wall, against the cliff-face. On the northern side of the ramp is a shaft and passage leading to a chamber below the pyramid, containing an empty wooden coffin and a linen-wrapped statue of Mentuhotep in Sed festival regalia. A sloping passage from the rear court led to a granite-lined chamber below the shrine. This was the actual burial chamber, but it had been entered in antiquity and there was little there beside the alabaster and granite shrine that originally held the king's burial.

Between the podium and cloister was a row of six shrines and beneath them six vertical shafts leading to small chambers containing the burials of ladies of the royal family. Their entrances had been obscured by modifications to the original plan and their contents (notably the superbly carved limestone sarcophagi of queens Kawit [114] and Ashayet) remained intact.

A platform and the line of an unfinished causeway in a similar bay just to the south indicate the beginning of a similar construction by Mentuhotep III, but Mentuhotep II's monument remained unique until Hatshepsut built hers alongside. It represents a hybrid between the local *saff* tombs and the pyramid tomb. The portico and courtyard come from the *saff* tomb, and the smaller tombs of nobles alongside the causeway reflect the subsidiary burials in the *saff* courtyard. On the other hand the pyramid is clearly inspired by the Old Kingdom tradition, although it is superimposed on the funerary temple instead of behind it.

With the removal of the XIIth-dynasty court to a northern capital (Ithet Tawy) we are back in pyramid country proper, and it is no surprise to find that this form of royal burial became once again fashionable. Ammenemes I retained something of the Intef tradition by building his pyramid at Lisht [41] on a terrace above the funerary temple, but in other respects it follows the plan of VIth-dynasty pyramids, as does the better preserved tomb of his successor. Sesostris I's valley temple has disappeared but the causeway, originally lined with Osirid statues of the king, leads to a cloistered court which contained ten statues of the king set against the rectangular pillars, and now in the Cairo Museum. Behind this lies the mortuary temple, a range of long store-rooms around a small courtyard containing five now empty statue niches in front of a sanctuary which backs on to the pyramid. The solid mass of the pyramid itself is divided diagonally and crosswise by massive stone walls into sixteen compart-

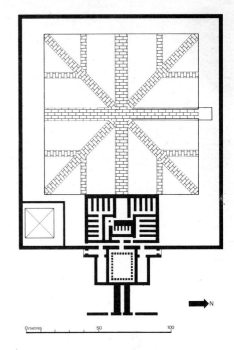

41. Plan of the pyramid of Sesostris I at Lisht, showing the arrangement of the mud-brick walls that reinforce the mass.

42. Pyramidion or capstone from a pyramid, inscribed with the name of Ammenemes III, found beside his pyramid at Dahshur. Grey basalt, length of base 1·85 m., height 1·4 m. Now in the Cairo Museum.

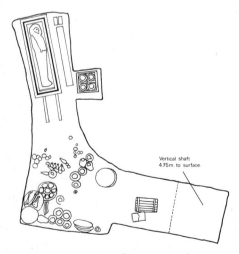

Vertical shaft
4·75m. to surface.

43. Plan and section of the tomb of the lady Senebtisi at Lisht, showing the position of the body and funerary provisions. A wall was built across the corridor at the bottom of the shaft and the shaft was filled with rubble. Early XIIth-dynasty.

ments. These are filled with rough blocks of local limestone and cased in fine Tura limestone. A narrow passage leads from the north face to the burial chamber, now submerged and inaccessible because of a rise in the water-table. Around the pyramid is a courtyard enclosing nine subsidiary pyramids, each with its own mortuary chapel.

Sesostris II reverted even more closely to Old Kingdom practice by building himself a mastaba at Abydos as well as his pyramid at Lahun, where he built on an existing outcrop, but, contrary to custom, put the entrance on the south side. As well as a rock-cut cenotaph at Abydos, Sesostris III built a pyramid at Dahshur. It had a core of mud-brick, and was protected by a maze of subterranean passages, approached from an entrance away from the pyramid on its western flank. Ammenemes III took this method of protection to its ultimate conclusion in his pyramid at Hawara, where the funerary temple covered a vast area (forty-six hectares) with, according to Strabo, a separate court for each nome so arranged that the building was dubbed the 'Labyrinth' by the Greeks. The pyramid itself lay to the north of this maze, and the subterranean burial chamber was approached by a complex passage, with confusing dead ends, leading through traps in the roof blocked by heavy sliding stones, and past dummy wells and chambers filled with stone to trick plunderers into time-wasting excavation. The chamber was a single block of quartzite $7 \times 3 \times 2$ m. high, hollowed out to form a box. The chamber was capped by three slabs of quartzite beneath two relieving chambers and was so arranged that the third slab could be slid into place from the antechamber after the mummy was installed in its quartzite sarcophagus. However, even this ingenious stratagem did not defeat the persistence of the plunderers [42].

The *saff* tombs of the Intef rulers contained burial chambers for their courtiers in the side porticoes. In the same way, the bay of Deir el-Bahri was treated as a large *saff* courtyard and the nobles of Mentuhotep II were buried in rock tombs ranged alongside the causeway to his monument. The usual construction was a long corridor, opening high in the cliff-face and running back to a square room, from which a passage descended to the burial chamber. In front, the face of the cliff was smoothed to a gradient, marked off by mud-brick walls.

Away from Thebes, the nomarchs continued the earlier tradition of rock-cut tombs, with local variations [43]. The most distinctive are at Qau el-Kebir, where they are built on a terrace plan, with a causeway leading to a colonnaded court and, on a higher terrace, a hypostyle hall in front of the tomb chapel. These may have been the link between the Old Kingdom pyramid complexes and the final layout of the Deir el-Bahri monument.

At Beni Hasan the rock-cut tomb chapels are arranged along a ledge about half-way up the cliff-face, with vertical burial shafts cut in the slopes in front of them [44]. The chapels themselves are remarkably spacious and fine polygonal columns, which purport to hold up the roof of solid rock, were left standing during the cutting of the chamber. Other rock-cut tombs were made at El-Bersheh and Meir.

The style of decoration employed in these tombs also reflects the local differences and the standard is not even constant at any one place. For instance, the tomb of Djar at Thebes is contemporary with, and similar in plan to, the tomb of Mentuhotep's vizier, Dagi, but its decoration is crude compared with the fine work in Dagi's tomb. The work at Aswan, El-Bersheh and Beni Hasan is competent but less good than the fine reliefs at Qau el-Kebir, Assiut and Meir.

56

These were executed according to the Memphite tradition established by crafts-men who had worked on the Old Kingdom tombs in these centres. The sunk relief work on the coffins of Kawit [114] and Ashayet shows this technique at its best. The outline is cut sharply at an acute angle to the surface, giving the firm line that Egyptian craftsmen admired. In the low reliefs on the shrine of Sesos-tris I at Karnak and on his pyramid temple at Lisht this outline is still clearly defined. The background is perfectly flat and the reliefs rise abruptly from it [46].

The subject-matter of the tomb painting varies little from the Old Kingdom motifs of agricultural and herding scenes, hunting in the swamp with throw-stick and spear and, in the desert, bird-trapping and fishing. One new subject is weaving and spinning, and there is reference to the political troubles in scenes of sieges and battles waged between two groups of Egyptians.

The servant figurines of the Old Kingdom are replaced by sets of model figures in painted wood, engaged in the same tasks as the figures in the wall-

46. The reconstructed shrine or processional temple of Sesostris I at Karnak, almost the only Middle Kingdom religious building to survive.

47. Granite statue of King Sesostris III from the temple of Mentuhotep II at Deir el-Bahri. Now in the Cairo Museum. Present height 1·48 m.

paintings. A particularly fine series was found in the tomb of Se'ankhkare''s chancellor, Meketre'. Squads of model soldiers are also found arranged in orderly rows and carrying their shields and weapons [92].

Another new feature, a direct result of the pride of the nomarchs in their local achievements and prestige, is the portrayal of individual or historical scenes related to specific events, not just the daily routine work on the estate. The most striking of these show the transport of a colossal statue (in the tomb of Djehuti-hotep at El-Bersheh) and the arrival of a group of western Asiatic nomads (in Khnumhotep's tomb at Beni Hasan). Also in Middle Kingdom work we find irregular division of the wall space. Although registers were still used, the wall was designed as a whole, with dominant figures of the owner of the tomb and other important people in prominent positions, and held together by a running frieze, usually depicting desert hunts, along the top. The remainder of the wall was filled with the traditional type of scene arranged in conventional registers.

The non-funerary monuments of the Middle Kingdom have almost completely disappeared, but enough remains to indicate the grand scale on which they were executed. One of the two granite obelisks that stood in front of the temple of Sesostris I at Heliopolis, which was dedicated to Re', remains. Another obelisk, with a rounded top, lay broken at Abgig in the Fayyum (but has now been erected just outside Medinet el-Fayyum), and some massive granite papyriform columns survive from the Sobek temple of Ammenemes III in the Fayyum. Also in the Fayyum, at Biyahmu, were two colossal statues of Ammenemes III, of which only the huge bases are now extant.

The plans of the Montu temple of Sesostris I at Tod and those for the larger building of Sesostris III at Medamud show that the general plan of the great cult temples had now been worked out. The small shrine of Renenutet erected by Ammenemes III and IV at Medinet Ma'adi on the western edge of the Fayyum is still well preserved, showing a porch with papyrus columns in front of a hall and tripartite sanctuary. However, the most famous of Middle Kingdom buildings is doubtless the limestone kiosk of Sesostris I, reconstructed from blocks that had been re-used in the Third Pylon of Amenophis III, at Karnak [46]. Ramps rise up to opposite sides of the base, on the four sides of which stand square pillars, connected by a low round-topped balustrade, supporting a flat roof. In the centre stand four more pillars around a stone pedestal, on which the barque of Amun might have rested during processions, but the meticulous carved reliefs and inscriptions indicate that it was originally built as a pavilion for Sesostris's Sed festival.

Other buildings at Thebes have not survived so fortunately. Work began on the great temple of Amun at Karnak under Sesostris I, but little more than the foundations survive. A small cult temple was also erected on the cliff-top at the opening of the Valley of the Kings, consisting of a 10 m. square mud-brick chapel in an enclosure which opened towards the river through the earliest recorded pylon gateway.

ART

One of the finest legacies from the Middle Kingdom is a series of truly great royal portraits. Like the relief carving, the early XIth-dynasty pieces are comparatively free from the traditions imposed by the Memphite School, although the reunion of the Two Lands meant that these were soon reasserted. The realistic approach of the Theban artists did not, however, succumb, but combined with the technical ability of the Memphis craftsmen to produce several masterpieces.

The massive sandstone statue of Mentuhotep II from his funerary temple is perfectly preserved and shows its fine painted finish [*Pl 6*]. The skin is black, the crown red and the robe white. Other portraits, such as the limestone series of Sesostris I from his pyramid temple at Lisht, show the king wearing the *nemes* headdress, and Sesostris III and Ammenemes III are sometimes represented in sphinx form.

The summit of the sculptor's skill is achieved in these portraits. The artist well characterizes Sesostris III's grim determination and strength, although some of the later statues that this monarch erected at Deir el-Bahri show a more careworn face. The Ammenemes III portraits were made in considerable numbers in the royal workshops and tend to follow a more rigid set of conventions. Even so, they are powerful portraits of a strong individual [47].

There are comparatively few examples of statues of private individuals from the Middle Kingdom. A VIth-dynasty worthy, Heka–ib, was a kind of local saint at Aswan and several later nomarchs dedicated statues to him which reflect the realism and vigour of the royal portraits. Most of the private sculptors, however, are in the form of block-statues, in which the body is sculpted in a squatting position, covered by a long garment, and inscribed on the flat surfaces with the man's names and titles [48].

The few large-scale works that survive are often badly damaged, such as the seated limestone figure of Senet, wife of Antefoker, vizier of Sesostris I, and the over life-size figures of nomarchs at Qau el-Kebir. The finest piece was found in Nubia: a seated figure of Sennuwy, wife of Hapdjefy of Assiut, provincial governor of Kerma. Although in the best Memphite tradition, it seems to have been made in local Nubian granite.

Other Egyptian statues were found in Syria–Palestine. Several sphinx statues of Ammenemes III and IV and of members of the royal family were presented to the local rulers at Ugarit, Qatna and Byblos; and statues of Egyptian individuals may have been brought along by diplomats such as Djehuti-hotep, nomarch of Hermopolis, whose statues were found at Megiddo. There may have been an Egyptian colony at Byblos, where several Egyptian objects were found, as well as inscriptions of local princes in Egyptian style. Other statues, found at Knossos in Crete, and Kurigen Kale and Adana in Anatolia, were probably taken along by traders.

At the end of the XIIth dynasty, there were a series of tumuli burials at Kerma in Nubia, the seat of the Egyptian colonial administrators. In each tumulus the dead man lay on an ivory inlaid wooden bed in a brick chamber, accompanied by several retainers who had been buried alive. The statues of Hapdjefy and his wife Sennuwy were found in one of these tumuli. He had prepared a magnificent tomb in his home town of Assiut, but it has been suggested that he may have died in office as governor and been buried according to local custom.

Foreign contact, however, was not all in one direction: a number of foreign objects of this date are found in Egypt. Most notable is the foundation deposit (see p. 200) below the temple at Tod, consisting of four copper boxes bearing cartouches of Ammenemes II and containing Asiatic silver ingots, vessels and other objects. Middle Minoan II Kamares ware has been found at Abydos and Lahun, and recently as far south as Aswan. This interchange continued into the Second Intermediate Period, for Middle Minoan III ware was found at Lisht, while so-called Tell el-Yahudiyeh ware is so commonly found in Lower

48. Block statue of a man named Snab inscribed with the offering formula. XVIth–dynasty. Now in the Gulbenkian Museum of Oriental Art, University of Durham. Height 52 cm.

Egypt that it was originally thought to be a distinctively Hyksos ware, instead of the Palestinian import that is now suggested.

THE SECOND INTERMEDIATE PERIOD

THE END OF THE MIDDLE KINGDOM

The last ruler of the XIIth dynasty was a queen, Sobekneferu, probably because there was no male heir, and lack of dynastic continuity was a major source of weakness in the XIIIth dynasty. Within 150 years there were about sixty kings, mostly of Theban origin, some of quite humble birth, relying heavily on their viziers who were more stable than their masters. The vizier Ankhu, for instance, has left monuments that indicate that he held sway during the reigns of at least five kings. This continuity of the central government meant that, at first, Egypt's prestige abroad was not at risk, as Egyptian objects from Semna in the south to Byblos in the north make clear. But there were also foreign influences working in Egypt, and by about 1720 BC, Asiatic intruders were strong enough to claim authority over the eastern Delta around Avaris. This pressure gradually increased until *c.* 1674 BC, when they occupied the northern capital of Memphis, and the remaining Egyptian rulers in Manetho's XIIIth dynasty were local governors and nomarchs.

In the western Delta an earlier secession took place at the beginning of the XIIIth dynasty, when an independent rule was established at Xois. This line of rulers forms the XIVth dynasty and their local independence was stoutly maintained until about 1603 BC.

THE HYKSOS

The pressure of Asiatic intruders on Egypt began in the First Intermediate Period (see p. 48) and the 'Wall of the Prince' was maintained throughout the Middle Kingdom. Nevertheless, some immigrants passed this barrier as the painting in Khnumhotep's tomb illustrates, and as the biblical story of Abraham records (Genesis XII, 10–20). The movement gained momentum rapidly during the weak XIIIth dynasty and, beginning in the eastern Delta, these intruders soon occupied Lower Egypt. The chiefs of these groups were called by the Egyptians *Hikau-Khaswet*, 'Rulers of the Foreign Lands'. Manetho applies this term, in a Graecized form 'Hyksos' and wrongly understood as meaning 'Shepherd Kings', to the people as a whole, a practice followed by Egyptologists.

The Hyksos rulers form two dynasties: the XVth and XVIth. The first of these was a powerful line of six kings, who continued Egypt's foreign trade contacts. Scarabs of the treasurer, Har, are known from as far apart as Kerma and Gaza and objects of Khyan, the third ruler, were traded in Knossos and Baghdad. However, from this time onwards Egyptian opposition, once more centred on Thebes, forced them to withdraw to their Delta enclave. Contemporary with these rulers was a large number of minor chiefs, who also used the royal titulary and are grouped together and known as the XVIth dynasty.

Although their domination was achieved by infiltration and not, as was once supposed, by sudden martial invasion, there must have been some conflict as pressure from the Hyksos developed. But after their control was established a *modus vivendi* evolved. The administration was not unduly oppressive: it was probably largely carried out by Egyptian civil servants and generally accepted. The picture of cruel destructive barbarians seems to have been mainly projected by later nationalistic propaganda.

Throughout this period, cultural life and artistic standards declined less than they had in the First Intermediate Period. XIIIth-dynasty rulers, though neither rich enough nor powerful enough to continue major building projects, did maintain the tradition of pyramid tombs, and the few surviving royal and private statues show that the craft schools were still operating. The Hyksos rulers patronized workers in the classical Egyptian style for their own monuments, and indicated their approval by copying good Middle Kingdom pieces or simply by usurping them (an even more sincere form of flattery!). Apophis II, for example, took over two sphinxes of Ammenemes II and two colossal statues of the XIIIth-dynasty king, Semenkhkare'.

The introduction of the worship of a Semitic god, quickly identified with Seth, no doubt entailed the construction of new temples and the Hyksos recorded their repairs and improvements to existing ones. Their nomadic origins meant that they had had no opportunity to develop their own architectural or monumental style, but they did expose the Egyptians to many other foreign influences and ideas. Their practical contributions include the introduction of the horse and chariot, the composite bow and vertical loom. They also forced the Egyptians to realize that their Asiatic neighbours could not be kept permanently at bay, and from this point onwards there were close cultural ties with western Asia, and people, objects and ideas moved constantly between the two areas.

THE BEGINNINGS OF RESISTANCE

When the court of the XIIIth dynasty returned to their home city of Thebes after the fall of Ithet Tawy it became the focal point of Egyptian nationalism and resistance. A new dynasty (the XVIth dynasty) emerged, which at first could not afford to antagonize its neighbours, and limited its ambitions to establishing its rule in Upper Egypt. The policy of mutual tolerance became more strained as the Thebans became stronger. The Hyksos ruler, Apophis, attempted to pick a quarrel with Seqenenre', and later Awoserre' wrote to the Nubian chiefs urging them to attack the Thebans. Although the Nubians had regained their independence during Egypt's weakness, they had maintained an Egyptianizing culture and came instead to the support of the Thebans and fought as mercenaries under Kamose, when he began the final stage of the war of independence.

The burials of the XVIIth-dynasty rulers are near those of the Intefs among the foothills of Dra Abu-el-Naga at western Thebes. A tomb robber of the XXth dynasty described in his confession how he and his companions:

. . . broke through the tomb of the king [Sebekemsaf] in the rear chamber. We found the deep shaft and took torches in our hands and went down. We broke down the rubble wall, which we found at the mouth of the passage, and found the god lying at the back of his tomb, and we found the tomb of his queen, Nubkha''a, . . . likewise. We opened their sarcophagi and their coffins . . . and found the noble mummy of the king with a scimitar. There were many amulets and gold jewels round his neck and he wore a mask of gold. The noble mummy of the king was completely covered with gold and his coffins were ornamented with gold and silver inside and out and inlaid with all kinds of precious stones. We collected the gold . . . and set fire to their coffins. We took the equipment which we found with them, objects of gold, silver and bronze, and divided it amongst ourselves . . . twenty *deben* of gold fell to each of us.

The XVIIth-dynasty rulers left little else in the way of monuments. Too much of their energy and resources was employed in fighting for independence to allow for monumental sculpture and large public buildings.

During the Hyksos occupation of northern Egypt there appear in the south, at a number of sites ranging from Assiut to Aswan, a series of round, shallow graves belonging to the groups of Nubian mercenaries brought in to assist the Theban rulers in the liberation struggle. During the XVIIth dynasty, however, their graves are distinctive both in shape and in the types of objects found in them. These include leather goods, belts, archers' wrist-guards and, appropriately for mercenaries, their own weapons—axes, daggers, bows and arrows—and a considerable quantity of jewellery. They have their own distinctive pottery and bead work. Bones and horns of a variety of animals painted with crude designs of rings, spots and crosses in red and black paint are also found in these graves. The excavators also reported a characteristic strong smell from an unguent used in the burial. By the time of the explosion of the Hyksos, these immigrants had become completely Egyptianized, and no distinguishable archaeological trace remains of the presence.

NEW KINGDOM

XVIIIth dynasty	*c.* 1552–1306	*c.* 1552–1295
Before the Amarna period:	*Date of accession*	*Date of accession*
Ahmose	1552	1552
Amenophis I (Amenhotep)	1527	1527
Tuthmosis I (Thutmose)	1506	1506
Tuthmosis II	1493	1493
Queen Hatshepsut	1490–1468	1479
Tuthmosis III	1490–1436	1479
Amenophis II	1438	1427
Tuthmosis IV	1412	1401
Amenophis III	1402–1364	1391
Amarna period:		
Amenophis IV (Akhenaten)	1374*–1358	1363*–1350
Smenkhkare'	1360*–1357	1349*–1346
Tutankhamun	1357	1346
Ay	1348	1337
Horemheb (Haremhab)	1344–1306	1333–1295
The Ramessides		
XIXth dynasty	*c.* 1306–1195	*c.* 1295–1184
Ramesses I	1306	1295
Seti I (Sethos)	1305	1294
Ramesses II	*c.* 1290	1279–
Merenptah (Merneptah)	1224–1214	1213–1203
Siptah	1203–1197	1192–1186
Queen Tewosret	1203–1195	1112–1184
XXth dynasty	*c.* 1195–1069	*c.* 1184–1069
Ramesses III	1193–1162	1182–1151

N.B. Two possible systems of dating are possible for this period. The available evidence does not make it possible to decide in favour of either one.   * Indicates co-regencies.

6

The New Kingdom

THE XVIIIth DYNASTY: BEFORE AMARNA

Kamose's struggle against the Hyksos was carried to its conclusion by Ahmose, who forced them into Palestine and besieged them at Sharuhen near Gaza for three years. He then turned his attention to restoring Egypt's control of Nubia, campaigning as far south as the Second Cataract. Amenophis I followed him into Nubia and the following king, Tuthmosis I, occupied Syria–Palestine as far as the Euphrates.

Egypt now had a new policy in Palestine: the old practice of establishing trade-links by setting up Egyptian merchant colonies in major towns was dropped in favour of an overt martial policy of control through vassal states paying annual tribute, and occasionally reinforced by a military presence. This, at any rate, was how the Egyptians chose to see the relationship. With the memory of domination by the Hyksos ever present in Egyptian minds, Syria–Palestine was made into a kind of buffer state between Egypt and the newly apparent threat from Mitanni, a kingdom occupying the area between the Euphrates and Tigris in their upper stretches.

Tuthmosis II was succeeded by his nine-year-old son, two older ones having predeceased him. His widow, Hatshepsut, acted as regent for young Tuthmosis III, but in the second year of his reign assumed full regal powers herself and became the dominant partner of a co-regency. She embarked on a massive programme of building and restoration and also of exploration and trade, including a large expedition to the fabled land of Punt on the African coast. This left little time for military activity and when, after twenty years, she died, leaving Tuthmosis III the sole ruler, he was obliged to undertake a vigorous programme of yearly campaigns in Syria–Palestine to win back and consolidate his control.

Both Tuthmosis III and his son Amenophis II claimed great prowess as sportsmen, particularly as crack shots with their immensely powerful bows, with which they could pierce a bronze target. This was a tense period for Egypt, for military 'policing' operations continued in Nubia and Syria, and though Amenophis might scoff at his enemies, calling one 'The Old Woman of Arpakh', forceful leaders were still required to maintain Egypt's pre-eminent position.

There was perhaps a slight hitch in the dynastic succession for the next king, Tuthmosis IV, seemed to find it useful to back up his claim to the throne with the story that he had been helped to it by Re'-Horakhty in return for restoring the god's image, the Great Sphinx at Giza, and clearing sand from it. He also embarked on a diplomatic marriage with a Mitannian princess, a practice which Amenophis III, his successor, took up with enthusiasm. Not content with a sister of the king of Babylon and another of Tushratta of Mitanni, he was

49. Amenophis II in his chariot shooting arrows at a standing target and at a target of copper; granite block from Karnak. Now in Luxor Museum.

negotiating for a daughter of each ruler when he died. He was well advised to seek alliances with these powers. Mitanni had been fairly subdued after the attacks of Tuthmosis I and III and further weakened by internal feuds, but these had given the newly emerging Hittite powers in Asia Minor an excuse to interfere, and Egypt felt threatened by these northern powers.

The effects of being an imperial power were soon felt. Booty and tribute from the subject states encouraged a taste for luxury that contrasts with the earlier sobriety of taste in dress, food, art and life-style. Foreigners now settled in Egypt in great numbers, some as merchants, others as mercenaries and yet others as prisoners of war in various employment. Their language, their religion and other aspects of their culture were absorbed in large measure and, although Egypt dominated the Levant politically, she was culturally subject to much foreign influence.

MONUMENTS

The XVIIIth-dynasty rulers set a completely new trend in burial customs, abandoning the pyramid (although Ahmose built one at Abydos as a cenotaph) in favour of a less conspicuous tomb in the Valley of the Kings [*Pl 1*], a wadi opening just north of Dra Abu-el-Naga and running back behind the cliffs where Mentuhotep and his courtiers lay buried. The first tomb, for Amenophis I, was cut on Dra Abu-el-Naga, but from Tuthmosis I onwards the normal practice was for the funerary temple to be built on the edge of the cultivation, while the tomb was cut under close supervision in the guarded valley. Ineni, who cut the tomb of Tuthmosis I, records that he 'supervised the cutting of the tomb of His Majesty, all alone, none seeing, none hearing' and, what is even more unlikely, he did it without swearing!

There were some slight developments in the general plan of successive tombs. Essentially, however, they consisted of a dressed stone doorway leading to a long passageway sloping downward, divided by portals and short flights of steps, with a few small niches in the side walls to accommodate guardian statues. There is usually one right-angled turn in the passage: Amenophis III

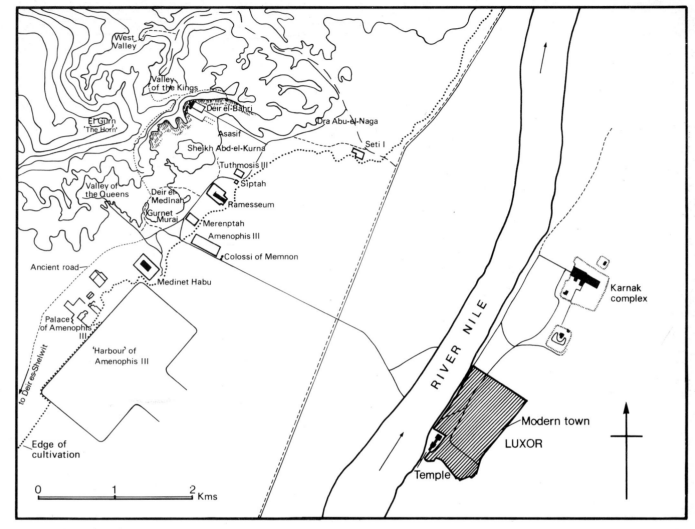

West Valley

Valley of the Kings

Deir el-Bahri

Dra Abu-el-Naga

El Gurn 'The Horn'

Asasif

Seti I

Sheikh Abd-el-Kurna

Tuthmosis III

Siptah

Valley of the Queens

Deir el Medinah

Ramesseum

Gurnet Murai

Merenptah

Amenophis III

Colossi of Memnon

Ancient road

Medinet Habu

Palace of Amenophis III

'Harbour' of Amenophis III

to Deir es-Shelwit

Edge of cultivation

0   1   2 Kms

RIVER NILE

Karnak complex

Modern town

LUXOR

Temple

and Tuthmosis IV had two, in opposite directions. The length of the passage varies from about 15 m. in the case of Tuthmosis I, to 184 m. in the long, curving corridor of Hatshepsut.

The burial chamber itself is approached through a vestibule and often has smaller rooms leading off it. In some cases, the corners of the chamber are rounded to give, in plan, the effect of a royal cartouche. The sarcophagus stood in a shallow depression, across the long axis of the room and away from the walls at the innermost end. The walls of the chambers and passages were decorated with texts and scenes from the funerary books, and are alive with monstrous demons among whom the king walks, guided by guardian spirits, to take his place in the great boat of the sun god.

Time has dealt harshly with the funerary temples erected in the main Nile valley to go with these tombs. Even the position of some temples is a matter of guesswork, but there is no doubt about the temple of Hatshepsut or of its place in the history of architecture, for it is a truly spectacular example of architectural skill. The man responsible, Senmut, a favourite of Hatshepsut, based his design on the temple of Mentuhotep II, which lay immediately alongside the site chosen for Hatshepsut's, and copied the design of the terraced

50. Map of Thebes, modern Luxor, to show the funerary temples and tombs of western Thebes, and the temples of Amun at Karnak and Luxor.

65

courts. Both temples are designed, not to challenge the height of the great cliffs behind, but to match their horizontal strata in the terracing and repeat the vertical striations and erosion lines in the colonnades. It is difficult to conceive of a design that could better suit so magnificent a situation and even enhance it [Frontispiece, *Pl 9*].

Hatshepsut's temple is on a larger scale than Mentuhotep's, with two large terraced courts approached by ramps and faced with double colonnades. Behind the colonnades are carved reliefs depicting events from her reign, such as the transfer of two obelisks from Aswan to Karnak [56], and a detailed account of the expedition to Punt with views of the native houses, loading of the boats and so on. Behind the northern colonnade on the second terrace a series of scenes recounting the queen's divine birth is carved: she perhaps felt it was necessary to support her rather dubious seizure of royal power by a fictitious account of the visit of Amun to her mother, Queen Ahmes, wife of Tuthmosis I, which resulted in her conception and birth as the god's daughter. A small chapel was built at either end of the second colonnade, with pillared forehall and shrine cut into the rock-face; at the north end is the chapel of Anubis, where the original colouring of the reliefs is least damaged, and at the south end is the larger chapel of Hathor. The centre of the third and uppermost terrace was occupied by a colonnaded hall behind a double colonnade of sixteen-sided columns and colossal Osirid statues of Hatshepsut. To the south was a mortuary chapel for Hatshepsut and her mortal father Tuthmosis I. To the north was a new feature in mortuary temples, a chapel open to the sky dedicated to Re'. The rock wall at the rear has a row of statue niches and a shrine, cut back into the rock, that was added or re-dedicated in Ptolemaic times to Imhotep and Amenhotep, son of Hapu.

Hatshepsut originally had a tomb sited away from the Valley of the Kings and equipped with a heavy quartzite coffin, but as 'king' she had a new tomb cut in the valley. However, her plan for a long corridor through the mountain, giving access to her burial chamber just behind her temple, was defeated by difficulties of working the rock.

The remains of a causeway running between the two large temples lead past the Hathor chapel to a terrace against the cliff face, where Tuthmosis III had erected a now much ruined festival temple. He and later rulers built their mortuary temples down by the cultivation, more or less in a line running from north to south [50]. Amenophis III also built a temple for his mortuary cult at Memphis, but his description of his temple at Thebes gives some impression of the sheer opulence of the age. It was built in fine sandstone, ornamented with gold, the floor of the shrine was paved with silver and the pillars were sheathed in electrum. The whole building was adorned with stelai and statues of granite, quartzite and precious stones, and built to last for ever.

In the XVIIIth dynasty there were, as always, important private tombs in many sites; and like the stone-built mastabas at Sakkara, decorated with fine reliefs showing scenes of daily life, but long ago robbed for building stone. The most important by far are the nobles' tombs in the cliffs on the west bank at Thebes. For nearly 400 years, from the beginning of the XVIIIth dynasty to the end of the XXth dynasty, the hills of Dra Abu-el-Naga, Sheikh Abd-el Kurna and Gurnet Murai were honeycombed with over 400 tomb pits and chapels, often breaking into earlier cuttings and re-using them. The tombs are now hopelessly intermixed with the houses of the present villagers, who in the last century and until quite recently made their living by exploiting the riches

deception

51. Tombs of the New Kingdom and Late Period: (A) plan of the subterranean chapel of Sennufer, Superintendent of the Garden of the Temple of Amun, *temp* Amenophis II. (B) Plan of the tomb chapel of the Army Commander Amenemhab, *temp* Tuthmosis III, with pillared broad hall. (C) Plan of the tomb chapel of the Superintendent of Agriculture, Menna, *temp* Tuthmosis IV, with a statue niche at the innermost end. (D) Tomb of King Tuthmosis III, Valley of the Kings, Thebes. The tomb has a steeply sloping access with a right-angled turn to a sarcophagus-shaped burial chamber. (E) Tomb of King Tutankhamun, Valley of the Kings, Thebes. Tiny by comparison with other royal tombs. (F) Tomb of Seti I, Valley of the Kings, Thebes. The largest of the royal tombs at Thebes, shown in plan and section to indicate the deep drainage pit at the end of the first two slopes and the attempt to put off robbers by concealing the continuation of the passage beneath a fake floor in the first chamber. (G) Tomb of Sennedjem at Deir el-Medinah showing the relationship of the underground rooms to the tomb chapel above, surmounted by a hollow, brick pyramid. (H) Two sections through a typical tomb of the XXVIth-dynasty at Sakkara. The tomb chamber, built at the bottom of a deep pit, was approached by the narrow shaft when the body was laid to rest and the burial sealed by filling the pits with sand. (B) and (C) illustrate the T-shaped plan of XVIIIth-dynasty tombs. (A) is unusual in having a chapel deep underground.

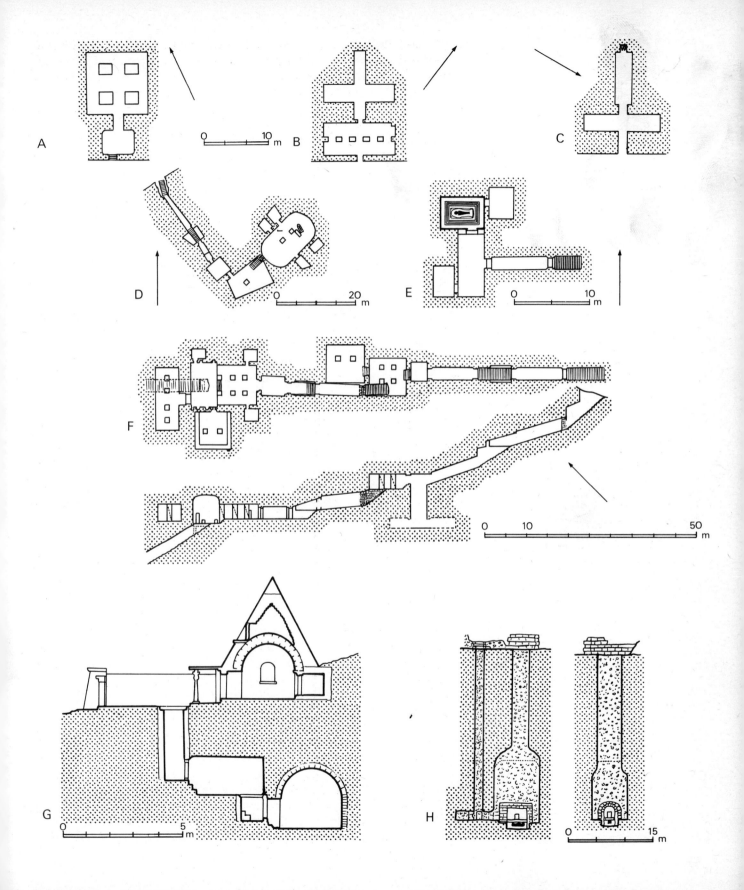

A

B

C

D

E

F

G

H

0   10 m

0   20 m

0   10 m

0   10   50 m

0   5 m

0   15 m

of the tombs and the naïvety of the tourists who visited them. Any attempt to excavate this area as systematically as Carter cleared the Valley of the Kings would mean destroying these homes and rehousing the people, a task which the government recently unsuccessfully attempted. Many of the tombs have been long known to the local population, and revealed only after all the removable items had been profitably sold: very few have been scientifically excavated and fewer properly published. There must be a considerable number still to be found [52].

The tombs vary in detail, but the usual plan consists of a walled courtyard against the smoothed-down cliff-face, behind which is cut a T-shaped chapel, the broad cross-piece of the 'T' being immediately behind the façade and the long 'stalk' running back into the cliff, terminating in a statue niche. Across the façade there may be a pillared portico. A shaft sunk in one corner of the courtyard leads to the subterranean burial chamber. Some contemporary illustrations show a small pyramid above the façade with a small stele in a niche on the east face. One painting even shows a garden and pool, but the difficulties of irrigation make this unlikely [51].

The size of the tomb varies. One of the largest is the tomb of Rekhmire', vizier in the time of Tuthmosis III and Amenophis II, which is a long hall, penetrating the hillside for 34 m. and gradually rising in height to 8 m. The tomb of another vizier, Ramose, who served Amenophis III, is unfinished but

53. Head of an unknown man, originally part of a group statue of the man and his wife. Mid–XVIIIth–dynasty. Now in the City Museum and Art Gallery, Birmingham.

has a spacious transverse hall 25 m. wide with thirty-two columns. Usually the tombs are more compact, and average about 10 m. across the transverse hall, with the long hall running back a similar distance.

The method of decoration in nearly all the tombs was by painting on a plastered surface, or on a gypsum wash if the rock surface was sufficiently good. A few tombs were decorated in a fine low relief, notably in the time of Hatshepsut and later in the reign of Amenophis III, but this largely depended on the quality of the rock, which was only suitable in some of the lower strata. Decoration in the painted tombs tends to change from brilliant colours on a light background at the beginning of the XVIIIth dynasty to quieter, more harmonious, even dull, colours by the time of Amenophis III. There is a similar tendency in the shape of figures which, at the beginning, are drawn individually and in sharp outline, but later they are grouped and overlapped and there are hints at perspective. Like contemporary sculpture, the drawing is detailed and refined and has a certain studied charm.

The decoration in the tombs is almost entirely restricted to the tomb chapel. The few actual burial chambers which are decorated have scenes from the *Book of the Dead* (see p. 209), although an exception is Sennufer's, mayor of Thebes in Amenophis II's reign, whose burial chamber is painted with scenes normally found in the tomb chapel.

These scenes are generally arranged according to a logical progression, beginning at the entrance with the tomb owner greeting the sun, then, in the broad hall, with scenes of his life, showing him supervising work on his estates and in his workshops, or relaxing at a party, or on a hunting expedition in the desert or marshes. The outer end of the long hall shows the funeral ritual, the 'Opening of the Mouth' (see p. 200), the funeral procession and the mourning relatives, while the innermost part of the chapel shows the man arriving in the Underworld, safely passing the guardian demons, surviving the great judgement and welcomed into the Afterworld by Anubis. At first, ceilings are painted in imitation of matting, but there is soon a change to colourful, geometric patterns incorporating stylized flowers, bucrania, and linked spirals. Sennufer again provides an exception, for much of his undulating ceiling was realistically painted with a beautiful vine, loaded with grapes.

The subjects of the paintings come from the now well established repertoire of tomb scenes, some of which were first met in the Old Kingdom mastabas. Now, the new craft of chariot-making is added and agricultural scenes often show field surveyors at work. Many of the officials are evidently proud of their political advancement and have themselves portrayed presiding over the reception of foreign tribute-bearers and ambassadors, or receiving promotion and the insignia of honour [Pl 30].

In addition to building their own mortuary temples, the XVIIIth dynasty observed their religious duty in building and embellishing the cult temples, in particular the two great temples at Thebes. The temple of Amon-Re' at Karnak, founded in the Middle Kingdom, now ruined, began to grow into a complex organism. Tuthmosis I built in front of it a series of shrines and halls, surrounded by a new enclosure wall faced with two large pylons and a pair of obelisks. Hatshepsut added two pairs of obelisks, two on the east side, now fragmentary, and two between pylons IV and V, one of which remains *in situ*. Tuthmosis III was a great benefactor of Karnak for, as well as venting his spite on Hatshepsut by roofing in her obelisks, he dug the great sacred lake, built the Ptah temple by the north gate and pylon VII on the south side, and commemorated his first Syrian campaign in the hall of another building behind the sanctuary, where he recorded with some imagination the flora and fauna of that country [57]. He also added an obelisk 33 m. high, which lay on its side until erected by Tuthmosis IV and now stands before the church of St John Lateran in Rome. Amenophis III erected pylon III, but his principal cult buildings at Karnak were the temple to the local god Montu, just outside the north gate, and to Amun's consort, Mut, just to the south, the home of the famous black granite statues of the lion-goddess Sekhmet, some 500 of which once sat or stood in the precincts [Pl 11].

Amenophis III's main building programme, however, was at the nearby temple of Amun-Mut-Khons at Luxor. The covered part of the temple consists of a series of pillared halls and vestibules leading to a shrine for the boat of Amun, and an inner shrine for the cult statue. The approach to this is remarkable. In front of the main cross-hall is a courtyard, 50 m. square, with a double row of pillars on three sides approached by a tall double line of pillars 16 m. high, and flanking walls. This fine courtyard with its elegantly proportioned pillars is entirely in keeping with the high standard of architecture already established by this dynasty at Deir el-Bahri [54].

Across the river, Amenophis III built the palace of Malkata, a huge estate incorporating parade grounds and small chapels, large audience halls richly

54. The southern end of the great court of Amenophis III in the temple of Amun at Luxor consists of a porch of columns four rows deep. Their capitals represent clusters of papyrus buds. Behind the porch, to the right of this view, stand the inner rooms of the temple, built on a slightly raised platform indicated here by the cavetto moulding.

decorated with painted walls, ceilings and floors, villas for government officials, offices, kitchens, workshops, and huts for the palace servants. Nearby is the great harbour of Birket Habu, 2·4 × 1 km., defined by the 12 m. high mounds of spoil excavated in its construction. It was almost certainly designed for ceremonial as well as mercantile use, but its identification with a so-called pleasure lake, whose construction is recorded on a large commemorative scarab, is now known to be mistaken.

Outside the capital city of Thebes the builders were also busy. There were large palaces at Deir el-Ballas, near Coptos, and Tuthmosis I erected a new palace at Memphis which served as the residence when the court moved to the northern end of the Two Kingdoms. Queen Hatshepsut claimed to have restored many monuments damaged during the years of Hyksos rule, and there are records of work on the Ptah temple at Memphis and the Osiris temple at Abydos, though little of this is visible today. Tuthmosis III erected a pair of obelisks at Heliopolis, which were removed in Roman times to Alexandria and much later to the Victoria Embankment, London and Central Park, New York. A number of temples were also erected in the cities of Syria–Palestine and in Nubia, where the Amun temple of Tuthmosis III at Gebel Barkal near Napata was especially famous.

STATUARY AND RELIEF

Royal statuary of this period was both monumental and numerous. Hatshepsut embellished her temple at Deir el-Bahri with over two hundred statues and sphinxes, most of them destroyed by Tuthmosis III; some of them twice life-size, some even larger, up to 8 m. high, but the truly colossal pieces are the statues of Amenophis III that stand before the site of his funerary temple. These statues, 21 m. high and each cut from a single block of stone transported from Heliopolis, are now usually known as the colossi of Memnon, after a Greek legendary hero [*Pl 10*].

The pieces all follow the established conventions and standard postures, although in the mortuary temples the dead king is now often depicted as a

55. Statue of Tetisheri, grandmother of Ahmose, the founder of the XVIIIth–dynasty, in limestone. Now in the British Museum, London. Height 37 cm.

56. Above: top of an obelisk of Queen Hatshepsut with a scene of the god Amun-Reʿ and the queen, who kneels before him wearing the Blue Crown of Pharoah. The figure of the god and his name were hacked out by Akhenaten's iconoclasts, but the damage was smoothed and the figure and name re-cut. XVIIIth–dynasty.

57. Right: some of the flora and fauna of Syria-Palestine depicted in relief in the Festival Hall of Tuthmosis III at the temple of Amun at Karnak in celebration of his campaigns in that area.

standing mummiform Osiris, an iconography first established in the mortuary temple of Sesostris I at Lisht. There is a noticeable tendency to idealize the subject and, by subtle altering of proportions, to achieve a better composition. Some of the kneeling statues, for instance, have overlong legs, but the portraits are probably realistic. There is certainly a distinctive 'Tuthmosid face', shared by Hatshepsut as well, and characterized by a prominent hooked nose. Throughout the dynasty the tendency to formalism increases and a highly calculated refined style is reached in the time of Amenophis III, with great attention paid to detailed work, reflecting the assured stability of a period that allowed opportunities for such precision. The tendency to an effeminate style that is often noted is perhaps due to the influence of Queen Hatshepsut's many works at the beginning of the dynasty [55].

Among statues of private individuals new types appear. The funerary statues now often stand at the inner end of the tomb chapel, carved *in situ* in a niche in the rock wall, while others show the deceased kneeling with a stele, on which is inscribed a short hymn to the sun. There are also votive statues, placed in the temples by permission of the king. These may be block statues or show the owner with an offering table or shrine.

The reliefs of the XVIIIth dynasty, like the statuary, continue the conventions and techniques of the Middle Kingdom with hardly any break. Most of the surviving examples are from the Theban area and those from early reigns are clearly influenced by the Middle Kingdom work in that area. Most of the work in the mortuary temples is now lost along with the buildings, but one may assume from the later Ramesside examples that the motifs were largely biographical, dwelling on the king's campaigns and his achievements in hunting and sport. The Hatshepsut Punt reliefs established her claim to extend Egyptian influence, and the obelisk relief reminded visitors of her devoted reconstruction work [56]. The flora and fauna of Syria, recorded by Tuthmosis III at Karnak, illustrate his military achievements and these are also recorded more explicitly on pylon VII in the same temple [57]; war scenes, however, do not occur as much as might be expected in a time of aggressive imperialism. Religious festivals and rituals are another important subject—for example, the Hathor festival depicted at Deir el-Bahri. Another interesting new feature are the two accounts of the divine birth of a ruler, Hatshepsut's at Deir el-Bahri and Amenophis III's at Luxor.

THE XVIIIth DYNASTY: THE AMARNA PERIOD
The campaigns in the early part of the XVIIIth dynasty brought considerable wealth into Egypt, much of which ended up in the hands of the priesthood of

Amun. The increased power of the priests became a serious threat to the stability of the throne and in an attempt to counteract this, various measures were taken: the city of Memphis was given increasing importance and political appointments were made amongst men who could be relied on to support the king in this conflict. New cults were developed and old rivals encouraged: the priesthood of the god Re' was advanced and chapels to him were erected even in the precincts of Karnak; and Amenophis III himself was actually worshipped as a god in the Nubian temples of Soleb and Sedinga. But these efforts were surpassed early in the reign of Amenophis IV.

The new king took up with fanatical zeal the worship of the sun, and in particular the life-giving disc or *Aten* of the sun. It was worshipped with increasing fervour throughout his reign, at first alongside other gods, then exclusively, and other gods were proscribed, their temples closed and their priesthoods disbanded. In the later stages temples and statues of other gods, especially Amun, were desecrated and their very names hacked out of inscriptions [58].

This was not just a political move, for if that were so the king had simply exchanged one set of priests for another. The source of much of the fanaticism and accompanying dogma and artistic tenets must be sought in the strange

58. Limestone relief found in the Royal Tomb at Amarna, probably a pattern for sculptors working on the chapel walls. Akhenaten leads Nefertiti and one of their daughters in worship of the Aten, offering bouquets of flowers to the god whose rays end in hands that give life to the royal family. The relief is carved in the supposedly realistic style of the king's early years, which seems in fact to result in over-emphasis of the king's singular physical attributes.

personality of the king himself. He appears from statues and other representations to have suffered from a glandular disorder usually diagnosed as Fröhlich's syndrome, although this is now impossible to check with certainty. The visible symptoms in the early royal portraits are a gaunt face and long jaw, large feminine breasts, abdomen and thighs. Together with this there was undoubtedly a highly developed artistic temperament and single-mindedness of religious purpose judged, according to one's viewpoint, as mental unbalance, artistic genius or prophetic vision [60].

The facts of the king's reign are few, and most of them are disputed. A few years after it began, possibly as co-regent with his father Amenophis III, he established a new capital dedicated to the Aten called Akhetaten, 'The horizon of the Aten', and changed his own name to Akhenaten, 'He who serves the Aten'. He later withdrew to Akhetaten, living there, with his queen Nefertiti and several daughters, a life apparently devoted to the worship of the Aten.*

Throughout the early period there was complete toleration shown by and to the Aten, but in Akhenaten's reign the Aten was elevated to a pre-eminent position and other cults were banned. It is likely that this was partly forced on Akhenaten by the priesthoods of the other gods, for had their opposition to the increasing challenge of Aten been successful, the crown, committed as it was to the Aten, might well have been in peril. It is less likely that this insistence on the Aten's supremacy was due to a monotheistic revelation received by Akhenaten, although this is how it is often romantically interpreted.

However, there was something of religious determination linked with these political pressures. Akhenaten's favourite epithet was: 'Living in [or on] Truth', which sums up his search for a closer relationship with nature, seen most clearly in the art style of Amarna and in his relationship with the Aten, with whom the king became closely identified. Akhenaten's attitude to the empire which his predecessors had built up in Nubia and Palestine is variously interpreted as an abandonment of reality or as skilled manoeuvring. In 1887 a series of letters, on clay tablets, in Akkadian, the *lingua franca* of the time, was found in the state archive at Amarna. Written to Amenophis III and Akhenaten from vassal rulers in the different city-states of Palestine, these letters describe the break up of the empire there [59]. Each vassal accused the other of plotting rebellion and threatening his security, and appealed to the king for military assistance. To some scholars it seems plain that many local rulers took advantage of the lack of Egyptian supervision to extend their own area of power, while pretending to the king that they were defending his interests. The assistance they sought was not forthcoming and the empire gradually slipped away, although some cities, such as Megiddo and Beth Shan, appear to have remained loyal. It is more likely that Egyptian policy was more subtle than this and that we see here the results of a carefully calculated policy of 'divide and rule', in which the various states were played off against each other.

Details of the family relationships and events at the end of Akhenaten's reign are as much of a problem as the chronology of its beginning. Smenkhkare', who was made co-regent late in Akhenaten's reign, may have been his brother or his son (or even Nefertiti in a new guise), but he outlived Akhenaten by only a few months, if at all, and was followed on the throne by his ·ten-year-old brother Tutankhaten.

The priesthood of Amun and the other gods had maintained a resistance to the Aten cult and were supported in this by the majority of the people, for the movement had swept away the established religious order that was the backbone

* On the site of Akhetaten are several modern villages amongst them el-Amarna and et-Till. Early excavators, used to the Arabic word 'Tell' for the mound marking the site of an ancient city, confusingly ran the two names together as Tell el-Amarna although there is no 'tell' on the site. The name 'Amarna' is now often used as an adjective describing the distinctive cultural and religious ideas of the period.

59. Two tablets from the group of letters found at Amarna, which were an archive of correspondence from rulers in Syria and Palestine to the XVIIIth–dynasty rulers. The letters were written in the cuneiform script and annotated by the Egyptian archivists in hieratic.

of the Egyptian way of life and had not replaced it with any tangible alternative.

Smenkhkare' may have been appointed co-regent to appease this resistance movement; and certainly Tutankhaten left Akhetaten to return to the old capital of Memphis and the gods of Thebes soon after his coronation. He abandoned the Aten cult and restored the temples to their rightful gods, emphasizing his change by altering his name from Tutankhaten (Pleasant is the life of the Aten) to Tutankhamun (Pleasant is the life of Amun). He began a considerable building programme and his general, Horemheb, soon re-established Egypt's claim to Syria, but before these projects really got under way the young king died and, more significantly in the light of later events, was buried.

He was succeeded by the aged adviser and priest Ay, who ruled for four years or so, and then by the general Horemheb, who was regarded as the first pharaoh since Amenophis III not tainted by the Aten heresy and therefore was later considered to have succeeded Amenophis III directly. The kings Akhenaten, Smenkhkare', Tutankhamun and Ay were regarded as never having existed. Akhetaten was abandoned and eventually destroyed by Horemheb's successors, and other buildings elsewhere were torn down to remove all trace of the Atenist episode.

MONUMENTS OF THE AMARNA PERIOD

Burial customs remained relatively untouched by this theological upheaval but the archaeological record is not as clear as one might wish. The so-called Royal Tomb at Amarna was sited in a wadi, 62 km. from Akhenaten's new city, and apparently intended for Nefertiti and her daughters Meritaten and Meketaten as well as for himself. It departed from the traditional XVIIIth-dynasty shape in having a straight corridor from entrance to main chamber. In the tomb were fragmentary pieces of funeral equipment inscribed with the names of Akhenaten, Queen Tiye, his mother, and Nefertiti. A tomb in the Valley of the Kings

at Thebes also contained damaged equipment bearing the names of members of the Amarna royal family, and it is possible that (during the reign of Tutankhamun) the bodies were removed from the Amarna tomb to Thebes, where they were later desecrated during the official anti-Amarna reaction.

The tombs of the Amarna nobles, cut in two groups in the cliffs surrounding Akhetaten, were similar in form to tombs of earlier XVIIIth-dynasty nobles, but the decoration is peculiar to Amarna. One of the most serious failures of the Aten cult was the absence of a concrete replacement for the Osirian Afterworld. Representations of this are completely missing from the tomb reliefs of Amarna, which consist solely of scenes showing the tomb-owner in his earthly relationship to the king: there was little to hope for beyond continuation of the sycophantic adulation of the king. The detailed accounts of royal appearances at which the tomb-owner played a part, and the proud record of his investment by the king, executed in the distinctive style of Amarna, are unmistakable, even without the constant repetition of the characteristic features of Akhenaten, who always occupies a dominant position, while the dead man is often comparatively insignificant.

During the reign of Amenophis III, the art style moves away from the consciously picturesque to a more realistic style, in which the sculptor is not afraid to reveal the obesity of the king or the lined face of Queen Tiye. With this went a more careful observation of anatomical details of bone structure and musculature. This appealed to Akhenaten's own brand of realism, although in the early recordings of his strange physique, portrayal was carried beyond the level of faithfulness to that of caricature. It is possible that Akhenaten's reforms were introduced so quickly that the artists had no time to adjust to the new realistic style but some of the early work, for instance the colossal statues from Karnak, is powerful, even in distortion, probably due to the innate ability of men like the master sculptor Bak.

These men showed distinct technical skill and a willingness to experiment, especially with different types of relief work. They executed raised and sunk relief in rock and plaster and developed a fine art form in which the traditional low relief was replaced by deeper carving that allowed for more delicate modelling. Their skill is also seen in the composite statuary where limestone bodies are fitted with quartzite heads. Features such as the eyes, eyebrows and headdresses would have been inlaid in glass or a different type of stone [*Pl 31*].

Some of the excellence of their observation may be due to the use, revealed in the workshop of the artist Tuthmosis at Amarna, of plaster masks [**61**]. These appear to have been cast from clay originals modelled from life and provide illustration of a dimension of portraiture otherwise unknown in Egypt. Tentative identifications are often offered but cannot be substantiated. From the same workshop comes the more idealistic painted limestone bust of Nefertiti, now in Berlin [**6o**]. It may have been the discipline of this sort of work that tempered the early tendency to caricature, for later in Akhenaten's reign the extremes were moderated and he was portrayed with a much more credible appearance.

There were similar changes in the work of the tomb painters, both in their choice of subject and the composition of their scenes. In addition to the ubiquitous portrayals of the king on state occasions, there are many scenes of his domestic life, in intimate poses that previously had not been used even for the portrayal of the lower classes. The king is shown with the queen sitting on his lap, or playing with his children, even weeping over the death of Meketaten.

6o. Above: sandstone colossus of Akhenaten from the destroyed temple of the Aten at Karnak. Now in the Cairo Museum. Height of complete piece *c.* 4 m. Below: an unfinished head of Nefertiti with eyebrows and other details picked out in black. Quartzite. Now in the Cairo Museum. Height 33 cm.

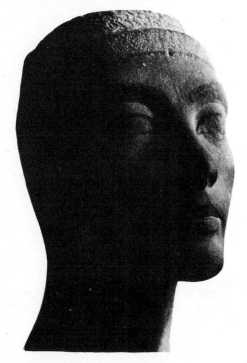

There is an interest in conveying actuality of events, with torches and braziers used to convey a sense of time and atmosphere, and also in the portrayal of scenery and landscape. This surpasses the realism of Middle Kingdom art, where actual events are portrayed but without reference to time or space [62].

The artists now make a conscious effort to compose their picture, using the whole spread of a tomb wall with only a limited use of registers, and figures are shown in relationship to each other, forming natural groups in a way which makes earlier paintings seem very stereotyped, as if peopled with cardboard cut-outs. Amarna people cluster about a central figure, follow gestures with their eyes and look at each other when they converse. This is not a complete innovation in the Amarna period but is carried out more extensively there. There are also tentative moves to give roundness to figures by shading, a development probably related to the increased amount of modelling in deep relief.

The Amarna style is most fully worked out in the city from which it takes its name, but its comparatively rapid introduction may be seen in some of the Theban tombs begun in the reign of Amenophis III but finished under Akhenaten. The best examples occur in Ramose's tomb, where one wall carries a traditional portrayal of the king as Amenophis IV with the goddess Ma'at, and opposite is a scene of the king and vizier with the Aten disc and rays overhead. This scene, too, was executed before the change of the king's name to Akhenaten, but shows the grotesque bodies with which courtiers were portrayed in deference to the ultra-realistic royal portraits [Pls 12–15].

Before the foundation of Akhetaten, monuments to the Aten were erected in the traditional cult centres, and blocks from these buildings have been found re-used in later constructions. From pylons II, IX and X erected at Karnak by Horemheb, and from the foundations of Seti's hypostyle hall, have come a large number of small sandstone blocks, originally used in several Aten temples on the Karnak site. They show signs of being re-cut as the nomenclature and theology of the Aten cult developed, but the use of the name Amenophis IV indicates they were used early in his reign.

61. Plaster head of an old woman, from the studio of the sculptor Tuthmosis at Amarna. Now in the Berlin Museum. Height 27 cm.

62. Wall-painting from Amarna showing two princesses sitting together on a cushion. The representation of shadow is unusual in Egyptian art. Now in the Ashmolean Museum, Oxford. Length 1·65 m.

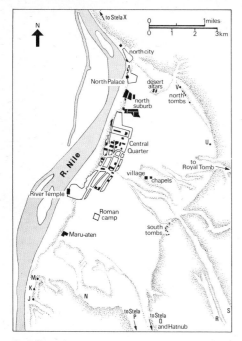

63. Map of the site of the city of Akhetaten, el-Amarna.

64. One of the fourteen great boundary stelai set up to celebrate the foundation of the city of Amarna and to define its limits.

Other groups of blocks have been discovered; some at Luxor and Medamud may have come from the Karnak temples or even from Amarna. Blocks from Hermopolis and Assiut in the style of the latter part of Akhenaten's reign probably came from Amarna, and others from Memphis suggest there may have been a temple there. Nubia also provides examples of work in the Amarna style.

Akhenaten's great city of Akhetaten now lies abandoned and destroyed, in the same state as it was left after the Ramesside officials had razed it to eradicate the memory of 'That Criminal'. Since it was built on a virgin site and abandoned before any redevelopment was undertaken, a clear picture of the layout is possible. Subsequent occupation was minimal, so the record is undisturbed [63].

The site is a large bay in the cliffs of the east bank near Hermopolis, 11 km. long and reaching back 5 km. from the river. Inaccessible except by river, its isolation was emphasized by stelai [64] which marked the boundary of this sacred area; its self-sufficiency was maintained by a food supply grown on the wide fertile plain on the opposite bank.

The centre of the bay was the site of the official city with the principal buildings: temples, palaces and government offices. Just to the south was the suburb which accommodated the great houses of the vizier, High Priest and other important officials, as well as the workshop of Tuthmosis. To the north was a middle-class residential and business area which also contained some poorer houses. East of the main centre lay a workers' village and within the bay were other palaces, pavilions and smaller housing estates. The areas along the riverside were linked by three parallel roads and much of the area between the river and the first of these roads is now lost below the cultivation.

THE AFTERMATH OF AMARNA

Tutankhamun describes in his Restoration stele (usurped by Horemheb) how, during the Amarna episode, the shrines of the gods were deserted and overgrown but when he came to the throne he restored them to their original condition, re-equipping them with new cult images of gold, lapis lazuli, turquoise and precious stones, and with a greater number of priests and servants. The principal remaining piece of evidence of this pious undertaking are the reliefs of the Festival of Opet, begun by Amenophis III on the walls behind his great colonnade at Luxor [65]. These were finished by Tutankhamun, although the credit was taken by Horemheb and Seti I who put their names in some of Tutankhamun's cartouches.

Tutankhamun's achievements have, however, been completely eclipsed by the richness of his burial. The discovery of his virtually intact grave by Howard Carter in 1922 and its methodical excavation must rank as one of the greatest triumphs of scientific archaeology [66].

The tomb is atypical in being very small and having four chambers grouped together instead of the more common linear plan. It is also undecorated except for the actual burial chamber. Probably the tomb intended for him was No. 23 in the Valley of the Kings, but before it was finished Tutankhamun died unexpectedly. Ay buried him in his own tomb and continued work on Tutankhamun's, which he later used himself.

There were two attempts at robbing: after the first the entrance corridor was filled with rubble and the second gang of robbers had to tunnel through that,

66. Howard Carter, watched by Lord Carnarvon and an Egyptian workman, opening the doors of the nest of shrines over the sarcophagus of Tutankhamun during the excavation of his tomb in 1922. The shrines are of wood overlaid with gold engraved with protective deities, their doors are secured by bars which pass through the hoops.

but were probably caught red-handed. Some of their loot was discovered, wrapped in a cloth on the floor of the antechamber, where the robbers had dropped it in their flight. A perfunctory attempt was made to sort out the chaos caused by the looting and the tomb resealed. It escaped further robbing because the entrance was buried, first under a group of workmen's huts, and later by debris from Ramesses VI's tomb.

The antechamber at the end of the entrance corridor contained much equipment that represented the daily life of the king. Although this had been ransacked by thieves and hastily repacked by officials, the boxes bore dockets which listed the contents from which it should be possible, once they are eventually published, to make a complete inventory. There were also three large ritual couches and two life-size figures guarding a plastered-up doorway. This led to

67. A group of emissaries from Libya and Asia in the presence of the King's Deputy Horemheb, who wears several gold collars and carries a fan and axe, perhaps as insignia of his office. From Horemheb's tomb at Sakkara. Now in the Rijksmuseum van Oudheden, Leiden.

the burial chamber that was almost completely occupied by four great gold-covered shrines, one inside the other, erected over the quartzite sarcophagus which contained the three gold coffins and the mummified king. In a smaller chamber beyond was another shrine, containing an alabaster chest divided into four compartments with human-headed lids, each holding a miniature gold coffin for the viscera of the king. Other chests contained a series of figures of the king or various gods. In a small chamber off the antechamber was more equipment for daily life and provisions of oil, wine and foodstuffs. This had been thoroughly ransacked and the officials had not attempted to restore order here as they had in the other rooms.

The tomb is important since it preserved for the first time, apart from Amenophis II's, the body of a pharaoh in its original tomb, and in this instance, with all the funerary equipment. A few parallels survive from the debris in other plundered tombs but here was a complete royal assemblage. Some of the pieces were mementoes from childhood, like an old and battered model boat; some were provided for future use, such as a fire drill, yet others were ritual equipment to ensure the future well-being of the king. Some pieces were presented by faithful retainers: some of the shabtis (see p. 208) and a beautifully carved small wooden figure of Osiris were given by the courtier who organized the funeral. Other pieces were appropriated from earlier burials, such as the second of the great covering shrines and the four miniature coffins in his canopic chest, which had had the original cartouche, probably Smenkhkare''s, altered. Some of the provision was simply makeshift: the lid of the sarcophagus, which was in granite and was cracked, had been roughly cemented and painted over to match. Two of the great beds show signs of hasty workmanship for the bodies, which bear ritual texts, have been married up with the wrong animal heads.

There is a strange mixture of artistic styles. The Amarna influence is very strong in some pieces, such as the designs on the gilded shrine and on the back of one throne, while the decoration of the burial chamber is very formal and orthodox. Some pieces show the successful development of the Amarna style and its adaptation to the traditional motifs, giving them more life and feeling.

A complete list and description of the objects has not yet been published and there is still much to be learnt from this discovery. In so far as it is possible to compare it with the few surviving parallels, the provision seems to have been both richer and of superior quality. Although the equipment has been removed

to the Cairo Museum, the body of the king lies in the tomb in one of his gilded coffins in the sarcophagus.

Ay's funerary temple, and Horemheb's, lay at the north-west corner of Ramesses III's temple at Medinet Habu and are now virtually completely lost. Ay had cut a tomb for himself at Amarna in the Amarna style, recording in it the great *Hymn to the Aten*, supposedly composed by Akhenaten himself. But, when he became king after Tutankhamun, Ay abandoned it for an orthodox tomb in the Valley of the Kings.

The Amarna heritage is finely developed in some of the work for Horemheb. A statue of him as a scribe takes up an early iconography, but the pose is relaxed and the expression is introspective. In the tomb at Sakkara that was made for him when he was a general, the working in relief was exceptionally fine. The tomb itself has been recently rediscovered after being lost for nearly a century, but the blocks with which it was lined are dispersed in many museums [67]. The reliefs are noteworthy for their vigour and expressiveness, as well as for several unusual subjects, such as the numerous foreigners [67]. Horemheb's tomb in the Valley of the Kings is also of interest, for in its unfinished state it preserves the different stages of relief carving, from the initial rough sketch to the finished work [*Pl 30*].

THE XIXth AND XXth DYNASTIES: THE RAMESSIDE PERIOD

Horemheb appointed as his successor his vizier Pramesse, who ruled as Ramesses I, first king of the XIXth dynasty, for just two years, before he was in turn succeeded by his son Seti I in 1318. Seti took as one of his titles the phrase 'Repeating Births', an indication of his intention to establish a national renaissance after the Amarna episode. Partly this renewal took the form of campaigns in Syria to reclaim those cities that had broken away under Akhenaten and to encourage those that had remained loyal; partly it was a cultural renewal or, more accurately, a continuation of the restorations of Tutankhamun and Horemheb. The Ramesside dynasty came from the Delta town of Avaris, the town of Seth, murderer of Osiris (see p. 197), and it was perhaps to dispel any doubt about their orthodoxy that Seti and his successors undertook extensive work at Abydos, the city of Osiris.

Pl 10. The 'Colossi of Memmon', statues of Amenophis III, originally more than 20 m. high, stand before his now-vanished funerary temple on the edge of the vegetation in front of the Theban hills. It is possible that a second pair stood farther north on the other side of the entrance. After it was damaged in an earthquake in 27 AD the northern (right) colossus used to give out a musical sound at daybreak and was therefore visited by many distinguished travellers until it was repaired in 199 AD and the sound ceased.

68. The central chamber of the Osireion, built by Seti I at Abydos. The plain post and lintel construction of the colonnade is perhaps deliberately reminiscent of the Chephren valley temple [cf. 23]. XIXth-dynasty.

Ramesses II succeeded his father in *c*. 1290 and maintained his work. He was troubled at first by invasions by the Sherden, the first arrivals in Egypt of the various groups of so-called Sea Peoples. However, the Sherden were defeated and many conscripted to fight alongside other mercenaries from Libya and Nubia in Egypt's wars in Syria–Palestine. The principal enemy here was the Hittites, as they attempted to extend their influence southwards from Anatolia. The major clash came in Ramesses's second campaign in his fifth year, when the Egyptian army, numbering four divisions, moved against the fortress of Qadesh. Misleading information encouraged Ramesses to press on with only part of his troops, but the Hittites were waiting for him and, according to Ramesses, it was only his personal bravery in rallying his troops and charging the enemy that saved the day. Although the king escaped, the Hittites were the real victors and extended their hold on Syria, but in Ramesses's twenty-first year the increasing threat from Assyria led both sides to draw up a peace treaty, subsequently sealed by Ramesses's marriage to the daughter of Hattusil, the Hittite king.

Ramesses II did nothing in a small way. He built temples and monuments throughout Egypt, Nubia and Palestine on a scale larger than all other pharaohs until, after reigning for sixty-seven years, he was succeeded by one of his one hundred or more children, Merenptah. This king's reign was marked by another attempted invasion by the Sea Peoples and Libyans into the western Delta. They were repulsed after a six-hour battle, leaving 6,000 dead and, apart from minor campaigns in Palestine and Nubia, Merenptah's reign was peaceful thereafter.

After Merenptah, the XIXth dynasty dissolved in a few short reigns in uncertain succession, ending with Siptah and finally Tewosret, who ruled as Queen Regnant. The Great Harris Papyrus, a list of benefactions bestowed by Ramesses III, describes these chaotic events and tells how order was restored by Sethnakhte, who died soon afterwards, having appointed Ramesses III as his successor.

The respite Merenptah had won was ended and the Sea Peoples made a desperate onslaught in Ramesses's eighth year. But they and their boats were trapped in the Delta swamps and defeated, and their threat to Egypt decisively removed. The Libyans were also crushingly defeated in the eleventh year of his reign and thereafter he enjoyed a peaceful and prosperous reign, marred at the end by a palace conspiracy when one of his minor wives, Tiy, attempted to replace him by her son Pentawer. Several high officials were involved and in the ensuing trial seventeen people were sentenced to death and seven more 'allowed to commit suicide'.

So ended the reign of the last great native pharaoh. Eight more Ramesses (IV–XI) followed in undistinguished order. Documentary records show administrative breakdowns, thefts and embezzlements amongst high officials, strikes by unpaid workers in the royal tombs, possible civil war in the reign of Ramesses V or VI and scandalous tomb robbery under Ramesses IX. The Palestinian colonies were lost soon·after the death of Ramesses III but Nubia remained in Egyptian hands. In Ramesses XI's reign, its powerful viceroy, Panehsy, challenged the growing power of the High Priest of Amun, Amunhotep, but was later disgraced in the tomb robbery scandals and withdrew to Nubia, where he set up an independent state. At the end of the dynasty the power of the king was so reduced that when a temple official, Wenamun, was commissioned to buy timber from Byblos he went on the authority of the new High Priest of

Amun, Herihor, who, within the Khonsu temple precinct at Karnak, even claimed a full royal titulary. Wenamun also sought the support of Nesubanebded, the actual ruler of the Delta. Ramesses XI himself was evidently of no consequence at all and administration of the kingdom was divided between Herihor and Nesubanebded.

ARCHITECTURE

Ramesses I reigned for too short a time to leave more than a small, simple tomb, No. 16 in the Valley of the Kings, but his successor, Seti I, cut the longest of all the tombs in the valley. For some 100 m. the tomb runs back into the cliff, in a series of stairs and sloping corridors, over a great pit designed to prevent flood damage and endanger robbers and, about half-way along its length, takes an (originally) hidden exit in an attempt to throw robbers off the scent. It contains several large pillared halls and a vaulted sarcophagus chamber, all decorated with fine, if somewhat brightly painted, reliefs of scenes and texts from various funerary rituals and litanies. Seti's sarcophagus, recovered by Belzoni and now in Sir John Soane's Museum in London, is a remarkable work of art in calcite, inlaid with processions of figures in blue pigment [Pl 29].

Beside this magnificent tomb most of the others seem unimportant. The passages are built on gentler slopes and, in the XXth dynasty, the low relief work was replaced by the more economical incised relief. Best preserved is the comparatively large tomb of Ramesses VI.

In this period other members of the royal family were buried in the valley behind Deir el-Medinah, now known as the Valley of the Queens. The most impressive of the eighty or so tombs is that of Nefertari, queen of Ramesses II. In places the decoration is in low relief, in others it is painted, but with a heavy outline that gives the impression of relief. The work is in brilliant colours, with elaborate details and great elegance, executed with fine technical artistry [Pl 25]. The tomb of Nefertari is unfortunately now in a very unstable condition, but other tombs illustrate the type well, notably those of Amenherkopshef and Khaemwese, sons of Ramesses III.

As Thebes recovered her earlier importance, the nobles' cemeteries on the west bank came back into use. Strangely, the influence of Amarna on the succeeding period is comparatively slight. The innovations were abandoned before their full promise was achieved as artists of the XIXth dynasty returned to the main stream of development. The subject-matter and style of the tomb-paintings continues the earlier tradition, but there are some changes. The colours are bolder and harsher than those of the XVIIIth dynasty and the soft grey background is replaced by a bright yellow. Early XIXth-dynasty tombs, like those of Userhet (No. 51) and Nebamun and Ipuky (No. 181) are very fine, with well-executed, detailed realism, but later work is often slipshod. Preparation of the surface was often skimped and the large acreage of wall space almost inevitably led to mediocrity, but there is still some imaginative work.

The tombs of the craftsmen at Deir el-Medinah, built on the western slope overlooking the village, were marked above ground by small, single-roomed chapels topped by sharp, hollow brick pyramids, often with figures of the owner carved on the limestone pyramidion and a small niche at the front containing a statuette of the owner. From the courtyard, stairs lead to one or two connected barrel-vaulted rooms containing some of the most brilliant wall-paintings of the funerary cult and the Afterworld [104].

The major kings of the Ramesside Period maintained the tradition of funerary

69. Head of a seated statue of Ramesses II wearing the Blue Crown reassembled from fragments from the great pit at Karnak. Now in the Museo Egizio, Turin. Height 1·94 m.

temples along the western limits of the cultivation at Thebes. Seti and his father Ramesses I shared a temple near the approach to the Valley of the Kings at Gurneh, but Seti and Ramesses II also built important temples at Abydos.

Seti's unique building is a seven-fold cult temple with seven parallel axes and seven shrines standing side by side, dedicated to Horus, Isis, Osiris, Amun, Re'-Horakhty, Ptah and Seti himself. The shrine of Osiris leads to an inner suite dedicated to the family of Osiris, Isis and Horus. At right-angles to the main temple is a further block of rooms, some for worship, others for temple offices and approached along a gallery inscribed with the famous king-list.

Just behind the temple lies another unique building, the Osireion [68]. A sunken central hall contained a lake, from whose waters rose a mound representing the mound-grave of Osiris. Beyond it is a tomb chamber where the king's body may have lain for a while after death and which later acted as a cenotaph.

Seti's unique temple was finished after his death by his son Ramesses II, and the Osireion by Merenptah: the decoration reveals this very clearly. The reliefs on the inner halls of the temple are in the technically perfect style of Seti I, in parts preserving their rich colouring: they are beautifully drawn and finely executed but lack the vitality of the earlier New Kingdom work. Ramesses II's work is much less subtle, with widespread use of sunk relief in which the surface of the block is not cut back to form the background, thus saving much labour. Ramesses II's own temple at Abydos is smaller and simpler than Seti's and also richly decorated, in a rather better style than that usually employed by this energetic builder [72].

Most of the Theban temples of the Ramessides have now disappeared but the Ramesseum of Ramesses II [70] and Medinet Habu, the funerary temple of Ramesses III, are sufficiently intact to give a fair impression of their original glory. The Ramesseum lies in a large enclosure 175 × 260 m.; much of the space on the north, west and south is taken up with long, brick-built vaulted magazines and minor offices. The main temple follows closely the plan of a cult temple with two open courts, a large hypostyle hall and series of smaller halls leading to the sanctuary against the west end. South of the first court, and connected with it by an opening through the south wall, was the king's residence, and behind it the houses where the court lived while on the west bank for events such as the valley festival. Flanking the north side of the hypostyle hall is a small temple of Seti I.

The front part of the temple was used as a quarry in Ptolemaic times, only the southern half of the first pylon and the west face of the north half of the second pylon survive but in the tumbled ruin of the first court lies a broken, 17·5 m. high, seated statue of the king in a single block of Aswan granite. It was allegedly the description of this statue that inspired Shelley's sonnet *Ozymandias*, the name being taken from the Greek form of Ramesses' name, Userma'atre' [72]. Two smaller statues flanked the central ramp leading from the second court into the temple building. The seven-ton head of yet another colossus was removed by Belzoni to the British Museum in 1816. The hypostyle hall beyond the second court is also damaged; its side walls, roof and several pillars are lost

Pl 11. View of the ruins of the temple of Amun at Karnak looking west from the south-east corner of the sacred lake. The principal structures in view are (left to right), Pylon VIII, erected by Queen Hatshepsut; the rear face of the southern half of Pylon I; the pillared hall and central clerestory of Seti I; one of the pair of obelisks erected by Tuthmosis I and one of the taller pair erected by Queen Hatshepsut. In the distance can be seen the cliffs of the west bank.

70. View eastwards across the second court of the Ramesseum: to the right of the row of Osirid pillars lies, on its back, the fallen head and torso of a colossal figure of the king. Thebes. XIXth–dynasty.

but in the next hall the ceiling blocks over the central aisle remain in position. The rooms behind are almost completely lost but the plan is decipherable.

The other great mortuary temple of this period was built by Ramesses III at Medinet Habu. The temple itself lies in a larger enclosure containing buildings of the Tuthmosids and later shrines, along with the temple well and lake. On the side facing the river a stone wall with crenellations stands in front of the enclosure wall giving a fortified aspect to the place, which is reinforced by the high battlemented gate that defends the approach to the temple [*Pl 17*].

The gate's design is based on the Syrian *migdol* or fortress, but the decoration of the rooms in the two upper storeys shows the king surrounded by his favourite girls from the harem and the building is plainly not intended to serve a military purpose. A similar gate in the west wall survives in ground plan only.

Alongside the eastern gate and extending in front of the wall lie the later additions to the XVIIIth-dynasty temple made in the XXVIth dynasty and later. Much of the enclosed area was occupied by offices and houses but in the south-eastern corner was a garden. A second enclosure wall lies within the main one and secludes the temple building and palace area. These follow, with only minor variations, the layout of the central area of the Ramesseum.

Seti built a small temple in the desert east of Edfu in the Wadi Abad, on the way to the gold mines and port of Berenice. It is cut into a rock bluff in a way that makes it a model for the Nubian temples of Ramesses II [**71**]. Besides the temple at Abydos, he also worked on the great hypostyle hall at Karnak which was eventually completed by Ramesses II, a great forest of 134 mighty columns in a space 103 × 51·8 m. [*Pl 18*]. The reliefs on the outer walls record the battles of these two pharaohs, setting the pattern for the most popular subject of reliefs in this period. Ramesses II added the first court and pylon at Luxor, built a second temple, known as 'The Portal', at Abydos and a temple of Ptah at Memphis, near which lie several colossal figures of the king. One is now re-erected in front of the railway station in Cairo. He also demolished the mortuary temple of Sesostris II at Kahun to provide material for a new temple at Heracleopolis, and stripped the granite casing from the pyramid of Chephren, while in the same reign Prince Khaemwese proudly recorded his restoration works on the pyramid of Unas.

It was in Nubia that Ramesses left his most impressive monument—in one of the largest rock-cut buildings in the world at Abu Simbel [*Pl 19*]. Behind the four, 20 m. high, figures of Ramesses, that form a three-dimensional projection of the usual pylon façade, lie the halls and shrine of a typical, though simplified, cult temple. The walls are decorated with scenes of the king's military successes

71. Small rock-cut temple with simple portico, constructed by Seti I as a shrine for gold miners on their way to the mines. This temple at Wadi Abad, about 56 km. east of Edfu, is built in a great bluff on which there are drawings of boats and animals dating from the Archaic Period.

72. A large granite statue of Ramesses II, about twice life-size, lying amongst the reeds and sand of Memphis.

and the shrine itself contains seated, rock-cut figures of Ptah, Amun, Ramesses and Re'-Horakhty. Nearby is the smaller shrine built for Nefertari, dedicated to Hathor, and other partly rock-cut temples were constructed at Beit el-Wali, Gerf Hussein, Wadi Es-Sebua and Derr. They doubtless served to impress the unsophisticated folk of Nubia with the power of their emperor. Another temple was built at Amara in Upper Nubia, where Seti I had founded a town which served as the seat of his local governor.

The Delta origin of these princes and the need for a base close to Palestine led to the establishment of a royal residence in the eastern Delta at Per-Ramesse ('The House of Ramesses' [biblical Raamses]). Two modern sites have been suggested for this, the city of Tanis, seat of the XXIst and XXIInd dynasty, which contains many monuments of Ramesses II, and the city of Qantir, 17 km. to the south, where there is a fine palace, begun under Seti I, richly decorated with faience tiles, and the foundations of a Ramesside temple. Of the two sites, Qantir is the more likely, since the Ramesside monuments at Tanis seem to have been moved there by the Libyan rulers from the buildings at Qantir and other sites.

With the exception of Ramesses III, who added several buildings to the Karnak complex, later Ramesside monarchs left little in the way of major monuments. Merenptah recorded his victory in a relief at Karnak, and Ramesses III depicted his defeat of the Sea Peoples in a vivid series of reliefs at Medinet Habu.

The New Kingdom was the era in which Egypt's imperial power was at its greatest. It resulted in enormous wealth and influence, but she maintained a resilience which enabled her to survive numerous subsequent foreign invasions.

The Later Dynasties

THE THIRD INTERMEDIATE PERIOD

THE TWENTY-FIRST DYNASTY

The XXIst dynasty was founded by Nesubanebded (called Smendes by Manetho), possibly a son-in-law of Ramesses XI, who ruled from the new capital of Tanis. It was a time of internal weakness and little political importance. Only near the end of the dynasty did Siamun feel strong enough to attack the Philistine city of Gezer in Palestine and form an alliance with Israel, then a strong power under Solomon (I Kings 9, 16). At Thebes, the dynasty of the High Priests of Amun, doubling as Great Commanders of the Army, likewise continued its undistinguished history, more or less independent of the northern regime but linked with it by marriage.

The royal burials of the dynasty were a complete departure from tradition. Some were found at Tanis, by Pierre Montet, in the precinct of the temple. Two small limestone chambers just below ground level were identified as the tomb of Psusennes; and his undisturbed body was found bedecked with jewellery and a gold mask in a fine anthropoid silver coffin with silver and gold vessels, canopic jars and bronze ushabtis (see p. 205). Also in this tomb was the mummy of King Amenemope in a wooden coffin in the sarcophagus of Psusennes' wife, Mutnodjmet: what happened to her body is unknown. Amenemope had been moved in with Psusennes from his own much smaller tomb nearby.

At Thebes, the depredations of the tomb robbers were causing such concern that the bodies of nine kings and forty other royal and priestly mummies were collected, together with what was left of their funerary equipment, and reburied in the tomb of Queen Inha'pi, wife of Ahmose, near Deir el-Bahri. The cache was rediscovered by local inhabitants in the 1870s and eventually by the Antiquities Service in 1881. Amongst the bodies recovered and removed to Cairo were those of Amenophis I, Tuthmosis III, Seti I, and Ramesses II and III.

About the same time as the first cache (and discovered ten years after it), another collection of mummies and funerary equipment, including 153 coffins, was buried in a collective tomb just north of Deir el-Bahri. Most of these were mummies of the priesthood of Amen-Re'. Yet another group of royal mummies of the XVIIIth and XIXth dynasties was found in 1898 in the tomb of Amenophis II.

The major works of the kings were at Tanis, where Psusennes I and Siamun were the principal builders. Psusennes erected the temple of Amun and its 18 m. thick enclosure wall, adorning the temple with several sculptures of earlier kings which he had transferred to Tanis and reinscribed. It was extended by

Pls 12, 13. Above: low relief of nobles and their wives at the funerary banquet. Below: unfinished (?) sketch of a group of Asiatics, from a set of scenes connected with Ramose's official duties. Reliefs from the tomb chapel of the vizier Ramose at Thebes. Late XVIIIth-dynasty.

Siamun, who also left his inscription on the Tuthmosis III obelisk at Heliopolis. Some work at Memphis was undertaken by the High Priests of Ptah. The High Priest of Amun, Pinudjem I, lined the dromos from pylon II to the quay at Karnak with ram-headed sphinxes, usurped from Ramesses II. The temple of Khonsu in the Karnak complex was completed, too.

THE LIBYAN DYNASTIES

THE TWENTY-SECOND AND TWENTY-THIRD DYNASTIES

When Psusennes II died without a male heir, power passed peacefully to his daughter's father-in-law Sheshonk, leader of the Libyans who had settled around Bubastis in the eastern Delta after their defeat by Ramesses III.

Two problems beset this dynasty. The growing empire of Assyria threatened the security of Palestine and Sheshonk I's enmity with Israel (see I Kings 14, 25) changed to alliance under Osorkon II, in the face of this threat, which was temporarily held off at the battle of Qarqar, 853 BC. The other problem was the power of the High Priests of Amun, which was dealt with by Sheshonk I when he abandoned the hereditary principle of this office and appointed his heir to it; but his strong line was not upheld and eventually the dispute broke out into open civil war in the reign of Takelothis II. A rival dynasty (the XXIIIrd) was formed at Leontopolis by a junior branch of the royal family which was accepted and supported by the Theban officials, with whom it was related. Neither dynasty apparently challenged the other, probably recognizing their own weakness. Local governors in most areas also enjoyed considerable independence.

Most of the rulers of XXIInd dynasty left their mark at Tanis, where new courts and gateways were added, often using buildings of the Ramessides as quarries. The earlier monarchs also built at Karnak, especially Sheshonk, who constructed the colonnaded forecourt with the Bubastite Portal on its south side [136], but other building work was on a comparatively minor scale. During the later years of the XXIInd and XXIIIrd dynasties, Tefnakht, the Prince of Sais in the western Delta, gradually expanded his control until he ruled a larger area than either of the contemporary pharaohs and began to exert influence as far away as Heracleopolis and Hermopolis.

The monuments at Tanis were mostly removed there from other sites and the decoration of tombs at the Theban necropolis was virtually given up, but several papyri show that the artists maintained their ability, and numerous sketches survive of great charm and humour. Some are similar to the caricatures of the XIXth and XXth dynasties from Deir el-Medinah, others show a new satirical streak, portraying animals in human situations and dress.

The finest products of this period, however, are those of the metalworkers. There are magnificent silver and gold vessels and a fine bronze statuette, beautifully finished with inlays of gold and silver, of Takelothis II's queen, Karomama, now alas partly damaged, but originally delicately inlaid with a feather design in gold, silver and electrum [73].

The young co-regent of Osorkon I, Heqakhepere' Sheshonk II, died prematurely and was given a lavish burial. His body, with a gold mask and decked with splendid pectorals, lying in a silver, falcon-headed coffin, was found reburied in the tomb of Psusennes. His canopic set was a group of matching silver coffinnettes.

THE NUBIAN DYNASTY

THE TWENTY-FIFTH DYNASTY

After the Ramessides Egypt had been too weak to concern itself with Nubia, where a separate kingdom emerged with a capital at Napata, near the Fourth Cataract, but Egyptian cultural influence remained very strong. About 760 BC the ruler of Nubia, Kashta, developed an interest in his northern neighbour and actually proclaimed himself 'King of Upper and Lower Egypt', but it was his successor, Piankhy, who put this claim into effect. With the authority of Amun expressed in his temple at Gebel Barkal, he advanced into Egypt to be welcomed by Amun of Thebes. He then returned to Napata but Tefnakht's expansion southwards forced him to come back north, and he eventually besieged and captured Memphis. Piankhy again returned to Napata and Tefnakht re-emerged from Sais, where he had withdrawn during Piankhy's attack, and took the formal title of pharaoh—although he did not challenge Osorkon IV of the XXIInd dynasty or the even weaker XXIIIrd dynasty at Leontopolis.

Between 725 and 716 the Assyrian threat was renewed. 'So, King of Egypt' (II Kings 17, 4), probably to be identified with Osorkon IV, last king of the XXIInd dynasty, proved a useless support for Hoshea of Israel, who was defeated by Shalmaneser V, and in 716 Osorkon IV himself had to buy off Sargon II, who had advanced to within 120 miles of Tanis.

The XXIInd and XXIIIrd dynasties petered out in the face of this aggression and Tefnakht's successor, Bakenrenef, was deposed by Piankhy's successor, Shabaka, who now occupied the whole country.

Shabaka maintained an uneasy peace with the Assyrians but his successor, Shebitku, sent a force under Taharqa to attack Sennacherib during his unsuccessful siege of Jerusalem in 701 BC. Taharqa succeeded to the throne in c. 690 and was in turn attacked by Esarhaddon in 674 and 671, when Memphis was temporarily captured. In 667 Assurbanipal again occupied the Delta and appointed Necho, Prince of Sais, as a vassal. After Taharqa's death, Tantamani recaptured the Delta and executed Necho, but Assurbanipal retaliated in strength and even captured and looted Thebes (Nahum 3, 8–10). Tantamani withdrew permanently to Nubia, and Necho's son Psammetichus was appointed a new Assyrian vassal in Sais and Memphis, although Upper Egypt was more or less independent under the mayor of Thebes, Montuemhat.

The Nubian kings were buried in their homeland at Kurru, although Taharqa began a new cemetery at Nuri. Most of the architectural work of the dynasty was at Gebel Barkal, where the XVIIIth-dynasty temple was restored and enlarged by Piankhy. However other rulers left several interesting monuments in Egypt, notably Taharqa's mighty colonnade in the forecourt at Karnak [74] and two smaller colonnades by the temples of Khonsu and Montu. He and Shabaka also added to the XVIIIth-dynasty temple at Medinet Habu.

The dynasty is marked by a strong archaizing tendency. The Nubian rulers revived the pyramid as a royal tomb, and Taharqa's temple at Kawa reproduces several Old Kingdom motifs in the decoration. Shabaka's careful copying of the Memphite cosmogony is another interesting witness of the concern felt by these foreign rulers for the traditions of Egypt.

A new movement may also be detected in the art style. There had been little interest in sculpture during the Third Intermediate Period, but now a renaissance began in this art form and lasted into the Hellenistic period. Many of the sculptures show what is often described as a 'brutal realism'. They are

73. Bronze statuette of the lady Takushit elaborately decorated with inlaid silver. XXIInd to XXVth-dynasty. Now in the Athens Museum. Height 69 cm.

93

Pls 14, 15. Above: painting of a group of professional women mourners, including an apprentice, part of the funeral process. Right: servants in the funeral procession carrying a bed and other equipment to be placed in the tomb. Paintings from the tomb chapel of the vizier Ramose at Thebes. Late XVIIIth–dynasty.

severe and unflattering portraits, with the frown of worried care and wrinkles of old age faithfully recorded, but in a way which emphasizes the impressive strength and authority of the subject. In the relief carving and statuary there is very careful attention to anatomical detail; muscular structure in particular is finely modelled.

THE SAITE REVIVAL: THE TWENTY-SIXTH DYNASTY
THE PERSIAN CONQUESTS: THE TWENTY-SEVENTH TO THIRTIETH DYNASTIES

About 656 BC Psammetichus emerged as the most powerful of the Assyrian vassal princes, and by having his daughter Nitocris adopted as the God's Wife of Amun, the title of the principal priestess at Karnak, he gained the loyalty of the Theban regime led by its mayor, Mentuemhat, so re-uniting Egypt. The Assyrians were preoccupied with their own problems as they succumbed to the Babylonians, who were in turn swallowed up by the Persians in 539 BC.

Although the Egyptian rulers were more or less independent at this stage, there were increasing numbers of foreigners in the country. To the Libyan settlers in the Delta were now added many Ionian and Carian mercenaries in Psammetichus's army, and the city of Naucratis, 16 km. from the capital Sais, was founded as a Greek trading colony, administered by Greek traders with their own temples to their own Greek gods. Later, in the fifth century BC, there was a Jewish colony sufficiently well established at Elephantine to have their totally unorthodox temple dedicated to Yahu, or Jehovah.

Necho II commissioned a band of Phoenicians to circumnavigate Africa, but other plans were less successful. He attempted to cut a canal linking the Nile with the Red Sea, and he and his successor Apries (Hophra in the Old Testament) interfered in Palestine, but without permanent effect (see II Kings 23, 29; 24, 1; Ezekiel 27, 11–21; and Jeremiah 37, 5). In 525, soon after the peaceful reign of Amasis, Egypt was occupied by the Persians under Cambyses.

The XXVIIth dynasty is formed by the Persian rulers, of whom Darius

74. View from the top of Pylon I in the temple of Amun at Karnak looking north–east to the court of Sheshonk with the sole surviving pillar of the kiosk of Taharqa. In front of the ruined Pylon II stands a huge granite statue of Pinodjem I as High Priest of Amun.

seems to have been the most enlightened in his treatment of Egypt. He completed Necho's Red Sea canal link, and carried out restoration work at several temples—even founding one to Amun in the distant Khargeh oasis. But revolt was always in the air, especially after the battle of Marathon (490 BC). Persian rule of a sort was maintained amidst increasing trouble and mutual suspicion until the death of Darius II in 404 BC. Manetho's XXVIIIth dynasty consists of one king, Amyrtaeus of Sais, of whom little is known beyond a brief mention in a document known as *The Demotic Chronicle*, a collection of miscellaneous data and comment, mostly of a historical nature.

The XXIXth dynasty was a line of four kings from the city of Mendes in the eastern Delta, whose main preoccupation was maintaining Egypt's state of rebellion against Persia. When an alliance with Sparta failed, King Achoris allied himself with Evagoras of Cyprus and the two were strong enough to withstand the Persian attack in 385, but Evagoras was eventually forced to submit in 380, and Achoris' son, Nepherites II, reigned only four months before the general Nectanebes founded the XXXth dynasty.

The XXXth dynasty consists of three kings, the first and last of whom have very similar names in the Greek form, namely Nectanebes (Egyptian: Nekht-nebef) and Nectanebos (Egyptian: Nekhthorheb). Each reigned for some eighteen years and, in spite of Persian threats, was strong enough to undertake a number of buildings and other projects; but, eventually, in 343, Nectanebos was forced to flee to Nubia and Egypt became a satrapy of the Persian Empire. Persian rule was finally ended by Alexander the Great, who was hailed in Egypt as a deliverer, formally installed as pharaoh and legitimized by a fine tale relating how Nectanebos had flown across the Mediterranean to beget him.

ARCHITECTURE AND ART

The royal tombs of the Egyptian rulers of the Late Period were probably amongst the sixteen tombs described by Herodotus in the precinct of Neith at Sais. These are now lost but there are some quite spectacular private tombs. In the last years of the XXVth dynasty, Mentuemhat, mayor of Thebes, built a vast tomb in front of Deir el-Bahri [*Pl 9*]. A huge mud-brick pylon leads to a forehall and sunken court, on two sides of which are small chapels; at the east end is a row of statues in niches and at the west a portico leading to the entrance to the burial chambers which are on a lower level. The badly robbed reliefs in the portico are based on several scenes from the XVIIIth-dynasty tomb of Menna, although the modelling lacks the vigour of Menna's paintings [Pl 21].

The tomb of Petamenope is even larger than Mentuemhat's. It follows a similar plan with a sunken court and burial chambers on a lower level. Winding passageways, lined with funeral texts, and false chambers were constructed in a vain attempt to mislead robbers and safeguard the actual burial chamber. Smaller, but similarly planned, tombs belong to other Saite nobles who were buried at Thebes, but a large number were buried at Sakkara, to the south and east of the pyramid of Unas.

No superstructure is recorded for these but the subterranean work is again impressive. The general plan is a shaft, anything up to 25 m. deep and 10 m. square, at the foot of which the burial chamber was constructed about a huge stone sarcophagus [51]. The lid of the sarcophagus was propped open and a roof built over the top. At the same time a pit, about 1·5 m. square, was sunk along-side the main shaft, connecting with it by a passage at the base. Through this the body was in due course lowered into the tomb and placed in the sarcophagus. The lid was then lowered into position and both pits filled with sand. In some tombs plugs in the roof of the burial chamber were removed and that, too, was flooded with sand. The sheer effort of removing such a vast quantity of loose sand usually discouraged even the most determined tomb robbers, and several of the burials were recovered intact. Unfortunately, burial customs at this period did not involve the deposition of much equipment with the deceased, although some fine jewellery was found on the bodies.

The archaizing tendency of the Saite dynasty is clearly illustrated by the way in which the burial chambers are decorated with funeral texts copied from the Old Kingdom examples in the pyramids nearby, which were investigated and restored. At Thebes, Mentuemhat's precedent was followed by a gentleman called Ibi, who copied large areas of the tomb scenes of a VIth-dynasty name-sake at Deir el-Gebrawi. Other forms of archaistic tomb design include the revival of the pyramidal form at Abydos and a copy of the Middle Kingdom cliff-tombs by the vizier and mayor of Thebes, Nesy-pe-ka-shuti, in the cliffs of Deir el-Bahri. The manifestations of interest in their cultural heritage are probably the result of a growing feeling of nationalism among the Egyptians, in the face of the large numbers of foreigners who were now settled in their country and the threat of foreign invasions [59].

The characteristic art form of these late dynasties is sculpture, particularly individual male figures. Group statues are rare and females, apart from the divine consorts of Amun, are almost unknown until the Ptolemaic period. There are, however, males in a variety of poses—the classical standing, sitting or kneeling positions and the crosslegged squat of the scribe are all found, as well as the extremely popular block statue (see p. 59). A number of influences may be detected in these sculptures. The archaizing style of the Saite dynasty is clearly recognizable, and the influence of the Old and Middle Kingdom work can be seen both in the forms and the details. An interesting departure from the older canon, however, is to be seen in the treatment of the human face; the confident smile of the Old Kingdom degenerated into a smug grin while, at the same time, the XXVth-dynasty trend of brutal realism was continued in other pieces.

75. Excavation of the tomb of Amen-tefnakht at Sakkara in 1941 involved elaborate staging and heavy work by a chain of basket-boys.

76. The inside face of Pylon I of the temple of Amun at Karnak. This pylon was never finished, the rough face of the stones was never smoothed and the brick ramps up which the stones were hauled have never been completely removed. Ptolemaic Period.

At the end of the Late Period we find a renaissance in architecture. Nectanebos began work at Philae and made additions to the temples at Ashmunein and Sais. At Karnak he built the great temenos wall, with its four gates facing the cardinal points, and decorated some of the smaller gateways. He also possibly began the unfinished pylon I, where even today some of the earthen ramp 'scaffolding' may still be seen [76]. In the First Court, Pinudjem's sphinxes, which originally extended to pylon II, had at some point been cleared away to one side, but the avenue linking Karnak and Luxor temples was lined with sphinxes and trees by Nectanebos.

Nectanebos' best memorial is his work at Sakkara. Since the XVIIIth dynasty at least, the dead Apis bull from the temple of Ptah at Memphis (see p. 101) had been buried just north of the Step Pyramid enclosure and, dating from Saite times, a large catacomb was excavated containing twenty-four vaults, wherein the individual Apis bulls lay in massive stone sarcophagi [135]. Other vaults, some connected with this series, others separate but in the same area, date back as far as the reign of Ramesses II. Nectanebos now erected the so-called Serapeum, a mortuary temple to Osiris Apis, who was better known by the contracted form of Serapis. The small temple lay at the end of a dromos lined with sphinxes and was discovered by Mariette in 1851, who worked from a description of the site in Strabo's *Geography*. More recent work nearby, by the Egypt Exploration Society, has revealed other galleries and catacombs containing the burials of the Isis cows, the mothers of the Apis, and of vast numbers of mummified ibises and hawks, as well as baboons and dogs. These galleries lie under the area of the Old Kingdom mastabas and often hit their shafts. Small temples mark their portals and in the surrounding area there was a large settlement for the priests and votaries, the stonemasons, scribes, embalmers, and others associated with the temples and catacombs. Since the site was renowned as an oracle, it attracted many pilgrims and throughout the Hellenistic period was a large and important religious centre.

Similar catacombs are known at other sacred sites, a notable example are the galleries at Tuna el-Gebel containing large numbers of mummified ibises and baboons—sacred animals of Thoth, the local deity. Here, deep entrance stairways lead to a kind of subterranean city laid out with streets up to 4·5 m. broad, covering an area of some four hectares or more.

At Armant the Buchis bulls, sacred to Montu, the local god, were likewise buried in a series of galleries, of which the earliest excavated is dated to the reign of Nectanebos, while others are dated as late as the Roman period.

THE LATER DYNASTIES

XXIst dynasty 1069–945 (Tanis) Upper Egypt controlled by the High Priest of Amun at Thebes

Nesubanebded		
(*Smendes*)	1069–1043	Pinudjem 1070–1032
Psusennes I	1039– 991	Menkheperre' 1045– 992
Amenemope	993– 984	
Siamun	978– 959	

XXIInd dynasty 945–715 (Tanis; Libyan origin)

		XXIInd dynasty		XXIIIth dynasty 818–715 (*Lèontopolis*)	XXIVth dynasty 727–715	XXVth dynasty (*Nubia*)
925	Sheshonk campaigns in Palestine	Sheshonk I	945–924			
		Osorkon I	924–889			
		Sheshonk II	*c.* 890			
		Takelothis I	889–874			
853	Egyptian troops at Battle of Qarqar support Israel and Syria	Osorkon II	874–850			
841	Assyrian threat in Palestine	Takelothis II	850–825			Alara *c.* 780–760
		Sheshonk III	825–773	Pedubastis 818–793		Kashta *c.* 760–747
		Pimay	773–767			Piankhky 747–716
716	Assyrian threat by Sargon II	Oskorkon IV	730–715			
671	Esarhaddon invades Egypt				Tefnakht 727–720	
667	Assurbanipal invades Egypt			715	Bakenrenef 720–715	Shabaka 716–702 Nubians invade Egypt
						Taharka 690–664
				663		Tantamani 664–656 Nubians withdraw from Egypt. Control in Upper Egypt by the mayors of Thebes

XXVIth dynasty 664–525 (Saite)

Psammetichus	
(*Psamtik*) I	664–610
Necho II	610–595

XXVIIth dynasty 525–404 (Persian)

XXVIIIth and XXIX dynasties 404–378

XXXth dynasty 380–343 (at Sebennytos)

Greek and Roman Egypt

THE PTOLEMAIC PERIOD 323–30 BC

Alexander's welcome interference in Egyptian affairs lasted only long enough for him to be accepted as pharaoh, consult the oracle of Amun at Siwa oasis, found Alexandria and appoint his governors, before he left to conquer the Persian Empire. In the settlement after his death in 323, power in Egypt was secured by Ptolemy, son of Lagus, one of Alexander's Macedonian bodyguards, who took over power as satrap and confirmed his accession in true Egyptian fashion by arranging the temporary burial of Alexander at Memphis before the body was removed to the tomb at Alexandria. When Alexander's son was murdered in 311, Ptolemy became *de facto* ruler and in 306, along with Seleucus in Syria and Cassander in Macedon, Ptolemy declared himself king. Thus began a dynasty of thirteen rulers who achieved a remarkable marriage between the conservative Egyptian world and their own lively Hellenistic culture.

In many ways the Egyptians and the Greek settlers lived their lives separately from and unaffected by each other, but it was also in this period that Egyptian culture was absorbed by the Greeks and, through them, has passed into the mainstream of Western civilization. For the bulk of the native population, there was little change from the seasonal round of agricultural toil. They remained underprivileged and overtaxed. The rights of citizenship in the self-governing *poleis* of Alexandria, Naucratis and Ptolemais, and other Greek towns such as Oxyrhynchus and Arsinoë were reserved almost exclusively for the Greek mercenaries and merchants who were settled there, or for the Hellenized upper-classes of Egyptian society. There was smouldering resentment between the two communities; local insurrection even led to the destruction of Thebes in 85 BC.

Nevertheless the rule of the Ptolemies was not without advantage to Egypt. On a purely materialistic level, the area of cultivable land was greatly increased by improved irrigation and drainage. Several new crops, including cotton and improved strains of grapes for better wine, were introduced and more luxury goods were made available by the increase in foreign trade.

The Ptolemies were tolerant in their attitude to Egyptian culture in general and Egyptian religion in particular. They made donations and granted exemptions to the priesthood and rebuilt and extended many temple estates. Many of these temples were new buildings on centuries-old sites and were no doubt designed to encourage acceptance of the foreign rulers, whose generosity was of course loudly proclaimed in the reliefs with which the temples were decorated. Nevertheless, they provided centres in which the religion of pharaonic Egypt, the backbone of the native culture, was able to survive. For us they now provide the best examples of Egyptian religious architecture. They appear to follow faithfully the general layout of earlier temples and the excellent preservation of the reliefs enables us to learn the uses of many of the rooms and chambers and understand something of the ceremonies that were performed in them.

We find similar enlightenment on other aspects of Egyptian culture, for there is so much documentary evidence available. Many papyri record day-to-day transactions, wills, tax receipts, leases, deeds, land surveys, census lists and the like, which serve to illuminate many of the perplexing problems of earlier periods.

These papyri also include many famous works of classical literature. The earliest surviving Greek manuscript, a late fourth-century text of the *Persae* of Timotheus, the Hawara manuscript of Homer and possibly Aristotle's treatise on the Athenian constitution were all found in tombs; and the rubbish heaps of Arsinoë, Oxyrhynchus and Tebtunis provided many more examples.

The cultured society of Ptolemaic Egypt was encouraged by royal patronage of learning. At the new capital of Alexandria were the world-famous Museum, where scholars were provided with free accommodation, and the Library, where books from all over the Greek world were copied and where bibliography and textual criticism were established. Definitive texts of classical authors were edited, and amongst the important works translated into Greek for the Library was the *Septuagint*, the Greek version of the Old Testament. This atmosphere of learning attracted many great scholars of international repute. Their work included the geometrical treatises of Euclid, the medical researches of Herophilus and Erasistratus, the measurement of the earth's circumference by Eratosthenes, and the discovery of the earth's rotation around the sun by Aristarchus.

Much of this work was Hellenistic in concept and execution, and the Egyptian contribution cannot be easily distinguished; but many of the subjects, such as geometry, medicine and astronomy, were those in which the Egyptians had long experience and their accumulated knowledge was doubtless utilized.

One conscious attempt to link the pharaonic traditions with the new Hellenistic culture is to be seen in the encouragement given to the cult of Serapis. Serapis was in origin Osiris Apis, or the dead Apis bull in his new existence in the Afterworld, but since Apis was the local god of the capital city Memphis, he was adopted by the Ptolemies as a kind of national deity. In deference to Greek ideas he was represented in human form as a bearded man and his cult soon became extremely popular, not only in Egypt but throughout the Greek and Roman world, even as far away as Britain. He was worshipped as a saviour-god of healing, fertility and the future life in a cult celebrated with mysteries like those of Mithras and Isis.

Apart from the Hellenistic buildings and monuments of Alexandria and other Greek cities, works in the traditional Egyptian style were also undertaken. By far the most impressive were the many cult temples that were now rebuilt following the start made by Nectanebos, including the great sanctuaries of Hathor at Dendera, Horus at Edfu, Khnum at Esna and Suchos and Haroeris at Kom Ombo and, reputedly most beautiful of all, the Isis temple at Philae, now partly submerged in Lake Nasser [77].

Also from this period are several smaller shrines, like the temple of Deir el-Medinah, the half-buried temple of Isis in the backstreets of Aswan, and the overgrown temple of Thoth, a little way south of Medinet Habu, known as Kasr el-Aguz. Yet others existed in such important centres as Coptos and Memphis, at Crocodilopolis in the Fayyum, and in the Delta, but these were destroyed long ago. The temple of Montu at Armant was used to provide the

77. The small chapel or *mammisi* at Philae, the so-called Kiosk of Trajan, as it appeared (top) before the island was flooded by the Aswan dam, (centre) in 1974 when it stood partially submerged in the reservoir between the old and the new dams, and (bottom) in October 1975, when the island had been surrounded by a cofferdam and the water pumped out. The temples were about to be dismantled and erected on the nearby island of Agilkia.

stone for a sugar factory in the mid-nineteenth century. Koseir was an important base for trade with Arabia and India and blocks of a Ptolemaic temple have also been found there.

Although the plan of these temples follows earlier convention, many of the details are now used on a large scale for the first time. The broken lintel, which had had a short-lived popularity at Amarna, is a characteristic feature of the main doorways and the screen wall with an open top area that forms the front of the first hypostyle hall is another trait. The pillars in these halls still have their capitals in the forms of plants, but they are much more ornate than the older examples. Lotus, papyrus and palm patterns are all used together but are carefully arranged in symmetrical pairs.

The greater part of the decoration of these temples is in uninspired sunk relief. The dynamic scenes of conquests of the New Kingdom are replaced by long, even rows of figures taking part in a solemn religious ritual, carefully marked off into panels by regimented lines of hieroglyphs. Only the wonted scene on the front of the temple pylon, of pharaoh smiting his enemies, calls for a dramatic posture; the rest of the figures shuffle along endlessly, interchangeable except for their insignia, with their smug smiles, dimpled knees, and doughnut-like navels. The subjects of the scenes, and to some extent even their position, is often repeated from temple to temple with some famous exceptions, like the scenes at Edfu recording the annual play celebrating the victory of the local god Horus over the wicked Seth.

The temples lie mostly in deep hollows in the centre of the present town, which in many cases still covers the outbuildings, although these can be seen at Dendera. It was possible to see a whole range of buildings on the island of Philae, in the magnificent setting of the First Cataract, but since the building of the first Aswan Dam this has been subjected to varying degrees of flooding. Even when the temple is finally removed to the new site on the nearby island of Agilkia, it is unlikely that it will be possible to reconstruct the original charm of Philae that many early travellers felt, for much of this lay in its island setting; the long colonnaded approach and the numerous small temples and shrines all added to the atmosphere of this holy island [77].

In the major shrines at Luxor and Karnak there was no great Ptolemaic rebuilding scheme, but Alexander's immediate successor, Philip Arrhidaeus, rebuilt the central shrine at Karnak in red granite with painted reliefs, and

78. Pylon and forecourt of the temple of Horus at Edfu; compare this Graeco–Roman building with the Ramesside pylon of the temple of Amun at Luxor [140, 141]. In the foreground, the remains of the *mammisi* or birth chapel.

Ptolemy Euergetes finished the gate in the south wall. It was probably one of the early Ptolemies who held a great spring-cleaning at Karnak and gathered together many statues and other items that seemed outmoded and dumped them in a great pit which Legrain found in 1903. From its murky depths he recovered over 17,000 bronzes and 751 stone statues and stelai. Many of the finest pieces in the Cairo Museum came from this cache including the statue of Ramesses II, illustrated on p. 89. At Luxor there was only minor new work but a pylon was added in front of the XVIIIth-dynasty shrine at Medinet Habu.

The Ptolemies were buried at Alexandria, near the *sema* of Alexander where the Mosque of the Prophet Daniel now stands, but the burials are either destroyed or await discovery.

79. Nubia between the First and Second Cataracts, an area extensively surveyed before work began on the High Dam at Aswan in 1960.

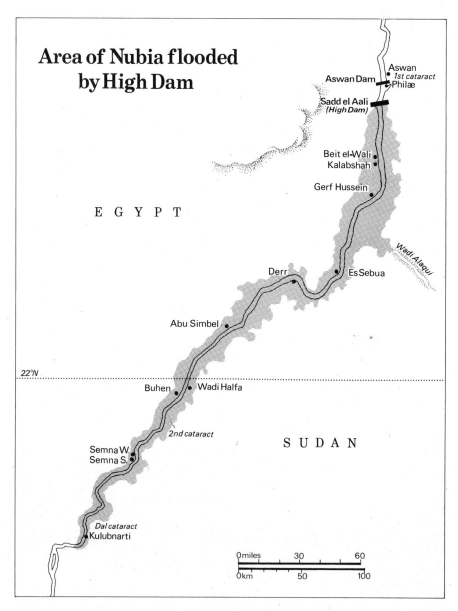

Many private burials have been recovered, usually comparatively poor, with few funeral gifts unceremoniously buried in earlier tombs. The cemetery of Tuna el-Gebel, however, provides an example of the wealthier burials. Here, near the ibis catacombs, there grew up a small town of house-tombs for the rich Greeks of Hermopolis. One of the earliest tombs is that of Petosiris, roughly contemporary with Alexander's occupation. The superstructure is built like the forehall of a small temple, and the burial lies in a deep shaft in the centre of the chapel. A porch, fronted by a screen wall, stands in front of a small pillared chapel [80]. The interior walls are decorated with well preserved painted reliefs which present an interesting combination of figures in Egyptian conventions, engaged on the traditional activities of Egyptian tomb-paintings but strongly influenced by Greek style, especially in the portrayal of details such as drapery and the occasional three-quarter or full-face view of the human figure [81].

Some of the later tombs had façades more like a house than a temple and a few have small stone lattice windows, possibly a sign of Near-Eastern influence. They are painted inside in a style fundamentally Egyptian in choice of subject and iconography, but with very strong Greek influence in colour and detail.

ROMAN AND COPTIC EGYPT: 30 BC–AD 641

After the battle of Actium and Cleopatra's death, Egypt was taken over by the Romans and administered as part of the imperial estate by a prefect responsible directly to the emperor. At first, efficient administration brought considerable prosperity but later there was a general decline, resulting from exploitation and increasingly stringent taxation; these burdens on individuals gradually undermined the economy and the morale of the population.

The emperors continued traditional building programmes and several Ptolemaic temples were eventually finished well into the first or even second century AD by emperors whose names, alphabetically transcribed into hieroglyphs, are duly recorded in cartouches on the temple walls. Some completely new buildings were undertaken, for instance the little Isis temple at Deir es-Shelwit, a few miles south of the principal area of occupation on the west bank at Thebes, and additions were made to others, such as the 'Kiosk of Trajan' at Philae. Considerable work was also done in Nubia, which the Romans partly occupied under Gaius Petronius in 25–21 BC, particularly in the temple of Kalabshah, built under Augustus.

They also destroyed and disfigured some of the older temples. The city of Coptos along with its temple of Min was destroyed by Diocletian as a reprisal

80. The tomb chapel of the priest Petosiris at Tuna el-Gebel, *c.* 325 BC. It resembles the first hall of a contemporary temple [cf. 137]; other tomb chapels nearby resemble houses.

81. Painted relief of a harvest scene from the tomb chapel of the priest Petosiris shows the influence of Greek artists in the portrayal of a standard Egyptian subject.

82. Relief from the rear wall of the temple of Hathor at Dendera showing (left) Cleopatra and her son Caesarion worshipping the gods Hathor, Horus Smatawy, Wennefer, Horus of Behdet, and Isis.

83. View from the rear of the temple of Hathor at Dendera illustrating the utilitarian design of these functional buildings compared with the decorative temples of Greece.

against a revolt. Luxor temple was made the centre of a *castrum*: the sanctuary was blocked off with an apse occupying the southern doorway of the hall behind Amenophis III's court, and this hall became the sanctuary for the imperial cult. Part of the painted decoration of the apse is still discernible.

In the Roman period there was much activity in the eastern desert, which was exploited for its mineral wealth. Abandoned workings and other debris in the form of crushing stones, gold-washing tables and spoil tips mark the gold mines, and walled encampments show stations along the roads to Qoseir (Leucos Limen) and Berenice on the Red Sea coast. Beryls and emerald-like stones were also mined and there are numerous quarries of Roman date: some, with trimmed blocks, marked with their destination, still awaiting transport.

Christianity was, according to Coptic tradition, taken to Egypt by St Mark but, although some Alexandrines may have been early converts, the new faith did not emerge as a recognizable force in the country until the second century, when its presence is confirmed by the discovery of papyri from Oxyrhynchus. The catechetical school at Alexandria attracted many students and was presided over by a series of distinguished leaders, notable amongst whom were Clement and Origen.

84. Portrait of Hermione, *grammatike*, a literary lady, painted in wax on wood, in the elaborate wrappings of her mummy. *c.* 2nd century AD. Now in Girton College, Cambridge.

Most of the early converts were Jews or Greeks but Dionysius, *c.* AD 250, encouraged the movement of evangelism amongst the native population. The poorer classes had long borne the brunt of the swingeing taxation and some had sought to avoid it by withdrawing their labour and abandoning their tenancies, choosing rather to live away from society in a tomb or cave on the edge of the desert. Intermittent persecution encouraged several Christians to follow this step. Foremost amongst them was St Anthony who, at the end of the third century, withdrew deep into the desert in search of seclusion. So great was the fame of his exploits of endurance and faith that disciples followed him, setting up their own cells near his, until an informal society developed which became the pattern of early monastic life. The sayings and deeds of these plain and unlettered men as recorded in the Coptic *Apophthegmata Patrum* or the seventeenth-century Latin folio, the *Vitae Patrum*, make stimulating and fascinating reading.

A more sociable form of monasticism was introduced *c.* AD 325 by Pakhom, who established the communal or cenobitical institutions that were copied in the European monastic orders. Pakhom, as befitted a converted soldier, laid down strict regulations for his followers and there is a military atmosphere about the great monasteries that they built in the fourth and fifth centuries [*Pl 20*].

Diocletian's onslaught on the Christians at the beginning of the fourth century produced many martyrs, whose faith attracted numerous converts. The church grew rapidly in numbers, which were swelled still further when Constantine made Christianity the official religion. Freedom from persecution encouraged theological speculation, and in the third and fourth centuries several heresies were developed, against which the Alexandrine bishops fought fiercely. But after the Council of Chalcedon (AD 451), the Egyptian Church was itself in schism from the rest of Christendom by reason of its espousal of the monophysite teaching. This may well have had a political motivation as much as a theological one: the monks were unlearned men not so much interested in the theological and philosophical niceties for their own sake as in using them as a means to express their dislike of the domination of the Byzantine rulers. Scholars like Clement and Origen were replaced by muscular bishops like Cyril, who used the fanaticism of the monks to establish religious and political separation.

The old pagan religion and philosophy persisted, though in decline, throughout this period in the temples and in the philosophical school of Alexandria. The temples gradually lost their personnel and their supporters and, their decorations defaced, were taken over for use as Christian churches. The last of them, the temple at Philae, was officially closed in AD 527 on the orders of Justinian, but still attracted pagan pilgrims from the south.

The term Coptic is often loosely applied to this period. It derives from the Greek word for Egypt, 'Aigyptios', and is best used, not to describe a period of history, but for the native population of Egypt and its culture through the late Roman or Byzantine period, as well as for the surviving Christian community after the Arab conquest. The study of Coptic archaeology has been on the whole neglected in preference for the great wealth of earlier remains, but is now a subject of renewed interest.

The principal remains of the period owe much to the Hellenistic and Byzantine influence. Their churches were generally built on the basilica plan and most of the relief decoration is of geometric or plant designs or scenes from the Bible. Tombstones are usually carved in flat relief with simple crosses and wreaths, or architectural designs, and the common Roman type, with a carved figure standing in a niche, was in use up to the sixth century. [155]

The classic period of Coptic culture is the period after Chalcedon down to the eleventh century. After the Arab conquest in 641 the tax system was arranged in favour of the Moslems, which was probably an important factor in the increasing number of Egyptians who eventually embraced Islam. Freedom of worship was allowed until the persecution in the eleventh century by the Caliph al-Hakim. Thereafter the Coptic community dwindled: some Christian villages preserved their identity and Coptic was spoken as a living language as late as the fifteenth or even sixteenth century in Upper Egypt, but it is now used only in the Coptic church as a liturgical language, the last surviving continuous link with the language of Ancient Egypt.

PART II

The Structure of the State

THE KING AND GOVERNMENT

Throughout the period from the union of the Two Lands under Menes to the death of Cleopatra, Egypt was at least theoretically a monarchy, although the power of the king varied from a strength approaching despotism in the Old Kingdom to short periods of almost total ineffectiveness. Nevertheless, for the nation, he was a divine figurehead in whose person the Two Lands were united, and continuity and stability of his government were highly regarded by Egyptian writers. It is perhaps too cynical to suggest that because they belonged to the government class they had a vested interest in such stability.

In practice, the king's rule was exercised by a highly developed bureaucracy, and in many cases the separate existence of the Two Lands was recognized by the establishment of two equal posts, with one official responsible for Upper Egypt, the other for the Delta. The principal official was the vizier, responsible for day-to-day administration, the treasury and the judiciary, although at some periods the real power was wielded by the priesthood of a major national deity, such as Re' or Amun.

For most of the time the capital was at Memphis, a huge site seventeen miles south of modern Cairo, greatly plundered and incompletely excavated. Its situation at the junction of the Nile valley and the Delta made it a good administrative centre. Thebes, the home city of the Middle Kingdom and the XVIIIth-dynasty rulers, was also a seat of the court. The Ramessides favoured their Delta homeland and built a capital at Qantir. Local administration was arranged under a series of districts called nomes whose number varied from time to time between thirty-eight and forty-two. They were run as separate economic units, and governed by a nomarch, with their own principal city usually built around the temple of the local deity.

ROYAL TITULARY

The titles of the king were developed in the Old Kingdom and eventually the full titulary consisted of a group of five names, each representing a different aspect of the monarchy. The earliest name was the one by which the king was known as the embodiment of the god Horus. In the Archaic Period it was frequently displayed in a *serekh*—a tall rectangle, the lower part of which was divided to represent the façade of a house or palace—surmounted by a figure of the Horus falcon [13]. To this was added the name used by the king as the incarnate form of the two principal goddesses of the two kingdoms, the vulture Nekhbet of El-Kab and the cobra Wadjet of Edjo, or Buto, in the Delta. The third name was used by the king as the Golden Horus, the fourth in his capacity as King of Upper and Lower Egypt, the fifth as son of the sun-god Re'.

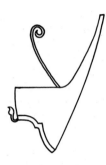

85. Royal crowns of Egypt: (top) the White Crown of Upper Egypt, (centre) the Red Crown of Lower Egypt, (bottom) the Double Crown.

These last two names are written in cartouches, frames formed by an oval loop of rope tied in a knot at one end. The loop has the Egyptian name *shenu*, based on the verb *sheni*, to encircle, and probably is intended to suggest that the king rules all that is encircled by the sun. Egyptian king-lists generally use the fourth name, but the kings are usually known to us by the last of their names, in the Greek form based on Manetho's usage, but occasionally in a transcribed form of the Egyptian. Some of the Egyptian forms were almost unrecognizably transfigured in their Greek guise: it takes considerable ingenuity, for instance, to recognize User-ma'at-Re', part of the name of Ramesses II, as Shelley's Ozymandias.

The word pharaoh is not a title but a circumlocution derived from the phrase *Per 'ao*, the Great House, applied to the palace or court and later to the person of the king who lived there. It is exactly parallel to our own way of referring to H.M. Government as Whitehall. Mention of the phrase was usually accompanied by a pious wish that the ruler should 'live, prosper and be healthy', written in an abbreviated form in three hieroglyphs ♀ ⚱ ∩ as a constantly repeated group on royal equipment.

REGALIA

Many statues of all periods show the king wearing the *nemes* head-cloth, which seems to be a piece of cloth worn over the wig and held in place by a band across the forehead and gathered at the back. It appears to be stiffly folded and the two lappets falling forward over the chest are often shown with many horizontal pleats. It is usually assumed to be of linen, but experiments show that linen does not hold its shape for long and leather is a possible alternative. It is often represented in stripes of different colours.

For special occasions a series of different crowns were provided. The earliest known of these are the White Crown of Upper Egypt and the Red Crown of Lower Egypt, frequently shown combined in a double crown to emphasize the dual nature of the kingdom.

The *atef*-crown, a form of the White Crown with a long plume on either side, occurs in the Old Kingdom but later is usually the headdress of Osiris. Likewise, the pair of plumes that form the *shuti*-crown, and which in the Middle Kingdom and Late Period are part of the royal ladies' headgear, are often associated with the gods Amun and Min.

The Blue Crown, first mentioned in the XIIIth dynasty, is common in the New Kingdom and is almost always shown in blue. On statues its surface is covered with small bosses, perhaps representing metal studs securing a leather cover to a frame or reinforcement, for in origin it was probably a military helmet.

At the front of the headdress there was attached a uraeus or model of the serpent goddess Wadjet, and sometimes also the head of the vulture goddess Nekhbet.

The crowns of the queens are also elaborate. They incorporate a long wig with lappets falling onto the breasts, while the headdress is in the form of vultures' wings with both the vulture's head and the uraeus on her brow. This may be surmounted by other emblems, such as the double plumes, or disc and horns, set in a circular base ornamented with a ring of uraei.

From the earliest times the king wore the tail of a giraffe or bull attached to the back of his belt. Occasionally it is shown between his legs in seated statues and Tutankhamun's was found *in situ*, wrapped in a bead net. The buckle at the front of the belt was often inscribed with the king's name and from the belt was hung an apron or sporran of strings of beads.

The false beard which the king affected was probably carefully braided and held in place by a band around his lower jaw. It was evidently an important part of the regalia—even Queen Hatshepsut is portrayed with one.

The king and some of the senior officials are sometimes shown with various staffs or sceptres which they carried as symbols of authority. One type of sceptre, which seems to have developed from an ordinary staff, has a forked foot and terminal in the shape of the narrow pointed head of the mythical dog-like Seth animal. The stick itself is straight in some examples, usually called the *was*, and wavy in others, when it is called the *djam*, but the terms are not always applied consistently. This sceptre is frequently carried by deities and, with the long hieroglyph for heaven, ⚊ often forms the frame around a ritual scene. A second type of sceptre is shorter with a long, broad, flat blade and a handle usually ornamented with papyrus or lotus-flower terminals. There are a variety of names for this sceptre, which is also seen in ritual contexts, where it is carried by the king as he makes an offering.

Two distinctive attributes of kingship and of Osiris as king of the Afterworld are the crook and flail. The crook is a shortened version of the shepherd's implement and men are occasionally shown carrying a full-length one, often with a simple bent-over top rather than the recurved type. Although the other implement is called a flail, it is angled, but not pivoted, at the top and has three loose streamers. It has been compared with the device used in other Mediterranean countries to collect the aromatic gum laudanum from the leaves of the cistus plant, but there is no evidence for this practice in pharaonic times.

In processions the king was accompanied by a fan-bearer who carried a large fan of woven grass-work or, later, ostrich feathers set in an ornate handle, about 1 m. long. Other insignia can be observed in illustrations or in extant examples, such as the two wands, one gold, one silver, surmounted by small figures of the king, found in the tomb of Tutankhamun.

Representations of the coronation ceremony show the king, wearing his regalia and a kilt, hailed by the leading gods. A second highlight of a king's reign was the Sed festival or jubilee, usually celebrated after thirty years of rule and thereafter at more frequent intervals. It may have been based on an earlier custom in which the king was subjected to a test to ascertain his fitness to continue in the arduous position of leader. If he failed he would be replaced by a younger leader, but during the dynastic period the test was commuted to a magical ceremony by which the king's powers were rejuvenated. The Step Pyramid reliefs of Djoser show him apparently engaged in running a set course [86], and the statue of Mentuhotep shows him wearing a long cloak that was part of the ceremonial robes.

86. Relief of King Djoser taking part in the ceremonial race, part of the Sed or jubilee festival. The delicately carved relief is one of three that stand in a corridor deep underground below the southern buildings of the Step Pyramid enclosure. Similar panels are found below the pyramid itself. The corridors are lined with blue glazed tiles imitating reed work.

SEALS

Delegated authority was made possible by the use of a seal, and authority to use official seals was the mark of a high official in the administration. Private seals usually bear the name and title of their owner and were evidently made to order; others have a geometric or plant design or the figure of a god. These could be bought ready-made and the design was presumably distinctive enough to be identified within the comparatively small circle of illiterate people concerned. Seals also seem to have been used as amulets, for many are inscribed with a motto or phrase wishing good luck. Many of the seals with a royal name

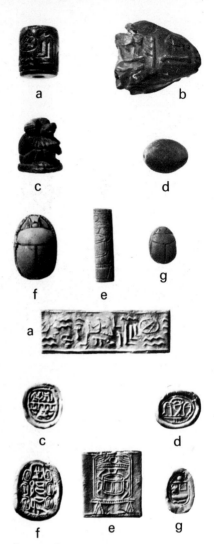

87. Group of seals and impressions: (a) Late predynastic cylinder seal, black steatite. (b) Mud sealing bearing an impression of a seal of type (a). (c) Middle Kingdom stamp seal, in the form of a squatting ape, green faience. (d) Middle Kingdom stamp seal in stylized cowrie, blue faience. (e) Middle Kingdom cylinder seal, ivory. (f) Hyksos-type scarab seal with characteristic scroll pattern around the inscription, blue faience. (g) New Kingdom scarab with design of Tuthmosis I, blue faience. Now in the City Museum and Art Gallery, Birmingham. Length of (d) 2·9 cm.

must come into this class, too, for there are large numbers that bear the cartouche of some popular monarchs, such as Tuthmosis III, some of which were made in the styles of later periods. An object bearing the name of a powerful ruler was probably as powerful as one with a god's name.

Egyptian seals may be divided into three main groups: cylinder seals, which were rolled over the sealing clay, and stamp seals, of which those in the form of the scarab beetle are sufficiently numerous to be treated as a separate group. Both the stamp seal and the scarab are often attached to a ring, sometimes worn as a signet ring but often too bulky or too flimsy for this purpose and these, like the cylinder seals, could be worn on a cord round the neck or tied to the belt. The seals were used on wet clay, which could be plastered over the lid of a jar or the door of a tomb, or, applied as sealing wax is today, over a knot securing a bolt, a lid or a rolled-up document [87].

Seal-makers are seldom referred to but their craft required great skill and artistry. Cylinder seals were often made in wood, as splits which show up in the impressions make clear, but few of these have survived. Others were made in steatite, haematite and, occasionally, copper or pottery. Stamp seals were made in semi-precious stones, but by far the most common material was glazed steatite. The colour of the glaze is usually blue or green. The fine stones tended to follow a fashion: amethyst was popular in the XIIth dynasty, carnelian and jasper in the New Kingdom.

Most common in the Archaic Period and Old Kingdom, cylinder seals were introduced from western Asia, where they were used to seal clay tablets. They were less suitable in Egypt, where the writing material—papyrus—could be rolled up and tied; it was more convenient to stamp-seal a small lump of clay over the knot. Cylinder seals persist as late as the Ramesside period but are comparatively rare after the VIth dynasty. In the Archaic Period they are about 1·5 cm. in diameter and 2 cm. long; later varieties are rather longer.

As the inconvenience of the cylinder seal became more manifest it was replaced by the stamp seal. Between the VIth and XIIth dynasties, the commonest variety was button-shaped, a disc with a small loop at the back, and the face inscribed with a stylized animal or geometric design, rarely a hieroglyphic inscription. In the late Middle Kingdom and the Second Intermediate Period a small rounded or oval seal with a plain humped back was popular; sometimes the back is hachured around the edge. The type persists, with higher, more elaborate backs, into the New Kingdom.

A few stamp seals of Middle Kingdom date have model animals carved in the round on their backs, but these are more common in the XVIIIth dynasty, when cats, hedgehogs, hippopotami, fish, frogs and ducks are popular.

In the New Kingdom, seals were often mounted on a gold ring or incorporated in a gold, silver or bronze signet ring, which, in the Ramesside and later periods, became the standard form. Faience rings of this type were probably not intended for use; it is more likely that they were given away as 'favours', distributed at banquets and similar occasions.

The origin of the beetle-backed stamp seal, the scarab, so-called after the name of the beetle (*scarabeus sacer*), is a matter of hypothesis. It was certainly a convenient form and incorporated various amuletic devices. The name of the beetle, *kheper*, enabled it to be used as the hieroglyph for *kheper*, meaning 'to come into existence' or simply 'to be'. It could then be linked with the idea of spontaneous generation, an idea which the apparent birth of the beetle from a ball of dung also supported. The figure of the beetle pushing this ball, which in fact was used for food, was likened to the god Khepri pushing the ball of the sun across the sky.

The typology of scarabs is extremely complicated: the material, the colour of the glaze (if any), the treatment of the back-markings and legs, the nature of inscription and general workmanship, all have to be taken into account. The earliest specimens are found in the VIth dynasty. Those inscribed with the names of Cheops and Chephren are usually of the archaizing Saite period. The design in the Middle Kingdom and Second Intermediate Period is often geometric, based on a twisted rope or pattern of whorls or plant design, but the amethyst and carnelian scarabs of the XIIth dynasty were too hard for the lapidaries to inscribe and the smooth base was often covered with a gold plate bearing the inscription. In most cases this plate has been removed and re-used long ago.

A great number of scarabs belonging to the Second Intermediate Period are found in archaeological contexts in Palestine, where they provide useful cross-dating evidence. Their non-Egyptian-speaking owners often had them inscribed with extraordinary combinations of hieroglyphs.

During the reign of Amenophis III a number of large scarabs were issued to commemorate his building achievements, marriage, etc. They are inscribed with a brief account of the incident and several copies were issued of each type.

Private names, royal names, expressions of good luck, animals and gods are all found on the New Kingdom and later specimens. The cartouche of Tuthmosis III was extremely common and is still popular with modern scarab-makers.

THE ROYAL PALACE

The Great House, or Palace, was perhaps the most ephemeral of Egyptian buildings. Private houses could be used by successive generations, and the houses of the dead and of the gods were built to last for eternity, but royalty must impress and each king attempted to outdo his predecessor by building a new, lavishly appointed palace.

The *serekh* indicates that early palaces were built with a niche design on the façade, probably at first structural and achieved by pillars of reed bundles, between which hung woven mats. Some of the pavilions in the Step Pyramid complex illustrate this in stone, and the early mastabas and sarcophagi also reflect this design. The so-called 'forts' of the Archaic Period cemetery at Abydos were based on castles of this type.

The palaces of the New Kingdom are the only ones that have survived sufficiently to allow some reconstruction of the original plan. Amongst the multifarious rooms of Amenophis III's palace at Malkata in western Thebes were four audience suites, based on a distinctive long hall containing a central aisle flanked by two rows of pillars leading to a throne dais, and approached by a short flight of steps. The dais was suitably decorated with paintings of bound captives and the rest of the hall painted to resemble a pool surrounded by plants, animals and birds.

At Amarna the principal palace, in the central city (see p. 78), was built astride the royal road. Its river frontage is lost, but west of the royal road lies a great pillared audience hall with over five hundred columns and a complex of smaller halls, courts, and formal gardens. A curious feature of this area is the use of ramps approaching the raised thresholds of the doorways as if to allow the passage of wheeled vehicles. This complex was connected by a bridge, with the smaller, private part of the palace on the east side of the royal road, where the royal family's apartments were decorated with murals of their family life. In the official residence, near the bridge, there was a large 'Window of Appearances', where the royal family made formal appearance on state occasions.

Outside the central city beyond the north suburb, lay the north palace. This was apparently designed for official occasions only, since it contains no living quarters. Two main courts, one behind the other, front on to the river; beyond the second, which contains a large pool, is a pillared hall leading to a throne room. South of these lay a range of halls and offices, and on the north side there is a large court with an open-air altar, a series of stables, and a small court with a central pool surrounded by cubicles decorated with paintings of birds in papyrus thickets. It connects with the throne room and is evidently for quiet repose and retreat.

A number of New Kingdom funerary temples at Thebes include, within the complex, usually just south of the main forecourt, a small residential area where the king could hold court during the Valley festival. Approached by a separate entrance, just left of the pylon, the area is composed mainly of a hall leading to a throne room, with a dais opposite a Window of Appearances overlooking the first court of the temple. A bedroom is situated just off the throne room, and small suites for officials are also provided nearby. This unit is most clearly seen at Medinet Habu [88].

Thrones were constructed on the same principles as chairs (see p. 118), usually heavily ornamented with gold and coloured inlays, symbols of the kingly occupant of the chair and the tutelary deities that were, hopefully, grouped around it. Lion masks or heads surmount the front legs and the arm panels might be carved in the form of protective wings. The framework of struts below the seat was made in the form of heraldic plants, the lotus and papyrus of the two regions of Egypt, intertwined around the hieroglyph ⚇, meaning union. Behind the throne a large fan or sun shade is usually shown. As well as actual examples found in the tombs of Tutankhamun and Tuthmosis IV (the latter in fragmentary condition), bronze model thrones were produced in the Late Period. The ceremonial throne was provided with a low footstool on which were represented the king's enemies, usually as nine bound Negroid and Asiatic captives.

WEIGHTS AND MEASURES

Weights and measures can be ascertained by computation from existing measuring-rods and containers, although there is some degree of discrepancy, perhaps due to different standards being in use in different areas or periods, or for different trades and commodities. The most noticeable discrepancies arise in the standards of weights. The principal units and approximate equivalents are as follows:

Capacity measure for liquids: 1 *hin* = 0·5 litre
Capacity measure for grain: 1 *heqat* = 4·5 litre
Weight: 10 *kite* to 1 *deben* = 91 grammes
Length (used in buildings): 1 royal cubit (divided into 7 palms or 28 digits*) = 52·3 cm.
1 short cubit (divided into 6 palms or 24 digits) = 45 cm.

* This unit is based on the human arm, the digit being the thickness of a finger and the palm being the width across the back of the hand.

88. The palace area lying on the south side of the first court of the temple of Medinet Habu used when Ramesses III visited the west bank for the Valley festival. The main throne room is built around a stepped dais flanked by two pillars, with a bedroom to the bottom left and bathroom to the top right. Other suites in the palace were used by the queen and courtiers. This photograph was taken from the top of the main pylon.

Long distances were measured by the *iteru* or river measure of 20,000 cubits, roughly 10·5 km. Area was measured by the *setjat* of 100 cubits squared, about 2,735 sq. m., and smaller areas in terms of a cubit, in this case a 1 cubit wide strip 100 cubits long.

Measurement of weight was done with a balance, held by a cord at the centre point with pans at either end. In the Middle Kingdom an upright stand supported the beam instead and a plumb line, hung against a rectangular board attached to the beam, made for greater precision. In the New Kingdom the board was replaced by a metal pointer. Weights are usually in polished hardstone, rectangular or dome-shaped. They are often unmarked and there was little accurate standardization.

As well as the cubit stick, a line was used when measuring long distances, such as field boundaries, and when setting out the foundations of a building. Jars and other containers sometimes bear a note of their capacity but actual capacity measures are rare.

The hours of sunlight were divided into twelve hours, which varied in length according to the season. They could be marked by a shadow clock, consisting of an upright arm that cast a shadow on to a calibrated horizontal arm. A water clock was developed in the New Kingdom in which the intervals of time are always constant, although in some examples there were different sets of calibrations for the different seasons. The exact time was important for religious ceremonies but otherwise it is doubtful if the Egyptians were particularly concerned and they probably judged the time approximately, relying on the position of the sun or the sharpness of their appetite. At night the passage of time was measured by observation of the stars, using a vertical staff with a narrow slit at the top through which the observer sighted on a plumb line. These two instruments were set up in a fixed position, usually on a temple roof and, using previously prepared tables, it was possible to mark off the divisions of the night by observing the positions of various stars. It was also possible to calculate the time roughly by looking in a north–south direction at a sitting person and using parts of the body as reference points for star positions.

Such calculations were dependent on careful observation and extensive records, which the Egyptians kept to the best of their ability, but they did not have sufficiently sophisticated devices for highly accurate work, in spite of what is often claimed for them.

The Egyptians at first appear to have marked the passage of the year by lunar months measured from one disappearance of the waning moon to the next, a period averaging about 29½ days. The recurring seasons were then linked with these months giving three seasons—Inundation, Spring and Summer—of 4 months each, and resulting in a year of 12 months or approximately 354 days. The year began with the coming of the inundation, which usually coincided with the heliacal rising of Sirius, or Egyptian Sothis, the brightest star in the sky apart from the sun.

The succeeding months were named by festivals dated by phases of the moon, but the last month of the year, the month of the festival of Sothis, was marked by a feast on the day of Sothis's rising, which was not related to the moon and therefore, if the 354-day year was not corrected, the festival would occur outside the month in which it was due to be celebrated. This was avoided by inserting an extra month every three, or sometimes two, years and since the months remained roughly in step with the seasons this calendar was used for the agricultural and festival year.

This practical but untidy arrangement did not appeal to the bureaucratic mind of the civil service and for administrative purposes a civil year was devised, consisting of three seasons of four months, each of thirty days to which were added five intercalary days. Since no allowance was made for the extra quarter of a day this year became progressively out of step with the true year and the Sothic rising (when the year was assumed to begin). This state of affairs was simply allowed to continue, although in a cycle of 1,460 years (4 × 365) the quarter-days amounted to a whole year and the two calendars briefly appeared to be in step again.

The civil year was set up during the Archaic Period and soon afterwards a second schematic lunar year was established, linked with the civil year so that its months coincided roughly with the civil months. All three calendars remained in use until the Christian period. The Romans added a sixth intercalary day each leap year and this is the Coptic calendar as used today.

The earliest method of recording the passing years, used in the Ist and IInd dynasties, was to name each year after an important event that occurred during it. For a time in the Old Kingdom the years were reckoned by the number of biennial cattle censuses that had occurred since the accession of the reigning monarch, so the year after the Third Cattle Census of King X would be the seventh year of his reign. In the VIth dynasty this was modified and the number of years that had elapsed since the accession became the normal method of dating events.

Since Egypt was a nation of producers rather than shopkeepers there was no incentive in dynastic times to introduce coined money. A barter system worked perfectly well and in the New Kingdom and later was regulated by a scale on which objects were valued in terms of weights of gold, silver or copper, or sacks of barley. Apart from a few fourth-century small silver coins in the Greek style and a few gold coins issued by Teos, penultimate king of the XXXth dynasty, coins were not used in Egypt before the Ptolemaic period, when the Attic silver standard was adopted. Gold and silver coins of the higher denominations carry the portrait of the king or his queen, or both, on the obverse, while the reverse most often bears an eagle on a thunderbolt. Lower denomination bronze coins were struck on a flan cast with a bevelled edge; the obverse, on the bevelled side, bears a head of Zeus and the reverse is usually a cornucopia or the eagle and thunderbolt with the legend: *ΠΤΟΛΕΜΑΙΟΥ ΒΑΣΙΛΗΩΣ*.

The isolation of Egypt in the Roman world was emphasized by the fact that a local coinage was ordered that was not circulated elsewhere in the Empire. The obverse usually bears the Emperor's name and title in Greek and his bust. The reverse may be a variety of types: the eagle and cornucopia continued in favour while others may be portraits of members of the Imperial house, divinities of the Greek or Egyptian pantheons, personified cities, buildings, animals and so on.

Very little coinage circulated outside Alexandria, where it was minted. Lead tokens are found in Middle and Lower Egypt in four main varieties issued at Akhmim, Memphis, Arsinoë and Oxyrhynchus, and in the Delta.

TRAVEL AND TRANSPORT

Distant travel for the common man is still a comparatively new feature of society, made possible initially by the advent of the railway. He may have travelled on pilgrimage or military service but not in the course of his normal life. This was no doubt true of the ancient Egyptians, but there were adventurous souls whose journeys took them far afield. Military campaigns took many men to Palestine and large expeditions were mounted to work the mines of Sinai or the quarries of the eastern desert. However, the Egyptian equivalent of the mysterious East or the wild West was undoubtedly the exotic South. Just beyond the barrier of the First Cataract were the riches of Nubia, and further south was the abundant store-house of Africa, with its gold, ivory, ebony and incense, and its strange animals and fierce tribes. To reach Africa, one either travelled up the Nile, like the Old Kingdom explorers Weni and Kharhuf, or sailed down the Red Sea to the east coast, the region of Eritrea, as Hatshepsut's men did. The rewards were great but so were the dangers; the Egyptians faced the fierce African tribes as military equals, without the advantages of gunpowder and steel that encouraged the explorers of Africa and America in our era.

Travel within the confines of Egypt was likewise restricted. Officials travelled on government business, dispensing justice, conducting audits and collecting taxes; rich landowners had estates in distant nomes which required occasional inspections; but of the poorer classes probably only the boatmen travelled far from home in the course of their work.

Transport was greatly helped by the shape of the country. Normally one would never be more than a few miles from the river and long journeys north and south could be undertaken fairly leisurely by boat. The downstream current helped the traveller to drift north and a reliable northerly wind provided the power for travelling south. So, for the Egyptians, the word for 'to go north' was simply 'to drift', and 'to go south' was 'to sail'. Their descriptive powers were taxed when they first met the 'upside-down' Euphrates! Heavy loads, such as the giant obelisks, also went by river and during the inundation period they could even be floated over the fields, and closer to their destination on the desert edge [90].

Roads therefore were not important. Dirt tracks were necessary in the towns for chariots, and pack animals followed paths along the dykes in the country, but paved roads were unnecessary. When Herodotus speaks of the paved way used for hauling stone for the pyramids, he was probably describing the funeral causeway connecting the valley and mortuary temples, although it may well have been built at an early stage in the construction for use as a service road. At Amarna there is evidence for parallel ridges of packed gravel which provided a firm base for rollers transporting heavy weights. They would be purely temporary and the traces would normally soon be obliterated.

The chariot was probably introduced into Egypt from Palestine during the Second Intermediate Period along with the horse. A XVIIth-dynasty model boat in the Cairo Museum is mounted on four-spoked wheels, and Egypt provides the oldest known complete examples of wheeled vehicles, from the funerary equipment of the fifteenth and fourteenth centuries BC. These chariots are beautifully and skilfully fashioned for lightness, using a frame of wood built well forward of the axle to increase stability, the sides filled in with a canvas overlaid with stucco and the floor with interwoven leather thongs. A single central pole, shaped by bending while wet, ran forward from the axle tree between the pair of horses to a yoke which rested on a saddle on the horses' backs. This was held in place by a girth strap and breast harness. The two wheels have four, or, after c. 1400 BC, six spokes, made of two separate pieces of wood glued together for greater resilience, and bound with leather ties.

The earliest bits, from about 1400 BC, consist of a bar of metal, sometimes hinged in the centre, with a loop at each end to which the reins were attached. Inside each loop threaded on the bar is a disc which keeps the bit in place. Later bits, in use about 1200 BC, have a jointed mouthpiece and flat oblong cheek-pieces with slots to take a strap running around the muzzle. Tutankhamun's horses were fitted with blinkers. Horses were occasionally used for riding and the riders carried whips, sometimes finely carved. Horseshoes were not used.

Carts were known in Egypt but goods were more often transported on donkeyback. Genesis (45, 19 and 46, 5) records that Pharaoh sent carts to transport Joseph's family to Egypt, and the Syrian who came to consult Neferhotep travelled with ox-drawn two-wheeled wagons. The invaders in the reign of Ramesses III brought their families in covered wagons in the true pioneer tradition!

The use of camels was limited. The Old Testament suggests they were known in the thirteenth century BC (Exodus 9, 3) and a camel's skull was found among neolithic remains in the Fayyum, but, apart from a thirteenth-century figure of a camel with waterjars from Memphis, there is little other evidence of their use.

Long after the wheel was in common use, heavy weights were still moved over short distances by sledge. Water poured on the ground apparently eased the task and the traction power was simply large numbers of men tugging on ropes and pushing with levers. The sledge on which the outer wooden coffin of Sennudjem was mounted shows signs of having been fitted with solid wheels, but this is quite exceptional. The wooden bases of bronze figurines are often sledge-shaped for this would be the way in which the larger figures of the god would be moved. The gods were also carried in procession on a framework of poles on the shoulders of men, who sometimes walked under a covering surround. There are a few examples of carrying-chairs, notably the richly ornamented one belonging to Queen Hetepheres, although the royal palanquin is frequently shown in representations of religious processions [Pl 23].

The dominance of the river in the environment led to the early development of sailing boats, shown on late Naqada pottery with cabins and square-rigged

masts. Sixty or so lines along the sides suggest large crafts with many rowers, unless the lines represent the wake of the boat. In dynastic times there are illustrations of boats in tomb scenes and temple reliefs, as well as model craft, chiefly from the Middle Kingdom. Some full-sized boats have survived; two from boat-pits by the pyramid of Cheops and six from Dahshur from the time of Sesostris III.

These surviving boats reveal some constructional details not clear from the reliefs of shipbuilding, such as those found in the Vth-dynasty tomb of Ti. The best preserved boat from Cheops's pyramid is built in cedar-wood, about 43 m. long and 6 m. wide. It has no keel but is built around a heavy beam placed on edge and running lengthwise just below the deck. Twelve frames are fixed to this and the planking of the hull and deck pegged together and lashed to the frames. There was a deck-house of wooden screens aft and columns for an awning amidships. There is no sign of a mast and the barge was probably towed; the six pairs of oars found in the boat would have provided steerage [89].

Most of the boats in the Old Kingdom illustrations are sailing craft, flat-bottomed with cut-off ends to the hull and with bipod masts well forward. These masts could be lowered into fork-shaped supports on the cabin roof when not required. When in use they were lashed against the beams and supported by several backstays. The sails were trapezoid on heavy yards, with the narrow end at the bottom to prevent them dipping into the water when rolling. Motive power was also provided by rowers sitting on the deck beams, and steerage by one or two long stern oars.

Changes in the hull form in the late Old Kingdom and the introduction of a lower, broader sail allowed the boats to sail close-hauled. The sail now had a boom, upturned at the ends, and the stern was built up above the level of the main deck. Steerage was usually with a long oar, lashed in a groove over the stern and again at the end of the stock to a heavy post in front of the steersman, who worked the oar by a tiller, a wooden rod socketed into the stock by which he could twist the blade. Alternatively, the end of the stock might move along a rope or pole stretched between two such posts. Most boats of the Middle and New Kingdom were based on this type. The so-called Byblos boats that ventured to sea, probably coast-hugging, to Byblos and Punt, were adaptations of the Nile sailing boat. They were given a higher and sharper stem and stern to ride the open sea better and were apparently strengthened by a 'hogging truss', a rope run from prow to stern over a pair of stanchions, and twisted tight with a stout pole. They were also adapted into fighting ships by the addition of a crow's nest for a sniping bowman or slinger, and by setting screens round the steersman and high bulwarks (with holes for the oars) to protect the crew.

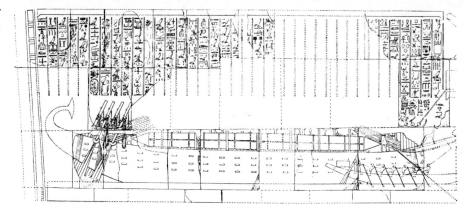

90. Line drawing, with restorations, of the relief showing the barge used for the transport of two obelisks from Aswan to Karnak. The obelisks appear to lie end to end on the deck. From the funerary temple of Hatshepsut at Deir el-Bahri, Thebes. XVIIIth–dynasty.

Large specially built transport barges were provided for heavy work, such as the removal of the great obelisks. Reliefs at Deir el-Bahri show two obelisks end to end on a great barge which the text describes as 120 cubits long (about 63 m.). It is not clear which of the four obelisks erected by Hatshepsut at Karnak they are, and the size of the human figures shows that the representation is not to scale. The barge is shown with three layers of beams protruding through the planking, probably set in equally substantial longitudinal timbers. Added strength is provided by five hogging trusses and motive power by thirty tugs, each with thirty oars [90].

Details of the rigging and other equipment is not always clear. Various curiously shaped pieces of wood on the models can be interpreted as cleats or similar features. In the absence of the pulley-block, the yards were hauled up by a topping-lift, apparently passing through a hole in the masthead or over a sort of miniature cross-tree arrangement. Numerous topping-lifts were provided for the boom as well, in order to maintain its upturned ends and so avoid the danger of its dipping into the water.

At all times papyrus boats were common, built of bundles of reeds lashed

91. Wooden model of a sailing boat, with an open–sided cabin. The man at the prow is sounding the lead, two others heave on quant-poles, two more haul on the rigging. The steersman squats on the after-deck holding the tiller of the heavy steering-oar. The owner sits in the cabin, with two trunks. On the cabin roof are painted two shields. XIIth–dynasty, from the tomb of Sebekhotep at Beni Hasan. Now in the British Museum, London. Length 69·8 cm.

together. They range from small skiffs used for fishing and wildfowling to substantial vessels with high upright prows and sharply curving sterns. Ceremonial boats often have these features even when made of wood, as if this were the traditional shape for such boats. They also have distinguishing ornaments, such as the ram's head at the prow of Amun's boat, and a canopy amidships to protect the shrine of the god. Funeral boats likewise have a canopy over the mummy on the river crossing [91].

THE ARMY

It was not until the New Kingdom that the government found it necessary to maintain a standing army of any size. Before that date a small army of professional soldiers was sufficient to maintain normal safeguards and levies might be raised by local nobles for specific duties. However, the problems of annual campaigns in Nubia or Palestine in the XVIIIth and succeeding dynasties demanded a large professional army with career officers, augmented by numbers of mercenaries, often foreigners and erstwhile enemies, particularly after the Ramesside campaigns.

The army that fought under the generalship of Ramesses II at Qadesh was composed of four divisions of 5,000 men each, comprising infantry regiments of about 200 men and chariots in squadrons of twenty-five. Amongst the regiments were both veteran soldiers and recruits; an élite corps of crack troops formed the king's guard. The companies paraded behind a standard, a rectangular board with a painted device, or a more elaborate carved ensign, and each division also had its special designation. In Ramesses II's army they were named after the gods Reʿ, Ptah, Sutekh and Amun [94].

There was some uniformity of dress throughout the army, although the mercenaries preferred their own distinctive weapons and armour. Egyptian soldiers carried a long shield, with a rounded or slightly pointed top, of rawhide with the hair left on for added strength. In the New Kingdom, scale armour was introduced, consisting of a short-sleeved leather tunic on to which some

92. Wooden model of a squad of soldiers: they are armed with spears and carry rawhide shields. From Assiut. XIth–dynasty. Now in the Cairo Museum.

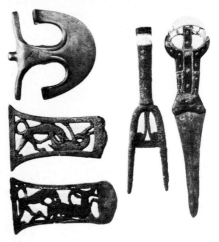

four hundred or so small leather (later bronze) plates were sewn. It had a leather collar at the neck and must have been a considerable impediment. A close-fitting leather helmet protected the head [92].

The earliest weapons, illustrated on the late predynastic palettes, were the bow and arrow, and the heavy stone mace. The simple bow with a single convex arc was used even after the double-convex bow with increased range had been developed. The Hyksos introduced the composite bow, of laminated wood and horn, which had a range of some 400 m. A few decorated bow-cases, and the occasional archer's bag containing spare arrowheads and 'strings' of gut or hide, survive. An important part of an archer's equipment was a metal or leather brace—a plate bound to the inside of the fore-arm to protect his wrist from the rub of the string. Arrows were about 75 cm. long, of wood or reed and flighted with bird's feathers. Flint arrowheads were common well into the dynastic period but bronze ones are also found, the long flesh-slashing types of the Middle Kingdom and early New Kingdom were replaced by short, thick, heavy types when armour was introduced. After the XXVIth dynasty they often had three wings instead of two and a few iron examples are known. The arrows were often carried loose, but in the Middle Kingdom a leather or basketwork quiver was commonly worn on the back or, in the New Kingdom, fixed to the chariot. Men are occasionally portrayed with slings, but the Egyptians do not seem to have used bands of slingers as did their Asiatic counterparts.

The mace was not commonly used after the Old Kingdom, although the ritual reliefs of the triumphant ruler that adorn the temple pylons usually depict him wielding one. It was replaced by heavy wooden clubs and by metal battle-axes. These had plain, D-shaped blades that fitted into a slot in the handle and were secured by a rawhide lashing. The Egyptians did not use a socketed axe-

93. Group of bronze weapons. Top left: Syrian epsilon-type axe from a XIIth–dynasty tomb at Abydos. Bottom left: open-work parade axes for ceremonial use, XVIIIth–dynasty. Centre: forked spear butt, XXth – XXIInd dynasty, Nabesha. Right: bronze dagger, with wood and ivory hilt, inlaid with copper. Middle Kingdom or Second Intermediate Period. Now in the Ashmolean Museum, Oxford. Length of dagger, 21·8 cm.

94. The army of Ramesses II in marching order with chariotry and infantry. Relief from the rear wall of his temple at Abydos.

head and, even in the Middle Kingdom, when they copied the epsilon-shaped socketed heads of the Asiatics, they developed a flat socketless version. The broad slashing blades were effective against unarmoured troops and a baton about 1 m. long, in which was set a long blade, was also used in the Middle Kingdom, but in the New Kingdom a narrower, waisted axe blade that would penetrate armour was used. A number of axes of both Middle and New Kingdom type carry a design in inlay or openwork and were probably made as parade axes for ceremonial use [93].

Daggers are rare before the Middle Kingdom, when they are quite short, with a wide blade, developing to a longer weapon, better described as a sword, in the New Kingdom. The handles in wood, bone or ivory were elaborately decorated. During the New Kingdom, the *khopesh* sword, shaped like a sickle but with a sharp outer or convex edge, was introduced from Near-Eastern

95. Massive mud-brick walls of the Middle Kingdom fortification at Buhen. The walls were some 4·8 m. thick and 11 m. high and stood behind a parapet and a ditch 7 m. deep. The site is now lost below the waters of Lake Nasser.

contacts. The amount of bronze needed for a sword made it a comparatively rare weapon. A company of model soldiers of Middle Kingdom date carry long spears with heavy heads, but the spears of New Kingdom date are shorter, about 1 m. long, with a lighter head and are more likely to have been used as javelins. Soldiers carry other weapons as well as the spear, which they probably discharged at a distance before closing with their foe [94].

We know little about the form of warfare. The accounts of the battles of Megiddo and Qadesh suggest that co-ordination and discipline were not strong points, but personal bravery was not lacking. Several long sieges of towns in Palestine are recorded. If the attackers could not successfully employ the ruse of Tuthmosis III's general, Djehuty, who captured Joppa by smuggling in troops concealed in baskets, they might have had to make a frontal attack using scaling ladders or a protective shelter, under which a battering ram could be wielded to breach the walls. Both these devices are illustrated in Middle Kingdom tombs, which also show the nature of the defences, with high walls topped by crenellations and strengthened at the base by a battered slope or *glacis*.

It is from the wall-paintings of the Middle Kingdom tombs at Beni Hasan that we have the most informative scenes of warfare, for Egypt was still unsettled following the anarchical First Intermediate Period, and warfare obviously played a significant part in people's lives. In many of the burials of this period the deceased took a bow or axe or some other weapon as part of his equipment to face the next world. Forts of this period in Nubia show that the Egyptians had to maintain strict military preparedness there. They are carefully sited, with an eye to a good defensive position and accessible water supply. The fortress of Buhen as rebuilt in the New Kingdom was on a much larger scale, with a perimeter ditch 6 m. wide and 2 m. deep in front of mud-brick walls 15 m. thick and 12 m. or more high [95].

Another weapon in the ruler's armoury was magic. From the Middle Kingdom there are a number of alabaster or pottery statuettes and a great number of pottery vessels bearing the names of enemies in Nubia and Syria–Palestine, whom it was thought would be weakened and defeated by the ritual cursing and smashing of the statuettes or vessels representing them. These 'execration texts' help to reconstruct the picture of Egypt's foreign campaigns by indicating the danger areas and the various lines of advance.

IO
Farming and Domestic Life

FARMING AND FOOD PRODUCTION

Ancient Egypt has been described as a 'civilization without cities', and in pharaonic times there were very few members of society whose lives were not closely linked with the agricultural cycle.

The farmers' year began with the arrival of the flood waters, about 19 July. During the three months that the water lay on the land the farmer could do little in the fields and some of the men were called on for corvée duty, doing the heavy haulage and labouring on pyramids and temples or on public works' schemes to control and conserve the flood water.

As soon as the waters began to recede planting started, for in a good season an energetic farmer might manage to raise two crops. The land was ploughed or roughly broken up and the seed broadcast so that it could be trodden in by herds of sheep or pigs. Then followed careful irrigation with water from the reservoirs where it had been stored [*Pl 22*].

Several crops would grow in the saturated soil without additional watering, but if more water was needed it could be brought by an intricate network of channels and dykes, fed by the *shaduf*, which was in use in the New Kingdom and probably earlier. The *saqia* or water wheel was not used in pharaonic Egypt.

The farmer's tools were heavy and crude. The fine soil required little ploughing and it was often only necessary to turn it over with a wooden hoe. These had either a pointed stick or a flat blade set in the handle and lashed in place with a rope. The plough consisted of a wooden share, later fitted with a metal shoe, fitted with two handles and a long shaft that was tied to a crude yoke placed over the animals' (oxen) horns. Harvesting was done with curved wooden sickles, set with flint blades, although bronze sickles became common in the New Kingdom [*Pl 21*].

Although Osiris and some other gods are shown carrying an instrument described as a flail, it is never shown in use in threshing scenes. That process was usually carried out by driving an ox over the piled-up ears of corn before it was winnowed, by tossing into the air with a wooden scoop, and sieved.

Although many of the traditional methods of agriculture are still employed in Egypt, there have been considerable changes in the crops grown, and there were several innovations during the long time-span of the pharaonic period. The basic cereal crop in the Old and Middle Kingdom was a barley, but in the New Kingdom emmer was the chief crop, and in the Hellenistic period winter wheat was grown in great quantity and became Egypt's principal export. Durra or sorghum was not grown on anything like the scale it is today. Ears of wheat were often placed in tombs as part of the funeral ceremony but, in spite of frequently repeated statements to the contrary, there is no properly documented account of any experiment in which these have successfully germinated in modern times.

The Egyptian method of agriculture was ideally suited to growing vegetables, of which odd rows could be planted in any available patch of soil. Several varieties of legumes have been found as part of the funerary provision and celery and cress have been identified in tomb scenes. The Israelites bemoaned the absence of the plentiful onions, garlic and leeks they had consumed during their bondage (Numbers 11, 5) and cos lettuces, thought to be an aphrodisiac, were provided for the upkeep of the god Min. Gourds of several different varieties, cucumbers and melons were also grown in quantity.

The *dom*-palm, the date and the fig (both the sycamore fig and the common fig) were the most popular fruit but several others were known, including the sidder, or 'Christ's thorn', *nabk* in Egyptian, as well as some whose Egyptian names have not been satisfactorily identified. Pomegranates were introduced in the New Kingdom; almonds, cherries, and possibly apples and pears, were brought in during the Greek period. Citrus fruits and bananas are not recorded although they are now popular.

Grapes were, of course, important for wine-making and there were extensive vineyards in the Delta and in the oases. The grapes were green or black and, as well as being made into wine, they were eaten fresh or as raisins or made into grape juice [*Pl 16*]. Another important crop was flax, which was grown for oil and for linen-making. Oil was also made from a number of other plants, including the castor oil plant, sesame, safflower, radish seeds, the balanos and the moringa nut, but the olive was not cultivated in Egypt until the New Kingdom and even then without success as an oil-producing tree. Rice and cotton were introduced in Hellenistic times.

Of the farmer's livestock his cattle were the most valuable. They were useful as draught animals and for treading out the grain at harvest time. They also provided him with milk and, eventually, meat. Two principal strains of cattle may be distinguished: a lean, tough variety called the *neg* and a heavier beast, the *iuwa*, which was imported in large numbers from the Sudan. Cattle were also imported in the New Kingdom from Cyprus and the Levant. As well as their more prosaic virtues, some cattle were regarded as incarnations of deities, and there is one ostracon from the New Kingdom showing a fight between two bulls that may have been a deliberately arranged sport or ritual.

In most of Upper Egypt grazing was poor and cattle were sent to the Delta for fattening, but sheep and goats could be maintained on the scrub at the desert edge. The type of sheep illustrated in the early dynasties is a large animal with horizontal twisted horns. These horns formed part of the insignia of the king and some of the gods, particularly Khnum and Herishef, but in the XVIIIth dynasty Amun took as his symbol the smaller fat-tailed sheep, distinguished by its thick curled horns. The sheep's wool was taboo as clothing for priests and the dead in spite of its common use elsewhere in the Near East, and the meat was likewise forbidden as an offering to the gods or as food for the priests. All these food taboos were probably subject to considerable variation from place to place and more carefully observed by the upper classes—particularly the priests—than by the mass of the people. The pig is another example, for it was associated with the wicked god Seth and therefore pronounced unclean, but debris from Deir el-Medinah shows that pork was eaten there.

The food supply was augmented and varied by the produce of professional fishermen, hunters and trappers. The Nile teemed with several varieties of fish, which were usually caught with a net trawled between two boats or two gangs of men working along each side of a pool. Stone or pottery weights were used as net sinkers. Smaller basketwork traps were set and light casting nets were used by individual fishermen; fish were also speared [*Pl 27*]. Numerous fish-hooks have been found of bone or metal: they are shown in Old Kingdom tomb scenes tied in groups to a line, but there are also illustrations of anglers fishing with a rod. Hatiay is even shown in his tomb at Thebes sitting on the fisherman's traditional folding stool but, surely unlikely, he is accompanied by his wife.

Catching the game birds that swarmed in the marshes of the Delta and riverside pools was another favourite relaxation of the upper classes. During the migration season there were many varieties of water birds, of which ducks and geese in particular made good eating. The sportsman went after them with bow and arrow or with a throwing stick [*Pl 27*]. Hunting arrows were of light reed construction with broad blunt blades, and unlike military arrows, their shape did not alter. Throwsticks were sometimes made of curved wooden blades that would return to the thrower; others are unevenly curved and would have had to have been retrieved. The gentleman sportsman is often shown with his wife and children in a flimsy skiff surrounded by fish and fowl of every description. One man has a cat, which is either used to put up the game or for retrieving it. Professional bird-hunters used a large clap-net, which they spread open in a carefully baited clearing before taking up a concealed position. At a given signal a sharp tug closed the net and, in the tomb-paintings, if not in real life, an enormous catch was always made. Some were killed at once, others kept for fattening [*Pl 16*].

Even the barren desert supplied some food for the table and sport for the hunter. On the fringes were the desert hare and the wild cattle, several kinds of small animals like the oryx, antelope and gazelle, together with the ostrich, whose feathers and eggs were valued. These animals were sometimes taken by trappers and traded in the market-place, but they were also hunted for sport, along with more dangerous animals, such as lions.

Honey was sometimes collected from wild bees and listed as a produce of the desert, but it was also taken from domesticated bees. These were kept in pottery hives and the bee-keepers drove off the bees with smoke before collecting the honey [96].

As well as raising vegetables and other food crops, the Egyptians were fond of flowers, which they wore as garlands or cut for decoration in their houses. Goddesses and ladies are shown carrying papyrus umbels, and garlands decorated not only the guests at a feast but also the wine jars and formed an important motif in architectural work and the decoration of minor objects. In the New Kingdom, cut-flowers for the table were placed in low open bowls, usually of blue faience with a dark blue line illustration of monkeys in a tree or fish in a pool. There are also stone and metal bowls, including one in bronze from the tomb of Rekhmire' which has a model Hathor cow standing in the centre.

The pools are reminders of the garden pools that the well-to-do liked to relax by and talked of so fondly in their poetry. Around them trees were planted in pits lined with clay and filled with soil. In the arid climate, irrigation was constantly necessary and it is an indication of the importance the Egyptians attached to their gardens that they were willing to go to this trouble.

The two favourite flowers of the artists were the papyrus and lotus, but the cornflower and pomegranate were also popular: chrysanthemums are also recognizable but too often the drawings are not faithful reproductions of nature.

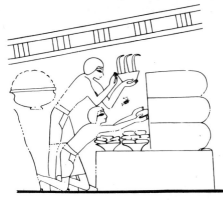

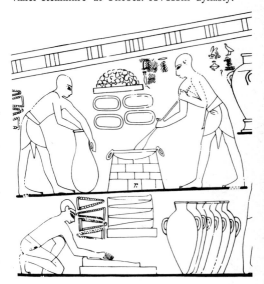

96. Above: collecting honeycombs from pottery hives, from which the bees are driven off by the smoke of a lamp. The combs are piled up in the bowl to allow the honey to drain out. Below: cooks at work preparing cakes. Line drawings of a wall-painting from the tomb chapel of the vizier Rekhmire' at Thebes. XVIIIth–dynasty.

Analysis of funeral wreaths has resulted in the identification of a large number of flowers, amongst them wild celery, cornflower, olive, blue water-lily, woody nightshade, mandrake, heliotrope, iris, convolvulus, ivy, mignonette, chrysanthemum, narcissus, poppy and immortelle. Several are not native to Egypt and were introduced in the New Kingdom or later.

FOOD AND DRINK

As befits a nation keen on the pleasures of good living, the Egyptians were fond of their food and drink, and from the earliest dynasties a focal point of the tomb decoration was the offering-table, piled high with all kinds of delicacies. These detailed representations, along with the lists of offerings and actual specimens, are our chief source of information about the Egyptians' diet, although care must be taken not to extrapolate too freely from these idealized pictures and ignore the often harsher realities of life. Famine was not unknown, especially in the year following a low Nile flood, and the diet of the lower classes was unvaried and not particularly nourishing, consisting of quantities of dried fish, bread and vegetables.

Meat was rare for all except the very rich, and the pictures of caged hyenas in Kagemni's mastaba may illustrate an attempt to increase the supply. Oxen slaughtered for sacrifice in the temples eventually ended up on the priests' tables, and the wild animals of the desert were also eaten. The plentiful game birds in the marshes were useful supplements to the supply of domestic fowl, such as geese, which are shown being forcibly fed. Fish was a very common food, although there were taboos in some areas and it was not usually regarded as suitable for offering to the gods. Goats were kept for milk, from which cheese and butter were produced.

The now-staple sugar cane was not known and honey was used as a sweetener, occasionally supplemented by syrup from the sycamore-fig or the extract from the carob. Most spices were imported from Syria–Palestine, as was olive oil.

As well as large quantities of fruit and vegetables, the offering scenes also show numerous varieties of bread and cakes in all shapes and sizes. Yeast was used in some varieties, which is why the tomb models often show the brewery

97. Wooden model of various domestic activities from the tomb of Khnem-Nekht at Beni Hasan showing (left) two women preparing dough, (centre) an ox trussed ready for slaughter, (right) brewer surrounded by vats and jars. XIIth–dynasty. Now in the Merseyside County Museum, Liverpool. Length 70 cm.

and bakery alongside each other; honey, spices, milk and fats were ingredients in other varieties.

The grain was pounded in a large stone mortar with a long, heavy, wooden pestle, then ground between a smooth rubbing-stone and a long, slightly hollow slab. A very small amount of sand was added to the pounded grain to assist the milling process and the resultant flour was therefore distinctly gritty, with a consequent disastrous effect on the teeth [99].

Baking was done in small, domed, clay ovens, fired by wood or charcoal, and grilling carried out over an open fire, although low metal grills are known, rather like modern barbecue stoves. Spit roasting is shown with the bird held over the fire on a long stick, while the cook fans the charcoal with his other hand.

Preserving food was important in the hot climate. There are several scenes of fish being slit open and of game being plucked and drawn before being hung up to dry in the sun. Salting was also practised. Salt was obtained from deposits in the western desert and also from sea water in the Delta, where the salt pans of Pelusium were a royal monopoly in Ptolemaic times. Salt bricks have been found, measuring about 20 × 10 × 5 cm., and analysis shows a high degree of

Pl 16. Wall-paintings of the vintage and bird trapping, from the tomb chapel of Nakht at Thebes. (Top) The grapes are collected and trodden in the wine press. Amphorae of wine are shown above, their contents labelled on the clay sealing. (Bottom) Wild birds are trapped in a clap-net operated at the signal of a man half-concealed behind a papyrus thicket. The birds are plucked, drawn and hung up to dry before presumably ending up in the jars shown in the picture. Watercolour copy by Nina de Garis Davies. Ashmolean Museum, Oxford. Original *c.* 1400 BC.

98. Pounding beans, which are piled up in a rounded heap and in baskets; the bean flour is sieved and will be made up into cakes. Line drawing of a wall-painting from the tomb chapel of the vizier Rekhmire' at Thebes. XVIIIth-dynasty.

purity. Besides its culinary use, salt was added to lamp oil to improve the flame and was used in the preparation of glazes and some medical prescriptions.

The domestic water supply for most families was obtained from the Nile, but wells were also sunk, especially in the precincts of the temple. They are usually covered and approached by a flight of steps. A huge well from which water was drawn in two stages from a depth of 35 m. was used to feed a large reservoir in the Ptolemaic cemetery at Tuna el-Gebel, and water for mining and quarrying parties was obtained from wells sunk in wadi beds in the desert.

As well as water, the Egyptians drank a great deal of beer and wine and were no strangers to the effects of over-indulgence, as several texts point out. Beer was the popular drink and the brewing process is often illustrated in tomb scenes, although not the malting process, which is not necessary and may have been omitted. Surviving examples of the mash show that barley was the most common grain used and the dried residue in beer jars has made it possible to identify the type of yeast. Date juice may have been added for sweetening but there is no clear evidence that anything was used to flavour the beer, as hops are nowadays.

Wine was chiefly made from grapes but dates and other fruits, such as the pomegranate, were also used. The grapes were trodden in a large press, and the last drops of juice extracted by twisting the remaining skins and seeds in a cloth. The juice was allowed to ferment in large amphorae, which were later sealed with a large clay sealing. The sealing or the jar wall were sometimes drilled with a small hole to allow gases to escape during further fermentation.

Considerable care and connoisseurship was exercised over wine. The vineyard and vintage were often recorded on the sealing or on the jar, and the colour and quality were also noted. One vintage is described as 'wine for tax purposes'.

HOUSES AND FURNISHINGS

So far as we can tell from the available evidence the houses of the villages differ little from those built in Egypt today. Flinders Petrie, while digging at Rifeh, found on the surface, above comparatively poor burials in the Middle Kingdom cemetery, a number of pottery model-houses which illustrate the sort of homestead one might expect to find in these villages, and others have since been found on other sites [100].

Most of these 'soul houses', as Petrie dubbed them, consist of a self-contained house and yard. In the yard are granaries and sometimes pools with canopies

99. Wooden model of a granary. A record of the grain is kept in the office (left) before it is stored in the large bins (right). From the tomb of Meket-re' at Thebes, c. 2000 BC. Now in the Metropolitan Museum of Art, New York. Height 36·5 cm.

above them. The houses vary in complexity from simple open-fronted shelters to elaborate structures with porticoes. The internal arrangement of rooms is not shown. Most have a flat roof, providing space for the household chores which could be carried out there, above the dirt and commotion of the farmyard atmosphere below, for that is where animals would be kept. As well as privacy the surrounding wall provided a windbreak and shade. Both house and wall would be built in mud-brick [99].

For town houses we have rather more information, particularly from Amarna, although care must be exercised before the evidence from that site is applied generally to the whole of Egypt. There, the builders had the advantage of a new site and almost unlimited space and so the tendency was to build sprawling houses in large grounds, whereas in most town sites land would be limited and compact house-design necessary.

The typical upper-class house at Amarna was set in its own grounds behind a high wall. The main gate opened into a garden with a pool, and trees growing in clay-lined pits. The path led past a shrine, open to the sky for Aten worship, to the main door set at the top of a small flight of steps. A porch and vestibule led into the reception rooms, the principal one being set in the centre of the house. It was lit by clerestory lighting as its walls were higher than the roof level of the surrounding rooms. The ceiling beams were supported by wooden pillars. Built against the walls was a low dais or divan, presumably covered in cushions when in use, and opposite it was a small brick hearth with a clay brazier.

From this central room doors led off in various directions, one to the backyard and servants quarters, one to another sitting-room and a suite of bedrooms. Another group of rooms, reached through a single door, are thought to be guest rooms that could be shut off when not in use. The master of the house had a suite of rooms to himself, of which the most important was a bedroom with an extra thick wall and a pottery container for valuables in the raised floor below his bed. Several of these suites were equipped with a lavatory (the traditional wooden seat supported on brick piers over a removable container or drain), together with a primitive shower unit, on the floor of which was a rectangular stone slab with a spout and channel leading to a soakaway to avoid damage to the mud-brick. The water supply was presumably a boy with a bucket. Other odd corners of the house were closed off to act as cupboards and from the main room there was a staircase leading to the roof [101].

Household servants lived in a range of buildings in the yard, which had a separate entrance from the roadway. Here also were the granaries and workshops, the kitchens, the stables and the dog kennel. Some houses were adapted to the specialist requirements of their owners; some merchants, for instance, had large store-rooms and offices, often approached by a separate entrance and kept apart from the living quarters.

The houses of the chief officials in the workers' village at Kahun have a similar layout, although they are more compact, but the average town house must have resembled those depicted in the tomb paintings of the New Kingdom. These show two or three storeys, the bottom occupied by the servants, the first and second floors used as reception rooms. Bedrooms are not shown. On the flat roof are granaries, space for drying clothes and food, and for other household tasks. Later this type of house seems to have developed into tenement blocks [102].

Care was taken in the disposition of these houses to take advantage of the prevailing, cool, north wind. The main reception rooms were on the north side

100. Clay model of a housestead set above a grave as a home for the deceased. The model shows an open-fronted shelter with a flat roof surrounded by a low parapet and approached by a flight of steps. In the enclosed yard stands a row of four granaries. From Buhen, Middle Kingdom. Now in the City Museum and Art Gallery, Birmingham. Length 33 cm.

Pls 17, 18. Overleaf: the great eastern gate of Medinet Habu, the mortuary temple of Ramesses III at Thebes, seen from the outer court of the temple. The gate, built on the pattern of a Syrian *migdol* or fortress, was erected roughly contemporaneously with the fall of the city of Troy.

Pl 18. View across the hypostyle hall of Seti I in the temple of Amun at Karnak. The columns are 13 m. tall and 8·5 m. in circumference, the two central rows are 19·5 m. tall and 10 m. in circumference. The extra height of the central rows provides the margin for the clerestory lighting, the stone grilles of which can be seen in this photograph.

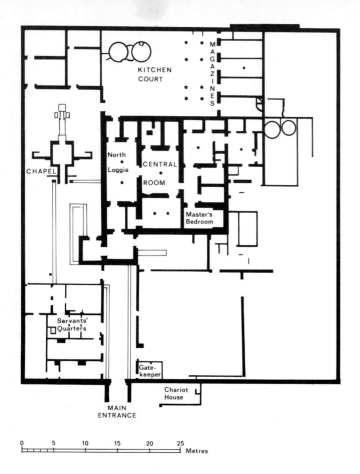

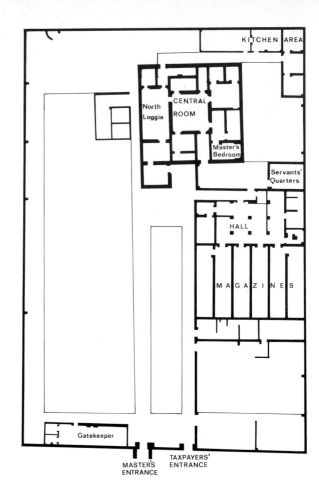

101. Houses from Amarna: Left: typical residence of an official from Amarna. The various features are not always uniformly arranged within the courtyard. In other houses the servants' quarters might be on the south side of the house, the place here occupied by a garden. Right: residence of a tax collector from Amarna showing how a typical house could be adapted to suit a specialist need. In this house, business and private visitors appear to have separate entrances and an extra door gives the householder easy access to his office. The magazines and large stockyard were necessary when taxes were paid in kind.

and at Kahun the houses on different sides of the street were planned differently, so that in each case the main courtyard faced north.

At Amarna the big houses were arranged along the main road grid, but the intervening spaces and odd corners were occupied by the haphazard buildings of the poorer classes. Other towns probably had no overall plan but developed organically about the temple or some other principal feature. The mortuary temples on the west bank at Thebes illustrate this, especially Medinet Habu, where the defensive outer wall offered some security in the troubled times of the first millennium BC, and the settlement persisted until the eighth century AD. Here the original planned layout was destroyed by overcrowding as houses were erected in almost any available space.

A different approach may be seen in the arrangement of workers' villages, which were planned for efficient administration and a high density of population. They were built to house the workers and their families, who were employed on large semi-permanent construction sites. Consideration of the comforts of the occupants and their individual wishes did not rate high among the architect's priorities, but they were probably no more unpopular than modern high-rise blocks or nineteenth-century working-class areas, and no less comfortable than the other contemporary housing.

The chief examples are at Kahun, Amarna and Deir el-Medinah. The first housed workers on Sesostris II's pyramid, the second on the tombs at Amarna.

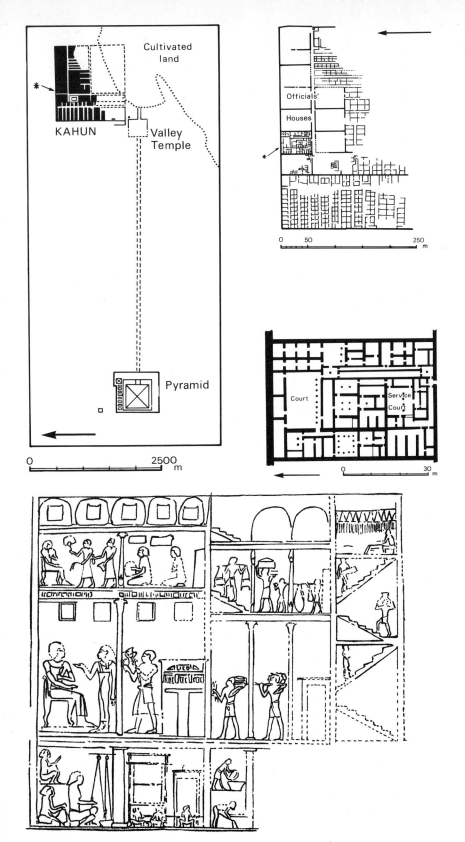

102. Left: general plan of the workers' village at Kahun which housed workers on the pyramid of Sesostris II. Top right: plan of the city showing positioning of the officials' houses to catch the cool north breeze. Centre right: plan of an official's house at Kahun, showing how the main court and reception room is placed on the north side, although the entrance is perforce from the south. Bottom: drawing of a town house, showing vertical disposition of rooms to conserve space; from an XVIIIth-dynasty tomb.

Cultivated land

Officials'

Houses

KAHUN

Valley Temple

Pyramid

0   2500
          m

0   50   250
                      m

Court

Service Court

0   30
            m

Pl 19. The rock temple of Ramesses II at Abu Simbel, in Nubia, faced with four colossal figures of the king, 20 m. high. The second figure from the left was damaged in an earthquake in antiquity. This photograph shows the temple as reconstructed after it was removed from its original position, which was flooded by the waters of Lake Nasser.

Deir el-Medinah was the home of the craftsmen employed on the royal tombs at Thebes and was occupied for several centuries, with successive alterations and extensions. The village of Kahun has not been completely excavated but it was probably laid out in a walled rectangle, the larger part of which was occupied by senior officials. The workers lived in much smaller houses crowded back-to-back on narrow streets. About twenty-five of these houses could be built on the area occupied by an official's mansion, which could house some fifty persons. The workers' houses vary in plan but most have a single entrance, leading past a small alcove in the hall to a larger room at the front of the house and a couple of smaller rooms at the back.

At Amarna, the village is 70 m. square with five streets running north to south, and all the houses except those on the west side have their doors facing west. The houses are divided crosswise roughly into three equal parts, the centre part being the large main room. The back is divided lengthwise into two to form a kitchen and bedroom, and the front third similarly forms an entrance hall and small room leading off the main room. A large house in the south-east corner was probably the house of the overseer, for the village was closely regulated. A high enclosure wall and single gateway aided supervision.

The village of Deir el-Medinah was founded in the reign of Tuthmosis I and two major extensions can be identified by the royal names stamped on the

mud-bricks used in the enclosure walls. The first phase was a single street

mud-bricks used in the enclosure walls. The first phase was a single street flanked by ten houses on each side running back to a thick enclosure wall. When the extensions took place, this simple plan was slightly altered and a number of houses were built outside the wall. At its largest, there were seventy houses within the walls, mostly occupied by descendants of earlier occupants, and another fifty outside. Here, rules were more relaxed and even animals were allowed inside the houses. Plainly, the enclosure wall ceased to act as a barrier in the later periods [103, 104, 105].

In this village the house plan was not dissimilar to the Amarna village. However, the kitchen area may have been an open yard; stairs indicate that the roof was used as additional space and small cellars were dug beneath the kitchen area. When these houses were rebuilt, they were not flattened to form a new building platform, as happened in other parts of the ancient Near East, but were rebuilt on the original floor level. This practice, and ostraca that illustrate periodic inspections, suggest a considerable degree of supervision.

The village was some way from the actual work-sites and the men did not waste time by walking there every day, but for ten days at a time they slept in the Valley of the Kings in rough shelters. An earlier example of these shelters lies behind the pyramid of Chephren, consisting of a row of 111 long, bare rooms, each holding about fifty men in barrack-like conditions.

Pl 20. The monastery of St. Simeon, more properly designated as the monastery of Anba Hadra (the Blessed Virgin), lies a short way out into the western desert slightly south of the rock tombs at Aswan. It was established during the seventh century, possibly in a deserted Roman fortress, and eventually destroyed in 1173 by Shems ed-Dulah, the brother of Saladin.

103, 104, 105. Plan of the New Kingdom workers' village of Deir el-Medinah, Thebes. In three phases of building the village grew from a single street to about twice its original size, but the cramped conditions did not improve. (104) General view of the village of Deir el-Medinah from the north-west, looking across the fore-courts and walls of the workers' tombs. (105) View along the main street of the village, looking southwards from the north gate. The Nile valley and the temple of Medinet Habu can be seen in the distance.

FURNITURE

Our knowledge of furniture is dependent on the examples that were provided as funeral equipment and the pieces illustrated in tomb scenes. A rich cache of furniture was found in Tutankhamun's tomb and Hetepheres's reburial incorporated several important items. The Deir el-Medinah tomb of the XVIIIth-dynasty Overseer of Works, Kha, produced more than thirty items that may be considered typical of the furnishings of an official's house, and there are several parallels for them in other tombs and in the tomb-paintings. However, little is known about the furnishings of the houses of the poor. Several stools were recovered from Deir el-Medinah, but it is unlikely that the poor possessed such items as tables and beds, for these could be 'built-in' as low mud-brick platforms.

138

106. Raised platform with steps and parapet thought to be a kind of family shrine where cult objects [cf. 146] were kept and where they received offerings. Several other examples are known from Deir el-Medinah, where they are found in the first room of the house. In the early XVIIIth-dynasty nucleus of the village they appear to be later additions but in the XIXth-dynasty areas they were built as part of the house, suggesting a change in religious practices, perhaps the result of the influence of the Amarna episode.

Several design features in Egyptian furniture have a long tradition, ranging from the time of Hetepheres to the Ramesside period and even later. These include the treatment of bed- and chair-legs as animal forms—legs in the shape of bulls' or gazelles' legs were popular in the Archaic Period but were gradually ousted by a lion type, which, in the New Kingdom, was surmounted by a Bes mask or, on royal thrones, a lion mask or, occasionally, a three-dimensional head. Plant forms were also used: bed- and chair-rails often end in papyrus umbels, and thrones have struts to the framework under the seat in the shape of entwined papyrus and lotus plants, symbolic of the united Two Kingdoms. Hieroglyphs, sometimes in long, inlaid inscriptions or in repeated groups of formulae inlaid or in fretwork, were another form of decoration; architectural features like the cavetto cornice and shrine-shaped top are used on chests and boxes.

The furniture is generally lightly constructed and some pieces appear almost flimsy, but the use of struts and lashings imparts considerable strength. The surface of the wood is often smoothed with a plaster skim and brightly painted with intricate patterns in imitation of the inlay work in stone and faience that adorns more expensive pieces. This applies particularly to chests and chair panels. Most of the pieces are in wood but some pieces are known in stone—for instance a calcite chest from the tomb of Tutankhamun—and some tables are made from woven and lashed reeds or rushes. The same materials, and the outer rind of papyrus, were occasionally used for boxes.

Chests, boxes and baskets were the basic containers for all household goods. Large cupboards, wardrobes and big chests of drawers have not been found, but boxes or chests up to about 80 cm. long were common for storing clothing, linen, jewellery, documents and similar items. Several have internal divisions specially designed to accommodate sets of toilet articles or wigs. It is rare that chests are fitted with cupboard-like doors. The opening is usually by a lid which may be hinged or slide on runners. Knobs in the shape of papyrus umbels were fitted to the lid and end wall so that the contents could be secured by tying the lid down and applying a sealing if necessary. Some have a shallow drawer fitted underneath the main compartment.

The chests come in a variety of shapes, usually oblong with flat, gabled or shrine-shaped tops. Tutankhamun had one in the form of a cartouche. They frequently stand on legs, either short ones about 10 cm. high, or longer ones, about 35 cm., the latter reinforced with lattice work or struts. Some are

Pl 21. Copy of a wall-painting from the tomb chapel of Menna at Thebes showing a sequence of harvest activities, beginning (bottom left) with scenes of cutting the corn, carrying it to the threshing floor and, returning along the top register, threshing with oxen, winnowing and finally measuring and recording the yield. Menna has arrived on the scene in his chariot and watches from a reed shelter, repeated in the centre of the top line. The little gleaners fighting, the workers resting in the shade of a tree and the lame old man watching the threshers add colourful details. This is a standard subject but receives detailed treatment in this tomb since Menna was Scribe of the Royal Fields. Water-colour copy by Nina de Garis Davies. Ashmolean Museum, Oxford. Original *c.* 1400 BC.

fitted with removable carrying poles that slide into bronze rings on the underside of the chest; others stand on sledge-like runners.

Stools are known as early as the Ist dynasty, but they are soon shown in statuary with low backs and chairs were quickly developed—although stools always remained more common than chairs. They are usually four-legged, often with rails about half-way up the legs. Three-legged stools are also known, probably for use in workshops, with outward-splayed legs and a heavy rough seat, semi-circular in plan. There are also folding stools, often with legs in the form of ducks' heads.

Illustrations of chairs in the Old Kingdom show them with very low backs or with backs of normal height and with or without arms that may be panelled. The simple box-type armchair often has a very wide seat and some are plainly intended to take two people. The backs are upright until, in the New Kingdom, a sloping back panel was provided that rested against a vertical strut, which continued the line of the rear legs and in some examples was made from the same length of timber.

The seats of both chairs and stools were made of interwoven rushes, reeds, linen cord, or leather thongs. Sometimes a piece of leather was sewn over the rails or, more rarely, lashed to the sides with thongs. In the New Kingdom many chairs and a few ornate stools have seats with a single curve, from side to side, or a double curve from front to back as well. These may have a leather seat or one of wooden slats. They appear distinctly uncomfortable but would obviously be used with a thick cushion. Illustrations of the earlier type of chair show that they were also provided with a thin padding which was draped over the back as well as the seat. A leopard pelt is sometimes shown draped over the seat of the folding stools.

The animal-shaped chair- and stool-legs have short, ribbed, cylindrical terminals sometimes shod with metal studs. Some of the legs are surprisingly

short: a number between 6 and 16 cm. long were found unattached in a Ist-dynasty tomb and may have come from foot-stools or beds, but Hetepheres's chair-legs are only about 25 cm. high and there are similar New Kingdom examples.

Beds are constructed with a slope, sometimes curving, from the head to the foot-board, which is almost always built up with three symmetrical panels, sometimes decorated with inlay [107]. No head-board is provided. The mattresses, made of tufted linen pads, lay on a panel of woven reed, cord or leather thongs, and linen coverings are found in some instances. Amongst the five beds of Tutankhamun was one that had two pairs of hinges in the side rails that allowed it to be folded in three, and a model bed in the Metropolitan Museum, New York, can be folded in two.

Instead of a pillow, a wooden or stone headrest was used, consisting of a curved neck-piece on a round or square pillar and an oblong base, usually made as two or three separate pieces fitted together. Occasionally animal shapes are adapted with skill and feeling. The headrest might well have been used with a cushion—one example still has its linen padding.

Headrests are frequently provided amongst the funerary equipment, often in the appropriate place in the coffin. As well as the deceased's name, the head-rest may be inscribed with chapters of the Book of the Dead, for the head, lying in the curve of the neck-piece may be regarded as the hieroglyph of the rising sun ☁, with its connotations of resurrection. Because of this magic symbolism the headrest was also a potent amulet [108].

Hetepheres's bed was found with the dismantled framework of a canopy that could be erected over the bed like a tent or large mosquito net. The woodwork was carved and covered with thin gold sheet, and the mortice and tenon joints were sheathed with copper. Copper hooks were provided to support the linen hangings, which were contained in a gold-covered box inlaid with faience.

107. Wooden bed with leather slings supporting a 'mattress' of folded linen sheets, one over 18 m. long; there is a wooden headrest instead of a pillow. Beside the bed is a cedar chest inlaid with ebony and ivory with silver fittings and compartments for a mirror and cosmetic vessels. The chest was made for the Royal Butler, Kemuny, *c.* 1800 BC. Now in the Metropolitan Museum of Art, New York. Length of bed 160 cm. Height of chest 20·5 cm.

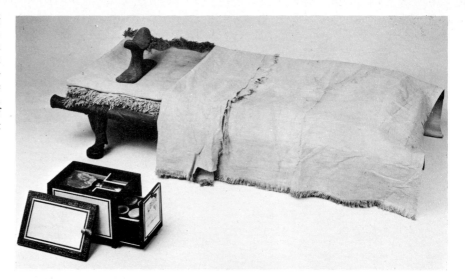

An illustration in the tomb of the IVth-dynasty queen, Meresankh III, shows attendants making up a bed under a similar canopy.

Tables are small, low and rectangular, with rails or struts for additional strength. They are usually of wood, but seldom ornamented apart from the occasional specimen bearing a line of hieroglyphs. In funeral stelai the funerary banquet is often piled on a circular table standing on a central flaring stem. Examples of these, with short stems, about 20 cm. high, and made from limestone or calcite, are commonly found in Old Kingdom tombs. Some tables have round holes in the top to support pointed or round-bottomed pots, and purpose-built pot stands are also known, with three or four splayed legs that also curve outwards at the top.

CONTAINERS AND EQUIPMENT

The study of pottery vessels has not been as enthusiastically undertaken in Egypt as in other fields of archaeological study, partly because it is perhaps thought that the abundance of inscribed material makes it less important for dating purposes and partly because of its general lack of aesthetic distinction. Much of the pottery that has survived may have been made deliberately for funeral use and that found on contemporary town sites is often cruder.

The pot types are mainly beakers, vases, bowls and amphorae, often with rounded bases suitable for standing in loose sand, but impractical without a pot-stand when they were stood on a hard surface. The comparative abundance of copper meant that many vessels were made in metal and these metal prototypes are reflected in many of the pot shapes from the Old Kingdom onwards.

Apart from the fine burnished and painted wares of the predynastic period the ordinary pottery is often very uninspired. Old Kingdom ware is mostly red with an ochre wash. Middle Kingdom ware is usually rough with a red slip and sometimes a decoration of white blobs. From Kerma at this time, there is a fine, highly burnished red and black ware that is very attractive, and a red or black ware decorated with incised patterns filled with white pigment is generally associated with the Hyksos.

In the XVIIIth dynasty the ware is well made, often with a good painted finish. Many vases have one or two loop handles on the shoulder and there are some attractive modelled vases with bodies usually in the form of a seated woman. There are also double vases consisting of two unequal types which look strangely awkward to use. The ware of Amarna is often quite large, with a fine flowing line to the tall slender vases, and painted with a pattern of flower petals predominantly blue on a cream slip background. The XIXth dynasty continues the virtuosity of Amarna in jars with several variously shaped handles and flasks. In the Late Period there was a fine drab ware originating in the Delta, made on a faster wheel and often with a human face modelled or incised on the side.

Foreign pot types were often imported into Egypt. As well as the Kamares and Tell el-Yahudiyeh wares of the Middle Kingdom, some storage pots of the Old Kingdom with small, wavy ledge-handles are thought to be Palestinian in origin, and slender red ware single-handled vessels of the New Kingdom probably carried Syrian imports. Small Cypriot flasks may have carried opium, advertising their contents by their shape as an inverted poppy head.

Faience was a popular material for *kohl* pots (see p. 147), finger bowls and the like. They are usually in deep blue or green with a design in a darker colour, most frequently of plant and animal motifs. Larger cups shaped like lotus flowers are known from the XVIIIth dynasty onwards and there are particularly fine pieces from the Late Period, modelled in low relief with animal figures or in the shape of a flower head. Several fine flasks in light green faience bear New Year greetings.

Amongst the specialist containers are brewers' vats, often illustrated in models and tomb scenes. At least one example is known, made of two hollowed-out sycamore logs, joined vertically with tenon and pegs, caulked with linen rags and sized and waterproofed by varnishing.

A common form of container was a basket made from the fronds of the date- or *dom*-palms, or from reeds, grass and straw. Randed baskets, i.e. those woven on stakes, are not known, the Egyptian method being to build up the basket from a bundle of fibres coiled round in a spiral, each new row being sewn to the row below with a strip of similar material. This strip was sometimes coloured to produce a geometric pattern.

Basketwork of this type is still common in Egypt. In dynastic times the popular type seems to have been a large rounded shape usually with a flat or pointed lid, but many other shapes are found—some with flat bases and some elongated or boat-shaped. Very fine baskets with intricate patterns are found from the New Kingdom, but the dry climate of Egypt has helped to preserve many specimens from all periods [109]. Some are women's work baskets, some are used as all-purpose domestic containers, or in building or agricultural work. The poor frequently used them as coffins. Basketwork techniques were also used to make sieves.

Some predynastic pots have a lattice-work decoration which suggests that they were carried in a string net. This is illustrated in some tomb scenes, where large pots are shown slung from a pole carried by two men. A few examples of these nets are known.

Matting was used for a number of household items as well as a floor covering. The false-door stelai show a rolled-up mat hanging in the doorway to be let down as a door or blind and the ornamental *serekhs* suggest that coloured mats were used, down to the Archaic Period at least, as a light form of wall or screen. The woven patterns on tomb ceilings suggest that a mat, covered perhaps with clay, could be used to form a roof. Fine matting was also used for beds and seats, for platters and for bags. The poorer classes buried their dead wrapped in matting.

108. Wooden folding headrest with leather neck-piece embossed with masks of the protective genius Bes. From Akhmim, New Kingdom. Now in the British Museum. Height 19 cm.

Pl 22. Copy of a wall-painting from the tomb chapel of Nakht at Thebes showing Nakht watching agricultural workers preparing the land and sowing seed. One man drinks from a goatskin bottle hung in the shade of a tree; sacks of seed and refreshments stand nearby. The painting is actually one continuous strip and the use of a curved base line for the upper part of the register, together with slightly smaller figures and trees gives a hint of perspective. Three men in the upper part appear to have no feet, which

. . . *continued*

Two types of matting were common. The fibres were either placed in bundles side by side and laced together by intertwining thread, or they were woven together in simple weaving patterns. Reeds, halfa-grass and palm fibres were the common materials.

Several miscellaneous items of domestic equipment survive. A large number of knives are known, with copper or bronze blades of various shapes, some curved, some straight, some double-edged. Even in the New Kingdom poorer households seemed to have made do with flint knives, and it is noticeable that flint workmanship in this period had degenerated from the comparatively well-made tools of the Middle Kingdom. Corn was usually ground on a saddle quern using a long heavy roller. Sometimes a large block of stone was used for the quern, the top surface of which sloped away from the grinder so that the flour was pushed into a trough at the lower edge. Deep stone mortars and pestles shaped like modern types were used for crushing other materials. Small wooden circular stamps were probably used to impress designs on loaves of bread.

Household brushes survive in fair number. They are fan-shaped, made of bundles of twigs or reeds bound together at one end to form a handle. Long wooden-handled brooms are not known.

The Egyptians had a reputation for cleanliness. In their frequent illustrations they used natron (sodium carbonate and sodium bicarbonate, which occurs naturally in the Wadi Natrun and other places in Egypt) and detergents, such as Fuller's Earth and pounded lupins. A scene from the tomb of the sculptor Ipuy at Deir el-Medinah shows laundrymen performing their trade, using large pottery tubs, and its dangers are described by one writer, who tells how it was performed on the river bank with a wary eye open for crocodiles. The washing was pounded with a wooden stick or mallet and afterwards 'ironed' with a wooden block.

Herodotus and Pliny refer to trade in large quantities of alum, which was mined in the oases. This was used as a mordant to fix dyes made from saffron, madder and other plants. Indigo was prepared in a solution with urine and the same writer understandably disapproved of the smell the dyer had to work in.

Firelighting was achieved by the use of a fire-drill. Any bit of hard wood rotated on a piece of softwood produces heat by friction and a wooden bit could be fitted to a carpenter's drill to achieve a fire most efficiently. Pieces of soft wood, with rows of holes to take the bit, and dry straw for tinder are occasionally found as part of the equipment in tombs. One assumes that the careful housewife would keep a small lamp burning to act as a pilot light rather than go through this elaborate and time-consuming process each time she wanted a fire and a good housewife would keep her lamp trimmed to ensure it remained alight.*

The tomb scenes of Rekhmire' show sacks of wood being brought to the furnaces. Wood and dried dung probably provided the fuel for the household ovens, which were simple brick domes open at the top, about 75 cm. high.

Lamps are rarely found in dynastic Egypt, although the tomb scenes and the standard hieroglyphic form shows a wick floating in a simple open dish, but these, when found, are not necessarily recognizable as a lamp. In the Graeco–Roman period the types common in Mediterranean countries were introduced. The fuel was usually vegetable oil or imported olive oil. Salt could be added to improve the lighting quality of the flame. The wick was probably a twist of reed, grass or old linen.

Another form of lighting shown in tomb scenes is a fat candle of some wax-impregnated fibre or a tall lump of tallow held in shape by a spiral band of linen or something similar. These could be placed around the house on a flat surface, and were carried in funeral processions as part of the ritual equipment.

DRESS AND PERSONAL ADORNMENT

Egyptian dress is deceptively simple for there are several varieties of styles. The working classes wore a short loin-cloth, while noblemen wore a longer kilt, carefully pleated and held by a belt, and sometimes a loose short-sleeved tunic, tied at the neck. At the end of the Old Kingdom a triangular pleated apron was introduced which, in the Middle Kingdom and later, was the traditional wear

may be because they are hidden by a slight rise in the ground in the same way that the ground appears behind the feet of their counterparts in the register below, or it may be that they are ankle deep in the soil. Watercolour copy by Nina de Garis Davies. Ashmolean Museum, Oxford. Original 1400 BC.

*cf. Proverbs 31, 18.

109. Samples of basketwork and matting, from a tomb at Beni Hasan. Middle Kingdom.

of the king. Women wore a tight-fitting sheath dress, reaching from below the breasts to the ankles, sometimes supported by broad shoulder straps. Both sexes occasionally wore a long garment often called a cloak, although it was really too light and thin to qualify for this description.

This basic dress was worn throughout dynastic Egypt but in the New Kingdom the taste for luxury made itself obvious, especially in the richer classes. Skirts were longer and fuller, cloaks became popular and more voluminous and a vast amount of time and effort must have been spent on the intricate goffering that was fashionable for both sexes, especially in the Ramesside period. The material was almost always white linen, set off to good effect by the colour of the skin and the bead necklaces, bracelets and belts, which formed solid blocks of bright colour. Some of the Middle Kingdom tomb models show dresses with woven patterns, and fragmentary examples of tapestry-woven designs were found in the tomb of Tuthmosis IV. Tutankhamun's shirts were decorated with needlework embroidery.

Quantities of textiles have been found in the cemeteries of Antinoopolis and Akhmim and other cities, dating from the late Roman period until after the Arab conquest. They are usually described as Coptic, but in fact the earliest examples show Hellenistic influences in the subjects and their treatment; recognizably Christian subjects do not occur before the seventh century.

The designs are worked in coloured wool, usually in tapestry weave and mostly in the form of bands at the neck and cuff and roundels on the shoulders. The earliest designs, mostly in purple wool on white linen, are inhabited borders and geometric designs based on animal and plant forms, but later more colours are used and human figures introduced.

During the dynastic period some classes did not follow changes of fashion. Children usually went naked and serving girls and 'musicians' wore little more than a belt. The office of priest was marked by a sash worn across the chest and the *sem*-priest wore a panther skin complete with head and claws. The vizier, too, is shown with a long plain tunic which had survived unchanged from the nobleman's dress of the Old Kingdom and was probably his official attire. Several funerary statuettes of Nubian servants, dancing girls and the like have tattooed patterns on the torso and limbs, and similar patterns may even be distinguished occasionally on the skins of mummies.

Many of the population went barefoot, others wore sandals with a sole of leather, wood or rushwork, the 'uppers' consisting of a T-shaped thong running between the toes and over the instep with a loop round the ankle. The word for this strap was phonetically similar to the word for 'life' and the strap sign ⚥ was used as the ubiquitous hieroglyph for life.

Most men carried a stick, either the stout quarterstaff of the donkey driver or a longer staff. One hieroglyph shows a figure carrying a stick that is forked at the base, and examples of such sticks have been excavated. Others have copper ferrules and ornamental knobs.

Hair styles varied considerably from period to period, although most members of the nobility had their hair cut short and wore a wig, usually of human hair. The Old Kingdom wigs were either short, closely curled and tight-fitting, or shoulder-length with a central parting and usually swept-back. Middle Kingdom wigs are longer but still fairly plain, and it is not until the New Kingdom that we find really elaborate creations composed of numerous long, curled or plaited tresses, ending in tight ringlets and falling well below the shoulder. The men's wigs are usually rather shorter than the ladies' and fall over the back

110. Calcite spoon for cosmetics, details in slate inlay; the girl's head and that of the gazelle are modelled separately and cemented in place. New Kingdom *c.* 1400 BC. Now in the Metropolitan Museum of Art, New York. Length 23 cm.

of the neck, but they have a lappet of small ringlets that comes forward across the collar bone. On festive occasions these coiffeurs were surmounted by a cone of fragrant oil that gradually melted, running down into the wig and on to the clothes. Flowers and small jewels were worn in the hair, and from the XVIIIth dynasty there are headdresses made up of numerous small roundels of glass inlaid into gold and stitched together in rows resembling a wig [Pl 24].

Priests had their heads completely shaven and children often wore their hair in a long, side plait. The lower classes are usually shown with their tight curls neatly trimmed or with a 'pudding basin' hair-cut.

Boxes of cosmetic implements and materials often form part of the funeral equipment and reveal what the sophisticated woman, or man, would use in her or his toilet. The equipment includes bronze mirrors, with ivory or bone handles in the form of lotus or papyrus plants, short fine-toothed combs, hairpins and round-ended sticks for applying *kohl*. Broad-bladed razors, bronze paring knives and small whetstones are also supplied, along with a small bronze implement consisting of a pivoting blade that fits into a channelled sheath, generally thought to be a hair-curler. Finely carved boxwood or ebony unguent spoons commonly had handles based on plant forms, or on the motif of a swimming girl [110].

The bronze mirrors are sometimes provided with their own brightly painted wooden or leather cases to protect the highly polished surface. Other cases, semi-circular in shape, were made for fans which were made of feathers set into handles like those of mirrors.

The eye make-up, *kohl*, made originally from malachite but later from galena, was ground to powder on a small palette and kept in small vessels, usually of calcite or another hard stone. Some elaborate containers were made in wood or faience in the form of a servant figure carrying a jar. Perfume oils may also have been kept in an ox horn, stopped with a wooden plug at the broad end and pierced with a fine hole at the tip, although some of them are more likely to have been used by workmen as oil-cans [111].

Most toilet sets include a number of stone, faience, or pottery jars containing the remains of fats, oils and liquids that were used as cosmetics [112]. Specimens of ground red ochre mixed with oil were probably intended to be used as lipstick or face-paint and mixtures of chalk and oil were perhaps cleansing creams. Henna was used as a hair dye. There are many references in the literature to the use of perfume, which was extracted from flowers or seeds, which were pressed and mixed with resins or oils.

Although, contrary to popular imagination, it is seldom the archaeologist's lot to find 'treasure', Egyptologists have certainly found their share. The treasures of Tutankhamun are world famous, but before that discovery several caches of royal jewels were found, notably those of the XVIIIth-dynasty Queen Ahhotep and of several Middle Kingdom princesses in the subsidiary burials at Dahshur and Lahun. The burials of nobles and other private individuals have also yielded their share.

Naturally the wealth of the jewels depends on the social standing of the owner. The ordinary people could seldom afford more than shell, bone or faience but for those who could, gold was the principal material or, more rarely, silver or electrum. Designs were worked by chasing, filigree or granulation or set with semi-precious stones such as lapis lazuli, carnelian, garnets and turquoise. Green felspar and amethyst were occasionally used, especially in the Middle Kingdom, and jaspers, crystal, obsidian and agate were also employed. Most of the stones were chosen for their colour (appropriately coloured glass or faience

111. Boxwood figure of a negress carrying a jar, one of a pair of elaborate cosmetic jars, the other is in the form of an Asiatic woman. XVIIIth-dynasty. Now in the Gulbenkian Museum of Oriental Art, University of Durham.

112. Group of cosmetic items, including a glass *kohl* jar, inlaid wooden jewellery box, bronze curlers and razor, bone and glass spoon, calcite ointment jar with sealing intact and glass and carnelian earrings. Now in the City Museum and Art Gallery, Birmingham. Length of jewellery box 9 cm.

113. Back of a pectoral of Queen Mereret from her tomb near the pyramid of Sesostris III at Dahshur. The front of the jewel is inlaid with carnelian, lapis lazuli and frit, but even the back is carefully finished with fine chasing. XIIth–dynasty. Now in the Cairo Museum. Width 10·4 cm.

could be substituted), since the colour was all important for its magical significance, green for growth, blue against the evil eye, red for flesh and so on. As well as providing magical protection, jewellery obviously also served as ornament and adornment. Some jewels were marks of honour, such as the Golden Fly, awarded for bravery in battle, and others have ritual or funerary significance.

There are distinct trends of fashion both in style and in the type of jewellery. For instance, diadems, shaped like natural wreaths, popular in the Old and Middle Kingdom, are replaced from the XVIIIth dynasty onwards by decorated fillets of linen, and ear-rings and studs do not appear before the Second Intermediate Period. Collars were popular at all times: the Old Kingdom favoured bead-work bands worn tightly around the throat in the form of chokers, or multiple strings of cylindrical beads on lunate or falcon-headed end-pieces. The Middle Kingdom preferred beads in the form of amuletic hieroglyphs and the New Kingdom fashion was for strings of multicoloured beads in the shape of flower petals and fruits [114].

Bracelets, armlets and anklets can only be distinguished from each other when found on the body. Old Kingdom bracelets were made of sections of tusk or of bead bands; the New Kingdom varieties were often hinged semi-circular plates, heavy with large carnelians, sards and other stones. Finger-rings, relatively common only in the New Kingdom, are mostly signets, horseshoe-shaped with a scarab on a swivel across the opening, and may well have been worn on a string round the neck rather than on the finger. Ear-rings and studs were worn by both sexes to judge by the pierced ears on various mummies. Pectorals are a typical Egyptian ornament. In the Middle Kingdom they were often of shell, or gold or silver in shell shape. The Lahun and Dahshur treasure contained several specimens in cloisonné fretwork which are part of the princesses' regalia rather than personal jewellery, as are those of Tutankhamun [113].

Much of the jewellery associated with the royal burials served a particular purpose as part of the regalia. Several pectorals are in the outline of a shrine

and show the king victorious over his enemies or bear his name, elaborately worked and ornamented with hieroglyphs expressing good fortune. Some of the rich pectorals of Tutankhamun are elaborate rebuses on his name and were probably designed for his coronation. Some jewels, for other monarchs, bear designs that refer to their jubilee ceremonies. Other forms of jewellery, such as the heavy bead collars and girdles, were worn on state occasions and ceremonials. Courtiers sometimes proudly record the fact that they were invested with the Award of Gold, the modern equivalent of which is probably a mention in the Honours List. Several New Kingdom scenes show this investiture, and the decoration seems to take the form of a necklace of gold disc beads.

A number of jewels were specifically made for the burial ritual and bear distinctively funeral motifs of Anubis and Osiris. Tutankhamun wore twenty-six pectorals, many of which have this type of subject.

TOYS, GAMES AND PASTIMES
Egyptian children had as many games to play as any other children. There is not a great deal of evidence, but passing references and tomb sketches show that they enjoyed games which tested their strength and skill. Running, jumping, leap-frog and wrestling were all popular. The tomb scenes from Beni Hasan show a whole series of wrestling holds and throws and a quarterstaff competition was arranged between Egyptian and foreign troops to entertain the court of Ramesses III. Reliefs from the Old Kingdom show what are probably inter-village contests between teams of boatmen fighting with their quants, but the ferocity with which they are waged makes it doubtful if they can be classed as sport.

Javelin-throwing and target-practice with bow and arrow were popular with boys and men, and girls played ball games with either leather balls stuffed with chaff or painted wooden ones. In their quieter moments, the children played knucklebones or marbles or with their various toys.

It is not always possible to be sure whether an object is a toy or a funerary model but some are buried with children, like the little gold doll's cup, 45 mm. high, and the tiny ivory palette belonging to Meketaten. Others are gaily painted or have moving parts, like the ivory dwarfs found at Thebes which dance on a base-board when their strings are pulled. The young Amenophis II is shown in a tomb-painting sitting on his nurse's lap playing with a toy set of enemy figures whose heads are moved by a string, and there are wooden crocodiles with moving jaws, clay donkeys carrying model sacks and dolls that no child could resist.

Grown-ups had their games as well, played on often beautifully made boards, the moves dictated, not by dice, which were in use but not common until the Greek period, but by knucklebones or by sets of ivory or wooden wands of differing shapes and decoration. The 'men' for the two most popular games, *senet* and *tjau*, were simple rounded shapes of pottery, clay, wood or faience, but occasionally they were delicately carved in more elaborate forms, such as animal heads in rarer materials: ivory, rock crystal and red jasper are known.

Several *senet* sets are known, often contained in a box with a board laid out on the top in three rows of ten squares, five of them specially marked. The method of play is not recorded. The boxes are sometimes laid out on another side for *tjau*, a game introduced from western Asia in the Hyksos period which was played on twelve squares down a central strip flanked by four more on either side at one end. Again the rules are not known. A third game, hounds and jackals, was popular in the Middle Kingdom.

Music played a great part in the entertainment of guests and also of course in temple services and rituals. Musicians were usually professionals, more often than not female, and frequently dressed, or rather undressed, in a manner certain to divert attention from any mistaken notes. The entertainment was enhanced by dancers, again more or less naked, who performed the acrobatic types of dance which we still associate with Africa today [*Pl 26*].

Musical instruments cover the whole range of the orchestra. A popular grouping was a harp and a lute, with a woodwind instrument such as a double or single flute. The percussion was represented by drums, tambourines, castanets of wood or ivory and sistra (rattles). Bronze trumpets are less commonly found and were principally used for giving military signals. The flutes, of course, preserve their ancient scales and it is possible to reconstruct the stringing of the instruments. From the Greek period there is at least one papyrus which preserves musical notation and attempts have been made to interpret this in modern times.

Pet animals were often found around the house. Cats were most popular and appear in several tomb paintings sitting quietly beneath their mistress' chair or devouring a fish stolen from the party food. They were also used in hunting, rather like retriever dogs if we are to believe the tomb scenes. Dogs were useful as guards for the house, in hunting, in battle and in police actions, but not apparently for herding. Several different types are known: basset hounds in the early periods, and a lean saluki-type derived from the jackal with a pointed muzzle, long pointed ears and upcurling tail. The New Kingdom dog was a mastiff type with a thicker muzzle and body and a hanging tail.

Monkeys also made good pets and several other animals appear to have been kept as pets or for food, but the experiments were not successful. In Mereruka's tomb there are gazelles, ibex and antelope wearing collars, and even hyenas apparently forcibly fed like Strasbourg geese.

II

The Cultural Life

LANGUAGE AND LITERATURE

One of the most fascinating aspects of Egypt is the hieroglyphic script, which for the layman today still has all the mystery and magic which the crafty Egyptian priests deliberately attributed to it to mislead and misinform their detested Greek conquerors.

The word *hieroglyphic* is strictly speaking reserved for the form of the script which preserves the pictorial element. This is almost without exception the form used for any inscription designed for public display—from the account of a king's victorious campaigns on a temple wall to the brief record of a man's name and title on a humble private statue. Based on this is an abbreviated form used for all kinds of jottings and notes and even for full-length books. This is *hieratic*, the cursive form of hieroglyphic, which has much the same relation to it as our ordinary handwriting has to Roman capitals. A third script, *demotic*, evolved from the hieratic *c.* 700 BC. It replaced hieratic as the ordinary day-to-day script of Ptolemaic and Roman Egypt and therefore, although its abbrevi-

115. Below left: hieratic script of the Old Kingdom. This papyrus is part of the records from the temple of the pyramid of Neferirkare' at Abusir and was probably written in the reign of Niuserre' or Isesi in the late Vth-dynasty: it is therefore one of the oldest papyrus documents known.

Below right: New Kingdom hieratic. This manuscript of *The Teaching of Amenemope*, a New Kingdom wisdom book, was probably written in the Ramesside period. It is set out in short lines corresponding to the form of the text, which is similar to the couplets of the biblical book of *The Proverbs*.

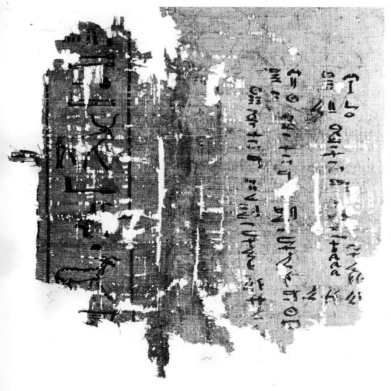

ated form requires specialist study even amongst Egyptologists, the texts are full of all the fascinating data of everyday life in that period.

About AD 150, the Greek alphabet was adapted, with the addition of a few extra signs for peculiarly Egyptian sounds, to form the language which we call Coptic. With the coming of Christianity and its emphasis on the importance of the Holy Scriptures this simpler script received a great boost in popularity, but the hieroglyphic script continued in use in the pagan temples—the last known inscription dating to AD 246 in the reign of Diocletian. Coptic died out as a spoken language in the sixteenth century but is still used in the liturgy of the Coptic Church.

In the hieroglyphic and associated scripts we find many of the stages in the development of writing as it were fossilized. Like the cuneiform script of Mesopotamia it began with the use of pictures to represent the sounds of language but the Babylonians, writing on clay, found it difficult to scratch the outlines clearly and soon reduced their pictures to increasingly stylized forms, while the smooth surface of papyrus enabled the Egyptians to preserve their pictorial characters.

The signs fall into three principal groups, some signs belonging to more than one group. The first group, *ideograms*, indicate an object by a picture of it, either in whole or part, for example:

$i \, \cdot \, 3 \, w$ = an old man.
pr = a house (shown in plan).

An extension of this is to indicate more complicated ideas by associated objects:

$hnkt$ = beer (a beer container)
$t \, 3 \, w$ = wind (a ship's sail).

Such signs can express basic ideas but any particular nuances are lost. The sign $\hat{A}$ can express worship, but which of the many words for worship (laud, glorify, adore, praise, magnify, revere, honour, and so on) did the writer intend? This can only be expressed by finding a way to write the sound of the word, and the second group of signs, *phonograms*, have a sound value rather than a pictorial one. Once it was established that $\square$ stood for the word *pr* for 'house', it was only a short step to use it for other words with the same two consonants, such as *pr* 'to go out'.

The Egyptians did not write their vowels, which were the distinguishing factor between identical groups of consonants when spoken, and to enable a reader to make this distinction a third type of sign was used, a *determinative*, indicating the semantic group to which the word belonged. The simplest of these is a stroke ι, which shows that the sign is an ideogram and is to be read at face value, so $\square \iota$ is to be read as 'house'. Others indicate categories of words; a pair of legs, for example, convey the idea of motion so $\square \wedge$ would be *pr* in the sense of 'to go out'.

Likewise, for example, the three words spelt $i \, 3 \, m$ can be distinguished as follows:

$i \, 3 \, m$ + tree determinative: $= a \, i \, 3 \, m$-tree (a type not yet specifically identified).
$i \, 3 \, mt$ + book roll, the determinative of an abstract quality: = charm, grace (*t* represents a feminine nominal ending).
$i \, 3 \, m$ + house sign, here acting as determinative of a building: = tent.

152

It is as if, in English, given a sign ♠, we might add a stroke determinative to indicate 'fir', an animal to indicate 'fur', a flame to indicate 'fire' and legs to indicate 'go far'.

Other determinatives reduce the possibility of ambiguity over the sound of the word. Most of the Egyptian phonograms have a value of more than one sound. Almost always these signs were accompanied by at least one phonetic determinative; so *pr*, 'to go out', is frequently written with ⊏⊐ followed by ◡, representing the single sign *r* followed by the motion determinative, i.e. ⊏⊐ ∧. By contrast, ⊏⊐ı for 'house' is not written with the complementary ◡, and is one of the few exceptions to this rule.

There are some 700 or so signs used in Middle Egyptian—not all in common use but many with two or three usages and one cannot begin to read Egyptian at all fluently until these are reasonably well learnt. The fact that many of the texts are in hieratic is yet another barrier for many students but this is overcome by publishing transcriptions into hieroglyphic, printed usually by photographic means from a manuscript rather than setting up in type which is prohibitively expensive.

Although knowledge of Coptic was kept alive by its liturgical use, the hieroglyphic script had long been forgotten and was the subject of much misdirected conjecture during the Middle Ages and later. The discovery of the decree of Ptolemy V Epiphanes, better known as the Rosetta Stone, opened up new possibilities when its trilingual inscription in hieroglyphic, demotic and Greek was recognized. The Swedish scholar Johan David Akerblad soon made some observations about the value of some signs. Between 1814 and 1819 Thomas Young identified the cartouche as the sign of a royal name and, by contrasting the contents of the cartouches with royal names in the Greek text, arrived at more values.

The solution was finally reached by Jean François Champollion, whose lifetime ambition was to decipher the script. All his reading had been to that end, including mastery of Coptic, which enabled him to take Young's work further, distinguishing types of signs and their values, until in 1822 he was able to claim in a famous letter to M. Dacier, Secretary of L'Académie des Inscriptions of Paris, to have discovered the basic principles of the script.

The decipherment of the hieroglyphic script brought to light a side of the ancient Egyptians that was quite unknown. Their literature shows them to be a lively people, interested in all forms of human knowledge, experiencing and sharing the whole range of human emotion. Their written documents range from medical treatises to love songs, from philosophy to curt replies to tax demands. Some are written to preserve and pass on knowledge; some to provide propaganda for a failing deity or to prop up a shaky throne; others arise from the unburdening of a heavy heart or delight in a tale well told.

The writers of these pieces are not always known to us. The compilers of the religious writings and the editors of the short stories are mostly, if not entirely, unknown. The work of writing the religious texts was probably limited to noting down the latest form of an age-old myth and many of the short stories may have had a history of oral tradition before they were committed to writing. On the other hand, most of the books of precepts are attributed to individuals, probably because the name of the writer adds authority and they express his own philosophy of life. The Egyptians were certainly aware of the lasting quality of the written word, which was celebrated by an unknown scribe of the New Kingdom in language echoed several hundreds of years later by Horace:

(The scribes) did not make themselves pyramids of brass and tombstones of iron,
They did not leave heirs and children to speak their fame,
But they made their heirs their writings and the books of teachings which they wrote.

The style of Egyptian literature is a major barrier to the modern readers. There is a tendency to use the same introductory formulae to each sentence, to use the same verb form in a string of sentences without feeling the need for variety, and to make a careful verbatim repetition of speeches that have already been recorded. These and other characteristics which we tend to find boring were to some extent relieved for the Egyptian reader by figures of speech which we cannot fully appreciate, like the puns which occur in all kinds of texts and which simply cannot be indicated in translation. In poetry the use of a refrain is common as it is in some Old Testament psalms, and much of the effect is achieved by the device known as parallelism which again occurs frequently in the Old Testament poems as well as in the nursery rhyme 'Old King Cole'. In this the effect is achieved by saying the same thing twice, but the second time the phrase may be turned round or a second idea added to it, or it may simply be repeated with a variation of wording [115].

In spite of our lack of a precise understanding of all the nuances of meaning, there is much about the literature that is immediately attractive. There is a direct appeal to the emotions, an apt selection of striking metaphor and a simplicity of story line that easily overcomes these barriers. The great variety of compositions caters for many moods and tastes and provides an intrinsic interest over and above the light they shed on the culture from which they spring.

THE SCRIBES' EQUIPMENT

The hieroglyph which is the ideogram for 'writing' shows the basic tools of the scribe's trade. It consists of an oblong palette with two small wells for black and red paint, a pot to contain water for moistening the cakes of paint, for washing his brush, and to wash out errors, and thirdly there is a brush-holder, in the shape of a lotus stem, opening at the top. Often the brush-holder and palette are combined in an oblong hollow box with an opening for the brushes to be slipped in. The majority are of wood but some are of ivory or some fine stone. Separate inkwells are also known, especially from the later periods. They are tall domes, with a small hole at the top, and are arranged in groups of three or four on a fairly solid base to prevent spillage [36].

Pens were made from rushes (*Juncus maritimus*) cut to a broad, flat edge so that thick or thin strokes could be made. In Graeco–Roman times it was pointed and split like a quill. The ink is usually black, prepared from carbon mixed with gum and, sometimes, iron oxide. The introductory words, chapter headings and other important words or phrases that the scribe wanted to single out might be written in red ink made from red ochre. An object with a handle like a mirror, and a broad, flat blade, might have been used to give a final burnish to the papyrus surface.

Scribes are often shown in tomb-paintings with a sort of duffle-bag, which they presumably used to hold this equipment. It appears to be made from an animal skin, the legs removed and a cord fitted round the neck. It is often brightly decorated [117].

The Egyptians had a much more fertile imagination than we have when it

117. Painted limestone statue of an unidentified scribe. The eyes are outlined in copper strip, the eyeballs are of crystal, the whites of alabaster and a copper nail acts as the pupil. VIth-dynasty. Now in the Cairo Museum. Height 49·5 cm.

came to finding writing materials. They invented paper, using strips of peeled papyrus reed placed side by side. More strips, also side by side, were placed across the first batch and the two layers pounded together. The height of a piece was therefore roughly the length of the average strip of papyrus reed, about 40 mm., but there was no rigid limit to the number of pages that could be joined to form rolls up to 10 m. or more long. The *recto*, or side that was first used by the writer was the one on which the strips ran across the face. The side where the strips ran vertically was less easy to use because the flow of the pen would be impeded by the joints. This side, the *verso*, was often left blank or used only for the tail-end of a text, or it might be used by a poorer scribe and contain a text quite different from the one on the *recto*.

The dry climate of Egypt is relatively kind to papyrus and large quantities of texts on that material have survived. Nevertheless it is easily torn by careless handling, as was the fate of the Turin king-list, and we are fortunate that many Egyptian documents were written on more durable material, such as flakes of limestone or sherds of pottery. To both of these is given the Greek name *ostracon* and they preserve for us whole series of administrative jottings, receipts, inter-departmental minutes, family letters and so on. Literary texts were also sometimes copied on ostraca; one imagines they were cheaper than papyrus—perhaps the equivalent of our paperback editions.

Sometimes schoolboys did their exercises on ostraca but often they used a writing board. These vary in size from about 15 × 20 cm., the usual size, to larger ones, about 30 × 50 cm. The boards were sometimes unprepared, but more often than not they were coated with gesso to give a smooth surface [118]. They could be washed clean for re-use and where this was done we have palimpsests—one text above another. It seems inevitable that it is the partially washed out text underneath that one wants to read, not the fresher one obscuring it!

ART AND ARTISTS

The forms and techniques of Egyptian art are dictated by the religious and magical purpose for which it was undertaken, for the idea of 'art for art's sake', although instinctively present, was not paramount in the approach of the Egyptian artist. The two major types of art which have survived in sufficient quantity for us to discuss, wall-paintings and sculpture, are found in either religious or funerary contexts and their purpose is to capture and make valid for eternity the effectiveness of an otherwise ephemeral act. An offering or ritual portrayed in a tomb or temple scene, properly consecrated by a form of the Opening of the Mouth ritual (see p. 200), which brought life to the figures and reality to the objects, was made effective for all time. So that nothing should be lacking from the act, the recording and communication of accurate and detailed information became a chief aim of the Egyptian artists.

This may at first seem a surprising statement when one considers the strange contortion of the human figure that is the standard Egyptian manner, but the information conveyed is based on knowledge not simply on observation and the artist draws what he knows to be there even if it is not visible from his position. In one scene the artist will use a variety of viewpoints, selecting whichever one suits his purpose. Consequently, in drawings of buildings, we find plan and elevation used together. The contents of a box may well be depicted as if resting on top of it, and the human figure is shown (with very few exceptions) in a mixture of profile and full-face views.

The depiction of the human figure was particularly subject to conventions

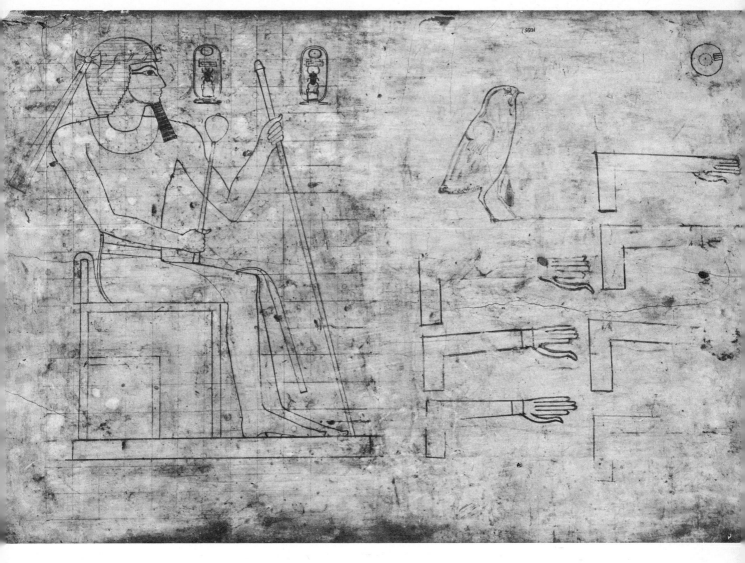

which were established at the beginning of pharaonic Egypt and lasted without major change to the Greek period. The proportions of the figures were worked out on a grid, nineteen squares high (more in the Saite renaissance), and for the important figures the angle of the legs and relative position of the shoulders and arms was also prescribed. Similar conventions influenced statuary: in standing figures, for instance, the left foot is nearly always advanced as if walking, although the figure is in fact depicted at rest, and a pillar is usually placed at the back, reaching up to the level of the neck, either as a structural feature to strengthen the piece or for some now unknown symbolism. Before the Amarna period, when it became a noticeable feature, there were, very few attempts to relate the figures to one another [*Pl 14*]. The important figure—the god, king, or owner of the tomb—is usually shown on a larger scale than other figures in the same scene and in family groups the man is shown slightly larger than his wife and both are much larger than their children, who are depicted, according to the same canon of proportions as miniature adults instead of being proportioned like children. The lower classes are depicted in more realistic

118. On this writing-board, of wood thinly covered with gesso, a scribe has laid out a grid in red ink and drawn a sketch of a king, named in the cartouche as Tuthmosis III. He has also practised drawing arms and a chick. XVIIIth-dynasty. Length 53.5 cm. Now in the British Museum, London.

attitudes and groupings, with less attention to the exact proportions and more characterization.

The same factors that dictate form and presentation also control the subject-matter of art. In both tomb and temple scenes the artists avoid details which would circumscribe the eternal effect they were striving to create. Portraits are therefore usually idealized and views and events generalized. Thus Hatshepsut's obelisk barges could be anywhere on the river between Aswan and Luxor [90]; we cannot tell whether Rekhmire''s workmen work indoors or out in the open. Even when specific historical events, such as the battle of Qadesh or the defeat of the Sea People, are recorded, the landscape is only perfunctorily indicated and the dominant figures of the kings are still in the conventional postures.

It is important not to be misled by this into thinking that the Egyptian artists were not skilled enough to draw differently. A number of ostraca, particularly a large group from Deir el-Medinah, show them in their free time, jotting down sketches, caricatures and animal studies, many of which are unlikely ever to have found a place in a commissioned work and were probably done for the pure joy of artistic expression.

The strength of the Egyptian artists lies in their draughtsmanship, which is authoritative and confident, the result of a long training in calligraphy in the scribal schools. In one flowing movement they can sketch a complete figure, even without the supporting grid, and in spite of the conventions they can impart character and mood with a deft flick of the pen. The compositions are dominated by a sense of symmetry and usually split up into a series of horizontal registers, thus bypassing the need for perspective, although there are a few suggestions of this concept. The individual scenes are often interspersed with panels of text to which the pictures seem to have the same relationship as the determinative signs in the individual words. The colours, which are limited and carefully chosen for effect, are applied as a flat wash—very seldom is there any attempt at shading—and the result is rich and warm [*Pl 22*].

A great part of the appeal of Egyptian art is its immediate accessibility. Although full of strange convention and peculiar details and attributes, it is on a human plane—homely, sympathetic and often humorous. Even the fantastic monsters, denizens of the underworld, seem within the realms of possibility and quite unfrightening [147]. In the composite figures the artists manage to marry two unlikely parts so fluently that at least one archaeologist, in an unguarded moment, has spoken of a life-size sphinx!

Of the artists themselves we know very little. They did not sign their work and in fact probably worked as a team rather than as individuals. They were regarded as skilled craftsmen and treated as such alongside the carpenters and metalworkers, and it is only rarely that we know who was responsible for decorating a particular tomb. A few artists and sculptors have left their own funerary stelai, which expatiate on their skill and achievements, and one may occasionally see how a particular artist has influenced the style of his period—Bak in the Amarna period is a good example—but normally their masterpieces remain anonymous and their innovations unattributed.

The principal artists seem to have graduated to their speciality after training as professional scribes. These men laid out the overall design and were responsible for the accuracy of detail in the insignia and texts. Less skilled men painted in the finished sketches and specialized stoneworkers carved the reliefs.

Unfinished paintings and reliefs show the different stages of the work. Several ostraca show how the artist either practised or experimented with the exact form of details for his projected work, although we do not have preliminary sketches of whole designs. Once the surface was prepared, the artist laid out his grid, paying particular attention to the area where his principal figures would come. He then drew the scene in rough on the wall and, having obtained the approximate positions, drew in the final outlines in detail. The painter then began to lay on the colour washes, beginning with the background, then the main blocks of colour, gradually working down to the small details. The final act was often to go over the outline once more in red or black [*Pl 30*].

The pigments that the artists used were usually finely ground natural mineral substances mixed with water and a binding agent such as egg white or gum from the acacia. Beeswax was used as a protective varnish and in Roman times as the medium for funerary portraits. Black pigment was usually made from lamp black or powdered charcoal. Blues and greens were obtained by powdering artificial frits that were compounds of silica, copper and calcium, or, more rarely, from naturally occurring minerals such as azurite and malachite. Brown, red and yellow were made from various ochres or iron oxides, and white from chalk or gypsum. Other shades and tints were achieved by mixing these basic pigments. Many of these colours are unstable and some have either altered significantly or disappeared with the passage of time, but the general impression left by the Egyptian wall-paintings is of almost unbelievable freshness and vividness [*Pl 16*].

From the beginning of the Ptolemaic Period there are a number of limestone plaques and sculptures in the round portraying several subjects, including animals and parts of the human body, especially busts, and, on the plaques, hieroglyphs. They have the appearance of being not quite finished, lacking a final smoothing and polishing, and often preserve the marks of the original grid on which they were based. At Sakkara a number of plaster casts were found, many of them of parts of animal and human figures. Although the parts of the body are sometimes described as votive pieces similar to those dedicated to Aesculapius in Greek sanctuaries, the other subjects cannot be explained in this way and are probably sculptors' trial pieces or students' practice work.

DOCTORS AND MEDICINE

The practice of medicine was the same mixture of religious, scientific and magical methods that exists even today. Wounds and injuries, and diseases that could be attributed to obvious causes, such as malnutrition, were intelligently treated; but illnesses were often regarded as the work of some hidden evil force or offended god, and amulets and ritual spells formed part of the treatment— possibly even effectively in psychogenetic cases. For this reason the men who practised as doctors were often also priests, usually of Sekhmet, goddess of healing. Doubtless great reliance was also placed on traditional family medicaments.

Many of the remedies and treatments are recorded in the dozen or so medical treatises that survive, by far the most important and scientific of which is the Edwin Smith Medical Papyrus (so-named after its one-time owner), attributed by the editor, Breasted, to the Old Kingdom sage Imhotep. The first part of this work is an essay on the heart, followed by forty-eight clinical observations on surgical cases, consisting of a description, diagnosis, prognosis and treatment. This part ends abruptly and is followed by a series of magic spells for exorcizing the pestilence-bringing winds and quack prescriptions for rejuvenating the aged.

The first section of the Edwin Smith Papyrus and parts of some of the other manuscripts illustrate the highly scientific approach of some doctors. The essay on the heart, while it does not describe the circulation of the blood, recognizes the pulse points and speaks of 'measuring the heart'. This could not be done accurately without a sophisticated timing device, but a practical observer could presumably judge excessive variations in speed or regularity. The descriptions often reveal clear understanding of anatomical and physiological details and the treatments are often basically the same as those carried out today. Cuts were stitched, burns anointed with oil, and fractures splinted and bandaged, often quite successfully, as numerous mummies show. Surgery was prescribed for some tumours which were incised and cauterized, others were left alone. The evidence for trepanation in Egyptian mummies is ambiguous, certainly it was not a widespread practice. Minor operations, such as circumcision, were possibly carried out with the aid of a local anaesthetic or under sedation from a drug such as opium.

The pharmacopoeia was extensive, and made use of those substances discovered by trial and error to be effective. It included herbs, often picked on certain days and under particular conditions, minerals such as copper salts (used as an antiseptic) and magnesia (used as a laxative), and other materials such as honey and wax. Modern research occasionally shows how some of the less likely substances were in fact effective, as in the case of ox liver, prescribed for night blindness and now known to contain the essential vitamin C. It is less likely that there was benefit in such items as dung, urine, or dirt from the fingernails. Many identifications escape us completely and some apparently magical potions, like 'Thoth's tooth', may be common names for useful plants, in the same way as the name 'foxglove' disguises the drug digitalis.

Prescriptions give precise details of the dosage according to the patient's age, when and how it is to be taken and for how long. This detailed care is typical of the professionalism of many practitioners, which is also illustrated by the extent to which some of them seem to have specialized in different aspects of their craft.

The general tone of the medical texts indicates a degree of superstition but also careful observation, intelligent treatment and, above all, the genuine concern which distinguishes the true doctor in every age.

12

Crafts and Industries

Almost every museum provides illustration of the vast quantity of artefacts produced in dynastic Egypt, many of which show an innate sense of good design and technical excellence; many others are mass-produced and ordinary. Along with tomb-paintings and tomb models of craftsmen at work they provide the bulk of our knowledge of Egyptian technology, for the tiny amount of written information that has survived is very difficult to interpret with confidence.

Of the organization of Egyptian industry we know more. There were no great manufacturing companies—most craftsmen seem to have practised, not privately or in guilds, but as employees of the rich nobility or in the great temple workshops. Those at Deir el-Medinah, employed on the kings' tombs, were divided into gangs with fixed work periods. Excuses for absence were noted, the weight of copper tools issued to each man was registered and a work diary kept. They were paid with rations of food, wood, oil, clothing and occasionally received a bonus of wine, salt, meat or other luxuries. They were not above going on strike if their pay was too much in arrears, as happened during the reign of Ramesses III. Other workers were doubtless similarly organized, including those at the temple of Amun of Karnak, who are depicted in the tomb of Rekhmire', the source of most of the line illustrations in this section. These workshops were controlled by high-ranking temple staff, such as Puyemre' and Nesamun, both Second Prophets of Amun in the reign of Tuthmosis III and Ramesses IX respectively, but there is no evidence that they had any practical skill. Distinguished craftsmen who reached supervisory grades, such as the Chief of Sculptors and High Priest of Amun in Sma Behdet, Ya (mid-XVIIIth dynasty), and the Royal Scribe, Minmose (*temp* Tuthmosis III), who supervised several temple building projects, seem occasionally to have been rewarded with priestly titles but not always in the main cult temples and the posts may have been sinecures.

Industries such as quarrying and mining came directly under the control of the State, and the gang of men sent on quarrying expeditions was organized as an army.

METALWORKING

COPPER AND BRONZE

Copper occurs in the eastern desert and in Nubia but was obtained mainly from Sinai, at Wadi Maghara and Serabit el-Khadim. When the supply from Sinai was exhausted soon after the beginning of the XVIIIth dynasty, copper was imported from Cyprus and other sources farther afield were tapped. Recent excavation at Timna in the Negev in southern Palestine has revealed extensive occupation in Ramesside times and evidence of the method of extraction. Nodules of copper ore were hammered out of sandstone outcrops and smelted in sophisticated furnaces of clay-lined stone construction, capable of heating to about 1,300°C. Finely ground ore was fed through on top of a charcoal fire and the molten metal sank down to form an inverted bun-shaped ingot at the bottom of the kiln. The slag was then run off into a stone-flanked tapping pit alongside and the furnace could be used again. Refining was possible only by repeated reheating in crucibles.

The alloy bronze—copper with between three and ten per cent tin—was introduced from Asia in the second millennium as one of the results of the increased contact with western Asia brought about by the Hyksos occupation. Egyptian metal technology was not as advanced as that of western Asia and the alloy was probably produced there and exported. The use of iron was also an Asiatic development: the few pieces of ironwork in Tutankhamun's funeral equipment were made in Anatolia and presented to the king. It was used for a few weapons and tools from the XXVth dynasty onwards, but is not in general use until Ptolemaic times. Very early pieces of iron, such as a series of beads from the predynastic cemetery at El Gaza, supposedly contained seven and a half per cent nickel, which suggests a meteoric origin, and many other early pieces are of dubious authenticity.

Although bronze figurines from the later dynasties survive in large quantities, examples of early metalwork are rare since worn, damaged or obsolete pieces could easily be melted down for re-use [119].

Copper workers began making tools and ornaments on a small scale in the late predynastic period. Smelting was done in small furnaces and the resulting ingot, small and brittle, was broken up and the pieces hammered into the required shape. The ingot was sometimes remelted in a crucible and rough casting in open moulds of stone or pottery could be undertaken.

The statue of Pepi I from the VIth dynasty shows that large works were undertaken in the Old Kingdom. The statue is made of sheets of the metal hammered over a wooden core. Vessels were raised by hammering from single sheets of metal, but too much hammering makes copper brittle, a state that can be relieved by annealing, or heating to red heat. On the other hand, a moderate degree of hammering hardens the metal and the cutting edges of tools could be treated in this way. Many accidental impurities also improved the hardness of the metal.

119. Metalworking: (top left) a man tends a small furnace while two men work foot-bellows; (bottom left) manoeuvring a crucible and (centre) pouring the molten metal into a many-spouted mould. The picture seems to suggest that they are making bronze doors, perhaps for a temple; two such doors are shown (top right). The text simply says that they are singing the praises of Tuthmosis III who makes monuments for the god Amun. The man emptying a sack of charcoal (bottom right) is the first of a line of men bringing up ingots of metal. Line drawing of a wall-painting from the tomb chapel of the vizier Rekhmire' at Thebes. XVIIIth-dynasty.

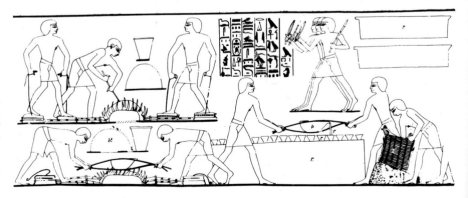

There is evidence for rough casting in an open mould being practised in the predynastic period. Petrie found a metalsmith's shop at Kahun, amongst the debris of which he recovered five open pottery moulds for chisels and knives. The copper boxes from Tod are amongst the earliest instances of casting in a closed mould. Some copper ewers of the Old Kingdom have their spouts attached by riveting, and parts of Hetepheres's funeral equipment show the use of hard solder, probably using natron (sodium-carbonate and -bicarbonate) as a flux.

Bronze could be worked in the same way as copper, which it gradually replaced. The bronze figurines of the Late Period were cast by the lost wax (*cire perdue*) process using a wax model, sometimes built up on a core of sandy material so that the resulting figurine was hollow and therefore used less metal. Some of these figurines are decorated with inlaid designs in silver or gold and there are occasional examples of gold plating [*Pl 28*, **128**].

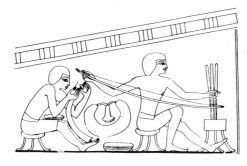

PRECIOUS METALS

Within the boundaries of Egypt, especially in the eastern desert, there were extensive deposits of gold, which were thoroughly exploited; and it was also obtained as tribute from Nubia. In the earliest periods it was obtained by washing river gravels but later the Egyptians mined quartz rock and extracted the gold by crushing and panning—an especially dangerous and heavy task in the desert heat, and therefore mostly done by convicts or the army.

120. Above: beadworking. Right: this man seems to be drilling with a bow-drill using three bits at once. Left: the beads are sewn together to form a heavy collar like the one shown between the two men.
Below: stoneworking. Drilling out a vase using a weighted drill with an eccentric handle [cf. **124**]. XVIIIth–dynasty. Line drawings of a wall-painting from the tomb chapel of the vizier Rekhmireʿ at Thebes.

The gold obtained in this way contained several impurities, especially silver and the alloy electrum, gold with about twenty per cent silver, which occurred both in the eastern desert and in Nubia, and was regarded by the Egyptians as a separate metal until the method of producing it artificially was discovered in the New Kingdom.

Silver, less common than gold and highly valued, was referred to as 'white gold'. The native sources available in the Old and Middle Kingdom in fact produced an alloy of up to forty per cent gold in silver and the purer silver of the New Kingdom was mostly obtained from western Asia, where the process of silver smelting had been discovered.

The finer skills involved in the making of jewellery and working of metals led to a high degree of specialization. There were different titles for the goldsmiths, lapidaries, faience-makers, bead-makers and necklace-makers, although there must have been some overlap between them. The techniques were essentially those used for working bronze but finer. Repoussé and chased work was well developed; sheets of metal were worked with hardwood or bone tools on a bed of soft material, such as wax, or over a wood or stone core. Working from both surfaces of the sheet, using the two techniques together, gave very high relief. Very thin sheets of gold might be hammered or stamped into dies to produce flimsy amulets, and *cire perdue* casting was also practised. Wire was probably cut from thin sheets with a chisel or flint tool, and sometimes smoothed by drawing through a narrow perforation in a hard stone. It was made in short lengths, soldered together, and from the Amarna Period onwards was also made by soldering beads together and rolling them under pressure [**120**].

For their soldering the goldsmiths used an alloy of silver and gold. They also knew the technique of colloidal hard soldering, in which the parts to be joined are stuck in place with a gum mixed with copper-carbonate, probably obtained from powdered malachite.

Cloisonné work was also popular for jewellery, especially in the Middle Kingdom. The cloisons were formed by strips of metal cut from a sheet and

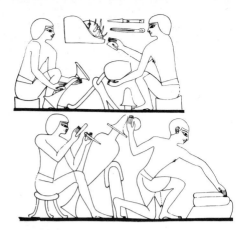

121. Gold and silversmithing. Top: two men polishing silver vessels; in the background a small furnace with blowpipe and tweezers beside it. Bottom: one man (left) inscribes a silver vessel while another (right) beats out a flat sheet of metal. Line drawing of a wall-painting from the tomb chapel of the vizier Rekhmire' at Thebes. XVIIIth-dynasty.

soldered on edge on a base plate. They were set with finely cut and polished stones but in the New Kingdom coloured glass was often substituted. Granulation was also a popular method of decorating jewellery; small round beads or granules of gold were soldered in patterns on to a larger sheet.

Beads were made of all kinds of materials. Gold beads were made in two halves and soldered, stone beads by boring with a bowdrill. They were drilled in their rough shape and polished afterwards. Beads could also be made from shells trimmed into discs and perforated, and some amuletic beads were made from teeth, horns and similar materials. However, faience was the most popular material. The paste was moulded over a core, consisting of a stick or thread, and scored with a knife to the required length. When fired the core burnt out, leaving a perforation.

As well as being widely used in the manufacture of jewellery, gold and silver were used for fine vessels, hammered into elaborate forms and often decorated by low repoussé or by tracing, usually with a floral design or a hieroglyphic inscription. Several fine XVIIIth-dynasty examples exist and even in the politically weak and unstable later dynasties of the first millennium the art of the gold and silversmiths was maintained [121].

STONEWORKING

Mud-brick is adequate for buildings for this mortal life, but for the permanent dwelling for the soul, and for the eternal houses of the gods, the Egyptians preferred to use the stone which was so readily to hand in the cliffs along the valley side. These are chiefly limestone of varying quality, including the fine white limestone of Tura, used for the Memphite reliefs and pyramid casings, and the calcite of Hatnub, used for stone vessels and often mistakenly called alabaster. Sandstone replaces the limestone cliffs from Edfu southwards. It was quarried in quantity at Gebel Silsileh and replaced limestone as the chief building stone in the New Kingdom and later. The great outcrops of granite at Aswan were heavily exploited and the surrounding deserts yielded the basalt, diorite, marble and porphyry which were valued for statuary, sarcophagi, facing-blocks, thresholds and the like.

Semi-precious stones were also found in the desert although it was sometimes necessary to go farther afield. Expeditions were mounted to Sinai for turquoise and lapis lazuli was imported from Afghanistan.

Probably the best-known ancient quarries are those at Aswan but there are limestone quarries at Tura near Cairo, a large calcite quarry at Hatnub near Amarna, and sandstone workings at Gebel Silsileh as well as numerous others along the Nile valley and in the eastern desert. Techniques are different according to the nature of the stone and its position: some of the Tura workings follow seams of stone like a mine, but most are open. Little evidence survives of the tools used by the quarrymen. Study of the markings on undressed stones and on the quarry face suggest that softer stones were cut with a pick similar in shape to the modern type, but no example is known.

Remaining traces at the granite quarries indicate how that stone was obtained. The rough surface of the outcrop was levelled by heating the rock surface with fire, then dowsing the fire with water, thus cracking the rock surface. Pounding with dolerite hammers reduced it to a plane. Test holes were made by pounding around a likely area to examine the strata and if it were flawless, a block was then separated by pounding out a trench around it. Large blocks such as the great obelisks were separated underneath by further pounding

but smaller slabs could be freed by cutting slots for wedges, which might be hammered in gently until the fracture occurred, or the wedges could be expanded by wetting and force the block free. With even harder stones like quartzite, the trench was made by pounding along a line of small drilled holes while in the softer rocks it could be hewn with a copper pick.

Much of the final shaping of the stone was done on the site, as a roughly finished colossus of Ramesses II at Aswan indicates. This reduced the weight of stone to be moved but meant that the workers may have had to stay in the quarry for some time. It took seven months to extract one of the pair of obelisks erected by Hatshepsut at Karnak [122].

The commoner stones, such as granite, limestone and sandstone, were used both for building and finer work throughout the dynastic period, but the use of other stones varied according to fashion and purpose. Diorite was used for statuary and vessels down to the Middle Kingdom but rarely later. Cosmetic oils and ointments throughout the dynastic period were kept in small jars of fine stone, usually calcite (calcium carbonate). The translucent veining that occurs in this is often cleverly used to enhance the appearance. Anhydrite was used only in the Middle Kingdom for small vessels, and quartzite was a favourite material for sarcophagi in the Middle and New Kingdoms. Porphyry was very popular in the Roman period.

Working the harder stones presented great problems to a people without iron and steel, but they were overcome at an early stage—in the predynastic period in fact. Although pounding might be adequate in quarrying, it could not

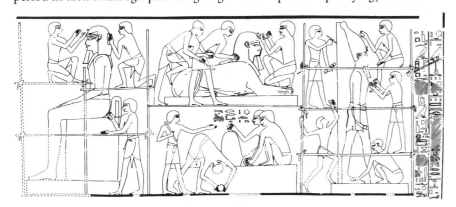

123. Teams of sculptors at work on two royal statues, a sphinx and a large altar. Some are doing heavy work with round mauls, others are using smaller polishing stones. A scribe writes the inscriptions on the back pillar of the large standing figure. Line drawing of a wall-painting from the tomb chapel of the vizier Rekhmire' at Thebes. XVIIIth–dynasty.

165

124. The hieroglyphic spelling of the Egyptian word for 'craftsman' uses the glyph of a stone drill, and this relief gives a clear drawing of the drill, showing the weighted top with the eccentric handle and the flint bit. From a fragment of relief from the mortuary temple of Sesostris II at Lahun. Now in the Fitzwilliam Museum, Cambridge. XIIth–dynasty.

produce the sharp, deep outline of, for instance, a hieroglyphic inscription or a clean-cut internal rectangle. The exact method is still a source of some mystery and much discussion and several unlikely theories have been advanced to explain it, including possession of a now-lost secret of tempering copper to the hardness of steel or the use of diamonds set in a cutting edge. Some unfinished pieces show the use of a saw to cut slabs of stone. The back of one of the Mycerinus' basalt triads shows clear saw marks, and the side of the granite coffin of Cheops does likewise, suggesting the use of a saw some 3 m. long. These particular marks are probably caused by an extra hard particle of the abrasive sand becoming accidentally and temporarily embedded in the blade rather than the deliberate use of a diamond-set saw. Much of the work was done using a drill with a crescentic flint bit or, for harder stones, a hollow tubular bit of copper or, later, bronze. None of these metal bits have been found but cylindrical drill cores survive, showing the regular grooving of the bit's cutting edge. A hollow bit reduces the amount of material to be abraded in a wide hole. Small perforations were usually drilled with a solid bit from both sides of the stone and have an hour-glass section. Both the saws and bits were probably toothed and used in conjunction with an abrasive such as quartz. Flint bits and blades would be sufficient to work the softer stones [123, 124].

Statues were usually brightly painted, though on the harder stones this was confined to details such as the eyes, headdress stripes and jewellery. Details were also supplied by using inlays, particularly for the eyes, where the whites might be represented by white quartz and the pupils by rock crystal, giving a striking life-like effect. The small cosmetic jars often had gold foil around the rim.

The first two or three dynasties saw the stoneworker's skill at its peak. Particularly notable are a series of dishes in slate and schist. These easily fractured stones have been carved into the most remarkable forms, suggesting that they are based on metal prototypes, with very thin walls, twisted and curved and deeply undercut. In the Ist-dynasty tomb of Hemaka at Sakkara, Emery found a number of stone discs of unknown purpose but of superb workmanship, beautifully inlaid with stones of contrasting colours. A great number of larger bowls and dishes from this era have also been found. Although they are made in stones like diorite, breccia and porphyry they, too, are finely finished and usually exactly symmetrical.

Many precious and semi-precious stones are to be found in the desert around the Nile valley; carnelian, jasper, crystal, agate, amethyst, chalcedony, chrysoprase, felspar, garnet and nephrite all occur in Egypt or close to its southern boundary in ancient Nubia. Turquoise was popular but involved a difficult journey from Sinai, and lapis lazuli had to be imported from as far away as Afghanistan. It is likely that faience and coloured glazes were developed as substitutes for these stones.

Unlike Mesopotamian practice these prized stones were seldom used in seal manufacture. Engraved gem-stones are not common before the Hellenistic period and most scarab seals were made of soft steatite hardened by firing in the glazing kiln.

WOODWORKING

Although wooden objects survive well in the Egyptian climate, it is not favourable to the growth of many trees and the material available for woodworking was very poor. Acacia, sidder, sycamore, fig and tamarisk are the principal native woods but they seldom yield long clean planks, and for most large-scale work the craftsman had to rely on imported timber, especially cedar, which was brought in large quantities from Lebanon. Other woods of western Asia, such as box, were used, but ebony seems to have been the only wood imported from Africa.

Woodworking developed with the use of copper tools in the early dynastic period. Several examples survive from the Old Kingdom onwards and include chisels, awls, axes and adzes. The bow drill with a copper bit is shown in use in Old Kingdom tomb scenes. Hammers were often rough club-shaped pieces of wood but the bell shape still used by stonemasons is shown in the New Kingdom tomb scenes.

Saws were set so that the cut was made on the pulling stroke and when a plank was rip-sawn it was lashed to an upright post and sawn vertically. Very smooth finishes could be achieved by careful use of the adze. Planes were not used until Roman times and the use of the lathe is generally discounted. Some XVIIIth-dynasty work appears to show signs of turning but the craft is never illustrated. Carpenters are often shown kneeling or sitting at their work and using a specially shaped block rather than a bench [125].

Scarcity of material taught the Egyptian craftsmen many tricks of economy. Knots were cut out and patched; irregular planks were roughly smoothed and fitted together with pegs or lashings, and battens. Deficiencies could be supplied with generous applications of plaster. The jigsaw effect of this use of short timbers is sometimes seen in tomb-paintings of small boats and in actual examples of cheaper coffins. Long planks for shipbuilding were sometimes made up by joining two lengths with scarf joints held by dovetail wedges. Another economizing device was to work with a framework of rails and stiles, filled in with veneered panels. An early, but rare, example of plywood is found in the IIIrd dynasty.

In construction work the common varieties of mitres, mortice, tenon and dovetail, are all found. The joints are sometimes strengthened by bentwood struts or by right-angled braces cut from naturally bent timbers. In the Old Kingdom joints were frequently lashed with leather, string or copper bands, sometimes passing through holes bored in the joint, otherwise lashed around the members. Wooden pegs were introduced later, and bronze nails in the

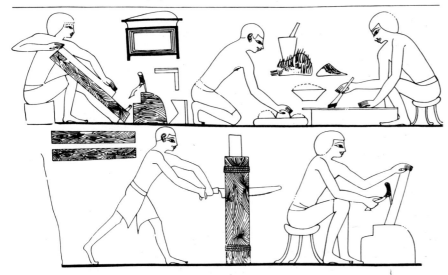

125. Woodworking. Top left: testing a plank with a straight edge; an adze and set-squares lie to hand. Top right: this scene seems to show the application of a plaster skim to the wood; the pot on the fire behind may contain glue. Bottom left: rip-sawing a plank lashed to a tree stump. Bottom right: trimming a plank with an adze. Line drawing of a wall-painting from the tomb chapel of the vizier Rekhmire' at Thebes. XVIIIth-dynasty.

126. *Kohl* jar in the form of a monkey (above) and chalice in the form of a lotus (below); both in faience. XVIIIth–dynasty. Now in the Fitzwilliam Museum, Cambridge.

XVIIIth dynasty. These were often made a decorative feature and capped with gold. Hinges of copper were used from the XVIIIth dynasty onwards but most lids were arranged to slide. They were secured by lashings around two ornate knobs, for locks were unknown—although some coffins were locked by irreversible tumbling devices, and one of Tutankhamun's chests had a fastening device operated by rotating a knob.

The fine woodwork was seldom left unadorned. Some of the New Kingdom pieces are very richly ornamented with faience and ivory inlay or appliqué work and held by glue or delicate dowelling. Veneered work was another way of disguising inferior timber and the carcase of some pieces like the XVIIIth-dynasty shrines of Tutankhamun were covered with gesso that was then modelled and gilded. There is some doubt about the exact way in which gold ornament was applied, for some pieces seem to indicate that a thin gold sheet was first worked in repoussé, then laid flat, face down, and the hollows filled with plaster. This plaster fill supported the raised areas of the gold when the sheet was stuck on to the surface of the wood. With Hetepheres's funeral furniture, the underlying wood appears to have been carved with the desired pattern and the thin gold sheet applied and rubbed into the hollows to reproduce the pattern. Woodwork was also painted and then varnished with a resinous shellac that often discoloured to a dark brown.

OTHER CRAFTS

GLASS AND GLAZES

The process of glazing was probably discovered by accident, but the effect was so attractive that efforts were made to repeat the accident and improve on it by experiment. Good glassmaking requires chemically pure ingredients, accuracy in measuring their proportions, and close control over the firing and cooling process. Without the means to achieve these, the ancient glassmakers had perforce to rely on their experience and instinct, although some of their accidents may have led them on to new developments. Most of the new techniques, and indeed the original discovery of the process, seem to have taken place in Mesopotamia, but Egyptian glassworkers have produced many fine masterpieces in this material.

The earliest form of glass in Egypt (dating from about 4000 BC) is as a blue or green glaze on beads. It is basically silica, usually in the form of sand, and an alkaline substance, such as potash or natron. Copper oxides, present as impurities in the sand, gave it its green colour and it was prized as a substitute for turquoise—the latter being valued for its magical properties. Without a tin or lead content the glaze contracts on cooling and does not adhere to clay which does not contain, in addition to the silicates usually present, free silica or silicon dioxide. Glazed pottery is therefore quite unknown in dynastic Egypt. However, the glaze does adhere well to steatite (hydrated magnesium silicate), which is easily carved and hardens when heated. This was the ideal material for beads and amulets and proved extremely popular.

Soon after the glazed steatite beads we find beads of faience. This term, as it is used in Egyptological literature, has nothing to do with the glazed pottery of Faenza but describes an artificial composition of powdered quartz, mixed to a paste with an alkaline binding agent such as natron in solution. The paste can be modelled, moulded or thrown on a wheel, and hardens on firing, although its texture varies according to the precise composition and degree of firing. The

127. Wooden model of a weaving shop, showing (left) spinning, (right) setting up warps, (centre) weaving on horizontal looms. From the tomb of Meket-reʿ at Thebes. Now in Cairo Museum. Length 93 cm. *c.* 2000 BC.

body is usually white but the surface could be coloured with powdered glazes painted on before firing, which also gave it a fine smooth surface. Alternatively, the coloured glazing material could be mixed with the body and would travel to the surface during firing. A similar synthetic substance is Egyptian blue, which is coloured throughout by the presence of copper calcium tetra-silicate. It is much less common than faience and used principally for small containers and amulets.

The early use of faience was for beads and small amulets, but small statuettes date from around 3000 BC and it was extensively used to glaze tiles decorating the underground corridors of the IIIrd-dynasty Step Pyramid. In the Middle Kingdom, vessels were made of faience and many small model animals were produced, including a number of hippopotami, charmingly painted with lotus flowers. The New Kingdom and later products are outstanding for the wide variety of colours and the delicacy of the modelling that was achieved [126].

About 1500 BC glass itself was introduced into Egypt, perhaps by a mistake in the proportions of silica and the alkali when making faience or, more likely, as one of the western Asiatic inventions that found their way to Egypt at this time. Glass vessels were made on a core of mud on which the body of the vessel was built up and, while still soft, decorated with threads of coloured glass that were then smoothed down to form an even surface. Zigzag decorations were also popular, formed by dragging a pointed tool through the coloured threads.

Although shades of green and blue were the most popular colours, experiment showed that other colours could be achieved by adding various oxides: cobalt for a deep blue, iron for yellow and red, and tin for white. There was considerable experiment in the New Kingdom, especially in the Amarna period, with new materials, and some very fine results were achieved. Glass and faience were extensively used for cosmetic containers, gaming sets, funerary statuettes (ushabtis) and jewellery [*Pl 31*]. Painted and inlaid tiles were popular architectural ornaments in palaces and temples and wood, ivory and bronze statuettes often had some distinctive feature, such as the Blue or Red Crown, added in the appropriate coloured glass or faience. Glass shapes were also inlaid in wood to decorate shrines and caskets, and in metal to substitute for precious stones in jewellery. These were usually cut or moulded separately and cemented or clasped in position in the cloison, but at least one piece of Tutankhamun's jewellery appears to show evidence of powdered glass having been fired in position in the cloison, which, if correct, would be the earliest known example of the enameller's art.

It is strange that after maintaining their first success for about five centuries, the Egyptians completely abandoned glassmaking in favour of faience until the sixth century BC, when the industry was revived. The difference between the sand core vessels of the early and late periods is principally in the shapes, which follow those of contemporary pottery vessels.

In the Graeco–Roman period Alexandria was a world-famous centre of glassmaking, and at this stage clear glass was developed and glass blowing was an established technique. Mosaic glass, formed of rods of coloured glass fused to form a pattern, was another introduction of the Ptolemaic period.

TEXTILES

Spinning and weaving were highly developed crafts in Egypt. At the beginning of the dynastic period all the variants of plain or tabby weaving known today were being exploited, although the linen weave, with single threads alternating, was the commonest. The best linen was made from better quality flax than that grown in Egypt today, and dentages of 160 warp threads and 120 weft threads to the inch are known; some of the Tutankhamun fabrics had counts of 280×80 to the inch.

After retting and beating to separate the bast fibres they were loosely twisted into roves and wound into balls. The balls were placed in heavy buckets and the roves passed through a ring in the bucket, which helped to maintain tension. No distaff was used and the thread was spun on a spindle, usually weighted with a wood, stone or pottery whorl. In the predynastic period and occasionally later the threads were doubled for added strength [127].

The earliest looms were horizontal, the warp being wound on two beams, each supported on a pair of pegs driven into the ground. Models from the XIIth-dynasty tomb of Meketre' show how the warp was set up on pegs driven into a convenient wall. It was then transferred to the loom, where alternate threads were lashed to a rod-heddle, which was raised to make the shed or space through which the bobbin carrying the weft was passed. On the return stroke the other threads were lifted by a shed rod. These two rods replaced the reed in the absence of which the warp threads are occasionally rather irregular. About 1600 BC the vertical loom was introduced. In Egypt the two beams were still used, fastened on an upright frame, whereas in most other countries the bottom beam was replaced by a row of weights. At the same time men replaced women at this work.

The introduction of the vertical loom coincided with the introduction of new types of weaving, probably also derived from western Asia. Tapestry weave was popular and the warp-faced weave used for braids. Some of the more complicated patterns required several heddles but might have been made on a ground loom with paired warp threads in two colours, the weaver selecting only the colour needed for the pattern while the other floated at the back.

Cotton was not used in any quantity before the Hellenistic period and wool seems to have been subject to a taboo of some kind. Herodotus records that it was forbidden for use in religious ceremonies or in burials. Few specimens

128. Left: ivory statuette of a queen or consort of Amun, XXVth-dynasty. Now in the Royal Scottish Museum, Edinburgh. Height 20·3 cm. Right: bronze figurine of the god Osiris. From Sakkara, Late Period. Now in the City Museum and Art Gallery, Birmingham. Height 12 cm.

129. Leatherworking: The hide is taken from a large pot, probably intended to represent the last stage of tanning, before the leather is cut and sewn into sandals. Line drawing of a wall-painting from the tomb chapel of the vizier Rekhmireʿ at Thebes. XVIIIth–dynasty.

survive from the Old and Middle Kingdoms, although it was widely used in the Christian period.

A variety of materials was used for ropes: flax, halfa-grass, papyrus and palm fibre were common and strips of leather are also known. Thin string was usually made of flax. Some predynastic pots have a painted lattice work design suggesting a carrying net and examples of such nets, finely and intricately knotted, are known. Several Middle Kingdom examples were found at Kerma and they are also illustrated in the New Kingdom tombs.

LEATHER

Leather was extensively used from the earliest times. Skins were used for clothing in predynastic times and tanned specimens are known from 4500 BC. Goat- and cow-skin are the principal sources identified and the tomb scenes show that the methods and tools of the leatherworker have changed very little. Acacia pods were a convenient source of tannin. From the colours in which model shields are depicted, it seems that the hair was often left in place—perhaps for added strength—but for other articles dyed or painted leather was used. Red, yellow and green are the usual colours.

Until the heavier weapons of the New Kingdom, leather could be used for armour. It provided protection without undue impediment and, as well as its use on shields, was strong enough to make the sides and floors of chariots. Quivers, mirror- and fan-cases, and bags were made in coloured leather sewn with leather thongs. Pieces of leather and interwoven thongs were used to make seats for chairs and stools, or stretched over a bed frame. Thongs of leather were used for lashings and made up into ropes. As well as rare examples of leather wrist-guards for archers and ritual braces, leather nets were worn as loincloths by workmen and finer specimens exist, which were used in some religious ceremonies. These are slit at very close intervals—each slit about 1 cm. long—resulting in a very fine meshed lattice. Pierced leather skirts or kilts ornamented with beads and fringeing are also found in predynastic graves.

Sandals provided an obvious use for leather, and consisted of a single piece forming the sole to which a thong was attached. This was stitched or knotted in place, though it has been suggested that some specimens were glued [129].

130. Cartonnage three-dimensional mask of a hawk, details in black and red, and fret-work appliqué element of a sea-horse in the same material, painted in green, red and yellow. The hawk is probably from an elaborately wrapped hawk mummy, the sea-horse may be from a coffin. Both Late Period. The hawk is now in the City Museum and Art Gallery, Birmingham. The sea-horse is now in the School of Archaeology and Oriental Studies, University of Liverpool.

IVORY AND BONE WORK

Ivory in Egypt was obtained from two sources, the hippopotamus and the elephant. The hippopotamus was revered as a representation of Tawosret, and objects made from its teeth seem to have been accorded special respect. It was the principal source of ivory for the curved flat wands, covered in magical symbols, that were used as protection against snake bites. Elephant ivory was more commonly used. There were plentiful supplies from the Sudan, and in the New Kingdom it was also imported from Syria. It was worked with flint tools—copper tools were not hard enough—and sometimes stained in bright colours. The style is often freer and more naturalistic than is usual in Egyptian work, and was probably much influenced by the flourishing ivory-carving school of Syria, but the tradition of high-quality workmanship reflects the fine pieces from the Archaic Period [16]. A variety of objects were made in ivory: writing palettes, pyxes, mirror handles, gaming boards and pieces are among the most popular.

Bone was used for similar purposes if there was a need for economy.

PLASTER AND CARTONNAGE

The poor quality of native wood often resulted in rough surfaces and imperfect joints, which could be hidden by a thin coat of plaster that made a fine smooth surface for painting. On wooden statuary the finer details could often be added by modelling on a thin coat of plaster.

The plaster was sometimes reinforced with a layer of linen and it soon became apparent to the Egyptians that two or three layers of linen coated with plaster could be moulded into any shape desired and would hold it when dry. This so-called cartonnage became a popular material for coffin cases, since these often followed the contours of the body. The head-piece in particular could be modelled, and then painted and gilded in a fair imitation of the much more expensive gold masks [130].

POTTERY

Pottery is first found in the Nile valley in the early neolithic cultures of the fifth millennium, when it is hand-made. A slow wheel was introduced by the end of the fourth millennium but it was probably no more than a pivoted disc that the potter moved round with one hand. This type of wheel, sometimes turned by an assistant, is still shown in the tomb scenes of the New Kingdom, and the fast foot-turned wheel was not in use much before the end of the dynastic period. The earliest illustration of a kiln is of a tall narrow type in a Vth-dynasty tomb, but the controlled firing of earlier pots suggests that the use of the kiln was well established by then.

The clay normally used was the ordinary river clay found throughout the Nile valley. This fires to a brown or red colour, but a finer calcareous clay, firing to a grey or buff colour, was used in dynastic times for finer ware. The latter is found in the region of Qena, still an important centre of the pottery industry. Black colouring could be achieved by exposure to smoke during firing, and a fine red colour, ideally obtained by good firing, could be produced by a red ochre wash or slip or simply by burnishing the brown clay.

Votive offerings, ushabtis and concubine figures for the dead, as well as figures that were probably intended as dolls or toys, were also made in pottery and sometimes from unfired mud or *beleezy*, the fine black silt that forms on the bottom of the irrigation canals.

BUILDING METHODS

Preparation for building began with the selection of a site and drawing of a plan. The site of a temple or tomb was probably dictated by tradition or oracle, although some sites, such as Deir el-Bahri, seem to have been selected for the sake of the natural setting. Several plans on ostraca and writing boards exist, sometimes of identifiable buildings such as the tombs of Ramesses IV and IX. They use a combination of plan and elevation and give measurements and other instructions in hieratic.

The sites of major buildings were carefully prepared. The rock platform on which the pyramids of Giza were built had been levelled at least along the sides of the pyramids, though many humps have been left in the centre. Levelling of this kind could be done by flooding a channel and noting the surface of the water. The orientation of the pyramids is amazingly accurate but could have been achieved by simple astronomy—bisecting the angle between the rising and setting points of a star will give a bearing on north. Several major temples seem to have been orientated on the Nile, which was apparently regarded as flowing from south to north even when it was, as for example at Abydos, actually flowing south-east to north-west.

Buildings were usually laid out in rectilinear form, though the Ramesseum and the forecourt of the Luxor temple show that this was not always the case. Unimportant buildings could be laid out visually, otherwise a rectangle could be obtained by simple geometry.

Buildings in the desert required little in the way of foundation if the underlying rock was reached and shown to be free from faults, but buildings in the lower parts of the valley were in danger of being undermined by the recurrent inundation. In 1899 eleven columns in the great hypostyle hall at Karnak fell because of this; and others were endangered and dismantled, providing an opportunity to examine the foundations. These were incredibly flimsy. A trench or pit packed with sand provided a firm level base, but between the sand and the ground level was a metre or so of small rotten stone blocks, which were easily decomposed by the damp and crushed by the immense weight of the walls and columns. Similar foundations were used in other buildings.

The masonry techniques were often not much better than the foundations. Temple pylons, for instance, were built with substantial facing blocks but the core was made up of blocks from older buildings that had been dismantled, and little attempt was made to provide any strengthening cross-ties or even to key the facing blocks to the core. On the other hand, joints between the blocks were cut with great precision. Rising joints were often cut at an oblique angle to the other faces. The top face was dressed after laying, when the blocks for the next row were offered and their positions noted. They were trimmed as economically as possible and not usually laid in regular level courses. The backs of the blocks were left rough and the face not trimmed until the whole wall was finished [76].

The pulley was unknown before the Roman period and the blocks were manoeuvred into position on wooden rockers. Scaffolding was used only on a small scale to provide a platform for men working on the final details. The stones were hauled into position up large mud-brick ramps, some of which still remain in position. Obelisks were similarly positioned by being hauled up a huge ramp and dropped bottom first on to a prepositioned base in a prepared pit.

The great casing blocks of the pyramids were set in a gypsum and sand mortar, which was mixed very thin and acted as a lubricant (and therefore

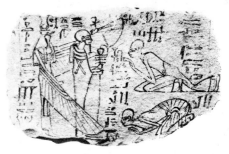

131. Ostracon with drawing of the god Ptah, protected by the goddess Merseger, with two workmen kneeling before him. *c.* 1160 BC. Purchased in western Thebes; probably from Deir el-Medinah. Now in the City Museum and Art Gallery, Birmingham. Length 12 cm.

132. Group of workers making sun-dried mud-bricks. Left: collecting mud from an ornamental pool, an unlikely source in reality; (bottom centre) kneading the mud; a workman tightens the blade of his mattock, pressing it against a wall; (centre top) laying out the bricks using a mould; (right) the dried bricks are carried off by workmen using a yoke and stacked in piles. Some of the workers have dark skins and fair hair, others have beards, suggesting that they may represent several different races, perhaps in Egypt as prisoners-of-war. Line drawing of a wall-painting from the tomb chapel of Rekhmireʻ at Thebes. XVIIIth–dynasty.

133. View upwards in one of the corbelled vaults of the Bent Pyramid at Dahshur. The vaults are over 17 m. high; each course of stonework projects about 15 cm. IIIrd–dynasty.

allowed fine adjustments) rather than as an adhesive to hold the blocks. Because it was so thin it was squeezed out of the horizontal joints and trickled into the rising joints giving the impression that they were thinly 'buttered' before laying. In constructions using smaller blocks less precisely trimmed, the mortar helped to provide a level bedding which distributed the weight evenly and prevented cracking. Although the edges of rising and bedding joints were trimmed to meet precisely, the surfaces were often pecked to provide a key for the mortar, like the frog in a modern brick. Wooden dovetails or butterfly clamps held the blocks in position until the mortar set, and then they were sometimes removed for re-use.

Almost all buildings except tombs and temples, but including palaces and fortresses, were built in sun-dried mud-brick. The mud was dug from the river bank, kneaded and mixed with straw, which acted as a binding agent, shaped in a wooden mould and left to dry in the sun—fired brick is not found until Roman times. The bricks were made to a standard size though this varied considerably from one period to another [132].

The main problem in the use of mud-brick was caused by shrinkage as the brick mass slowly dried out. To prevent cracking and collapse, mats of rushes, or even wooden beams in larger constructions, were placed along the courses at regular intervals. In the New Kingdom very long walls were laid in relatively short sections, with the courses running alternately level, concave or convex. This may also have been done to reduce the effect of shrinkage or to localize the danger of collapse. At times a wall was strengthened by building it along a wavy line rather than a straight one.

In a rainless climate this cheap and easily made building material is almost as permanent as stone. The brick walls of Archaic Hierakonpolis still stand today, along with many later monuments, such as the pylon of Mentuemhat's tomb at Thebes and the temenos walls of several major temples.

House roofs were constructed with beams of palm trunks overlaid with lathes and matting, but temples were roofed in stone, which caused several problems. As limestone blocks can span only about 3 m. without cracking, and sandstone will span about 7 m., the Egyptians were obliged to use numerous pillars to support the roofs of their temples. They were placed as far apart as possible, at the very limits of safety, with the consequent collapse of many roofs, but even so the temple interiors create the impression of a forest of columns. These halls, described as 'hypostyle' (from the Greek, literally, 'below pillars'), are a distinctive feature of Egyptian temples [Pl 18].

The pillars could have been avoided if the Egyptians had practised vaulting in stone, but their experiments in this direction were limited. Spaces were occasionally spanned by leaning two slabs against each other with ingenious locking devices at the top. Corbelled vaulting was also used [133]. This involves laying succeeding courses so that each layer projects slightly farther over the gap until it is sufficiently narrow to be spanned with a single block—the best-known example is in the great ascending gallery of the Great Pyramid. Both these forms of vaulting could be hollowed out underneath, making a false arch, but the true arch with a keystone was not used in dynastic Egypt. Brick store-houses in the precincts of the Ramesseum were constructed with vaulted roofs, using specially shaped bricks built up against an end wall.

Stairs within the houses were constructed with mud-bricks. In stone buildings the blocks forming the steps were sometimes cantilevered out from the wall and sometimes cut out after the block had been laid in position. In temple stair-cases the rise is often very gentle to allow for those carrying the shrine in processions, and the treads often have a slight slope from the back to the front of the step.

Doors and gates were not usually hinged but swung on pivots, the bottom one sunk in a hollowed stone, the top one also fitted into a stone block or heavy piece of wood. The pivots are sometimes reinforced with a metal plate. Large openings, temple doorways for instance, usually had double doors sometimes overlaid in bronze. They could be locked by vertical bolts engaging in the sill or lintel, or by a long rod sliding on staples on one leaf engaging in another staple on the other leaf or in a hole in the jamb [134]. Poorer houses had a simpler door of matting or rough cloth. The false-door stelai often illustrate such a rush mat tied up in a roll above the opening.

House windows were small grilles set high up in the walls. The light is strong in Egypt and sufficient light penetrated in this way, while at the same time the room remained reasonably cool. In the temples light was admitted through small slits in the roof, and from the XVIIIth dynasty onwards by means of the open upper part of the screen wall at the front; in the New Kingdom the hypostyle halls were lit by clerestories. The window grilles were occasionally fretted in the form of hieroglyphs or other symbolic devices.

Two decorative features are distinctive in Egyptian masonry. At the corners and along the top of temple pylons, shrines and even many of the false-door stelai is a rounded ridge on which are inscribed imitation cross-lashings. This so-called Torus Roll probably represents the bundled-reed framework of the earliest buildings and the cavetto cornice above it represents a line of palm fronds also derived from an early type of building. Along the tops of many walls can be seen a painted frieze of tall pointed signs, a so-called 'khekher' frieze from the sign's phonetic value. This may represent a practice, still to be seen in Egypt, when reeds are stuck into the tops of mud-brick walls and tied loosely together so that they stand above the wall, so increasing the shade it provides without adding to its weight or bulk. A khekher frieze is often painted on tomb walls just below the ceiling.

134. Top: bronze pivot from the upper right-hand corner of a heavy wooden door, inscribed with the names and titles of Psammetichus II. Now in the Royal Scottish Museum, Edinburgh. Length 46 cm. Bottom: heavy bronze bolt in the form of a lion, probably from the great door of a temple. The hieroglyph of a lion is used in the spelling of the word 'to shut', the design, therefore, incorporates this symbolism. Late Period or Graeco-Roman. Now in the Gulbenkian Museum of Oriental Art, University of Durham. Length 44·5 cm.

The Egyptians, like the Athenians, were 'in all things too superstitious'. What follows is a very abbreviated account of the part religious beliefs played in Egyptian life, with particular reference to the way in which they affected the design of temples and cult equipment and the organization of religious life.

⌐The gods of the early Egyptians were the strong forces in the world about him that he feared, admired or even loved. They included animals such as the lion and crocodile, the falcon and the beetle and the useful and friendly domestic animals, all of which it was to his advantage to placate or encourage. The great cosmic forces: the sun, the wind and the storm closely affected his well-being and he regarded other important factors in his life, such as the regular recurrence of the inundation or a fruitful harvest, as being under the auspices of a deity who could be cajoled or threatened, encouraged and thanked.

The inaccessibility of the cosmic forces early led to a form of symbolism and the development of anthropomorphism. The gods of the animal cults are often shown with human bodies, perhaps partly because the ritual involved the priest wearing the appropriate animal mask. Amongst the deities, specialized figures emerged, such as Hapi, whose obesity proclaimed the liberality of the flooding river, and Renenutet, the harvest goddess, who appeared in the form of a cobra, which must often have been found in the warm heaps of grain or basking in the sun on the threshing floors.

Many of the principal deities had special ties with particular towns or areas. The origin of this link lies in the predynastic period, when some of the gods' symbols appear on pots and palettes. The fortunes of the gods were linked with the political fortunes of their area. For instance, the rise of Re' of Heliopolis is associated with the Memphite dynasties of the Old Kingdom; and that of Montu and Amun with Thebes in the Middle and New Kingdoms. This position of power is often reflected in the appearance of the god's name as part of the king's name, hence the number of Old Kingdom names compounded with Re' and the *Mentu*hoteps and *Amen*hoteps in later periods.

Changes and amalgamations of political power also led to the syncretistic movement in the cults. As two areas formed closer links, so points of similarity could be found between their local gods. The process was helped by the fact that many of the gods were, on the whole, cosmic deities with perhaps some special local facet, but there were wide grounds for mutual recognition. This process, and their anthropomorphic character, led to several instances of gods and goddesses being linked in family groups, together with offspring. The Egyptian willingness to compromise, however, meant that even the animal aspects of the gods could also be included in this syncretism as peculiar localized forms.

Pl 23. The reconstructed chair and part of the bed with headrest of Queen Hetepheres set out in her wooden framed tent [cf. **148**].

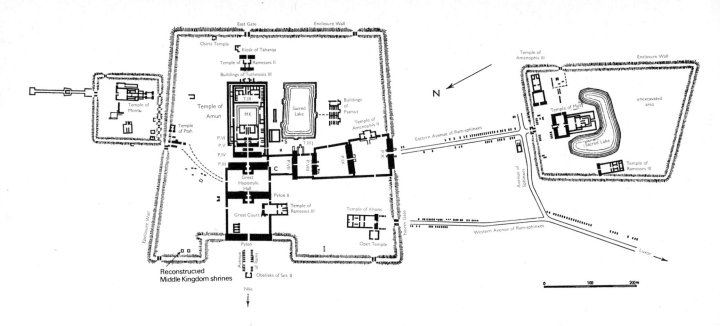

East Gate · Enclosure Wall
Osiris Temple
Kiosk of Taharqa
Temple of Ramesses II
Buildings of Tuthmosis III
Temple of Amun
Sacred Lake
Buildings of Psamut
T.III
MK
Temple of Montu
Temple of Ptah
Temple of Amenophis II
P.VI
P.V
P.IV
T.III
S
P.X
P.IX
Temple of Amenophis III
Enclosure Wall
Temple of Mut
unexcavated area
Sacred Lake
Eastern Avenue of Ram-sphinxes
P.III
C
P.VII
P.II/VIII
Temple of Ramesses III
Avenue of Sphinxes
Enclosure Wall
Great Hypostyle Hall
Pylon II
Great Court
Temple of Ramesses III
Temple of Khons
North Gate
Western Avenue of Ram-sphinxes
Luxor
Pylon
Avenue of Rams
Opet Temple
Reconstructed Middle Kingdom shrines
Obelisks of Set. II
Nile

N

0   100   200 m

Local loyalty might tend to work against syncretism but never to a serious degree, for the tradition of religious tolerance would prevent any clash between partisan supporters of different gods. A man might well have his own favourite god, but he was free to pray to any other if he thought this might be more effective in certain cases.

The principal hint of any rivalry over dogma comes in the various cosmogonies. Two of these, the Solar cosmogony of Heliopolis and the Hermopolitan story associated with Thoth and later Amun, involve a picture of primeval chaos, from which emerged a god who created other gods that were identified with different parts of the universe.

A more sophisticated approach was made by the priests of Ptah of Memphis, probably in the IIIrd or IVth dynasty, as a reaction to the increasing prestige of Re'. This story suggested that Ptah as the supreme primordial deity, had created the other gods, including Atum and Re', by his own word. This approximation to the Christian dogma was too intellectual a doctrine to be popular, but it remained in circulation and won increasing recognition in the Late Period, when Shabaka had it copied from a damaged papyrus on to a large basalt block, the so-called Shabaka Stone, now in the British Museum. Unfortunately this stone was later used as a millstone and much of the text was lost.

Perhaps the most exotic of the cults were those of the animal deities. The actual practice varied according to location: in some areas all representatives of a species were regarded as sacred and their dead bodies carefully mummified and stored in seemingly endless numbers, such as the ibises at Sakkara and Hermopolis, but in other cases one individual animal was the incarnation of the god and others could be treated ordinarily. The Mnevis bull who was the incarnation of Re' at Heliopolis, the Buchis bull of Montu at Armant and the Apis bull of Ptah at Memphis are the most famous examples. They were selected by carefully observed signs, rather as a new Dalai Lama is chosen in Tibet, and taken to the temple where they were pampered throughout their life and mummified and ceremonially buried at death, when the search for the new incarnation began. Even the mother of the Apis received special honours. These animal cults are known throughout dynastic Egypt but were especially popular in the Late Period when they could be used as a sign of nationalist superiority over dominant foreigners, for whom animal worship was quite incomprehensible.

Occasionally, distinguished individuals were deified, some like Heka–ib for a short while and in a limited area, others, like Imhotep, vizier of Djoser, gained national recognition. Imhotep's cult enjoyed great popularity in Hellenistic times and he was identified with the Greek god of medicine, Aesculapius.

The stability of government and the social order relied largely on the divinity of the king as the Horus, son of the preceding monarch who had on death become identified with Osiris (see p. 197). This concept of a divine king was in no way reduced by his evident mortality, and he was often referred to as the 'Good God' although his statue was only exceptionally placed in the temple shrine as an object of worship. He more frequently appears, in fact, as the officiant, and was theoretically the chief priest of all the gods. The idea of the king's continuing link with the previous ruler was more than a polite fiction and was taken very seriously, especially by those kings who had arrived on their throne by some devious method. In these circumstances it had its greatest value and effect.

⌈Religion was a powerful force in the stability of Egyptian life generally⌋

136. Plan of the great temple of Amun at Karnak.

135. One of the huge granite sarcophagi, each weighing several tons, used for the burials of the sacred Apis bulls in the Serapeum at Sakkara. Late Period.

The knowledge that the gods were receiving their due attention in the performance of the cult and that the efficacy of the myths was duly released in their re-enactment at festivals was a reassuring factor for all men. However, the relationship between religious belief and moral behaviour was not stressed and although many writers suggested that moral uprightness was desired by the gods they more often proposed a philosophical or pragmatic basis for morality. Personal involvement with the gods was seldom deep-rooted; the troubled times of the Late Period saw the writing of many hymns of personal devotion, but few among the common people came close to the gods, except at festivals. Their devotion was more often centred on a very localized deity, such as the goddess Merseger, the genius who inhabited the great peak that dominates the Valley of the Kings and who was worshipped by the Deir el-Medinah workers. There is also evidence that they were allowed to come to one of the minor gates of the great temples to present their petitions to the god of their own city [131].

The only persons to penetrate into the temple were the servants and priests of the god. Theoretically the king was the officiating priest at all times, but in practice his duties were delegated to local nobles and officials. These formed a non-professional priesthood which served according to a fixed rota, living an ordinary secular life in the intervals. In the New Kingdom the priesthood changed and became largely professional, but many priests still wielded great political power.

Pl 25. The main hall of the tomb chapel of Queen Nefertari, in the Valley of the Queens, Thebes. The decoration is in painted low relief and shows the queen (left) before Thoth, the ibis-headed god of writing and wisdom from Hermopolis, and (right) offering to Osiris. XIXth–dynasty.

Pl 24. Headdress of a queen of Tuthmosis III, reconstructed from fragments. Some 850 gold rosettes, set with green, blue and red artificial stones or paste are linked together and suspended from a central crown-plate of gold. When complete the whole headdress would have weighed about two kilogrammes. Height 37 cm.

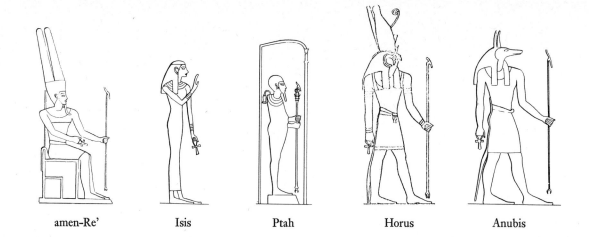

| amen-Re' | Isis | Ptah | Horus | Anubis |

The hierarchy of priests was detailed and carefully ordered, especially in a large temple. The principal priests, the 'Servants of the God', were actually numbered First, Second, Third and so on in rank, and other senior officers had specialist titles, such as the 'Father of the God', and the 'Lector Priest', on whom devolved the responsibility of correct recitation of the ritual. Minor parts of the ritual were undertaken by the *Wab*-priests, or 'Pure Ones'. Others formed the choir, carried the god's shrine in processions and performed other small duties.

THE TEMPLE: PURPOSE AND DESIGN

The temple building was a home for the god and a stage for the re-enactment of his rituals. It therefore contains the basic components of the house, but the layout is planned to allow for processions. Therefore the sanctuary, which corresponds to the main bedroom of the house, is placed at the end of a straight axis that passes through a number of courts and halls, which themselves correspond to the garden and reception rooms of a house. This applies to all the principal types of temple: the cult temple, the funerary or mortuary temple, where the place of the cult image of the god was taken by the dead king, and the sun temple, although the latter were open to the sky and the cult image was the squat obelisk or *benben* with its gold- or electrum-covered apex.

As well as the great cult temples of dynastic Egypt, several were founded in the Greek period or even later. These were often new foundations on sites of earlier religious importance and dedicated to the traditional deities, such as Horus of Edfu, Hathor of Dendera and Khnum of Esna. They are important for the study of the temple architecture and ritual for, unlike the great temples of Karnak and Luxor, their basic plan did not pass through centuries of alteration and addition, and many of them are very well preserved [137, 138].

The cult temples represent Egypt in microcosm. The twin piers of the entrance pylon recall the hieroglyph ⌴, representing the horizon or the limits of Egypt, and on their outer faces the king is frequently portrayed destroying his foreign foes [40]. Within, the hypostyle halls were originally designed as huge papyrus thickets, the floors painted as water, the bases of the plant-form pillars decorated with leaves, while overhead the ceilings were painted with stars. The symbolic plants and gods of Upper and Lower Egypt are arrayed on opposite sides of the principal axis and every part of the temple is given ritual significance.

Thōth   Mīn   Hathor   Reʿ-Harakhti   Osiris   Khnum

The sanctuary area is raised on a mound, probably symbolizing the primeval mound that figures in the creation myths as the site of the initial act of creation. It is emphasized in several temples by a cavetto moulding that runs around the outside of the rear walls of the temple at about 1 m. in height, as if making a kind of dais. It can be clearly seen in the temple of Luxor, and at Medinet Habu it is represented by a slope or batter for the first few courses of stonework.

137. Main building of the temple of Horus at Edfu, seen from the top of the pylon.

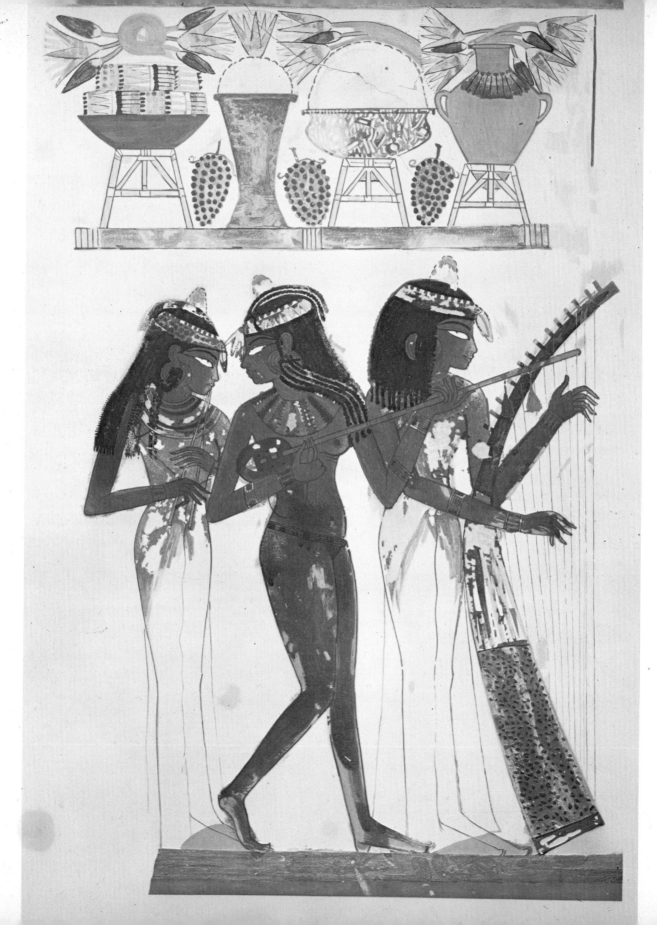

Great care was taken to isolate the temple, to keep it virtually uncontaminated by contact with the secular world. At the foundation ceremony the site was purified with a layer of clean sand, and a series of corridors or ambulatories, one within the other, ensured that there was no cross-wall connecting the shrine with the outer walls of the building. The foundation ceremony is recorded in detail in reliefs at Edfu and Dendera. They show the king, assisted by the gods, laying out the site; then he purifies it with incense, makes the first brick and lays the first block. Foundation deposits were often made, consisting of animal sacrifices, caches of model tools, faience plaques or inscribed stone vessels. There was another ceremony when the building was complete, which involved making a procession around it with incense and spices and formally presenting it to the god.

From entrance to sanctuary the air of mystery was increased by reducing the size of the rooms along with a series of rises in floor level, matched by a lower ceiling and by gradual diminution of the lighting. In the Graeco-Roman temples one passed from an open court to the vestibule, lit by the open top of the screen wall. In earlier temples the front halls were lit by a clerestory, but the sanctuary area was completely cut off from daylight. The narrow slanting beams of bright light from the clerestory or screen, followed by the flickering, leaping gleams of torchlight in the inner rooms, playing on the richly painted figures of the gods and the hieroglyphs, together with the singing and the incense, all combined to increase the air of mystery as the worshipper approached the sanctuary [143].

The roof was an important feature, especially of the Graeco-Roman temples, for some ceremonies involving the meeting of the divine image with the sun were carried out there. Elaborate stairways enabled the cult image to be carried up to the roof for this union, which would take place in a small open shrine [142].

Pl 27. The Royal Scribe Menna enjoying a day's sport with his family in the marshes. They are shown twice: as he spears a fish and as he prepares to hurl a throwstick at birds in a clump of papyrus reeds. The birds are put up by Menna's cat. Watercolour copy by Nina de Garis Davies of a wall-painting in the tomb chapel of Menna. Original *c.* 1400 BC.

Pl 26. A group of musicians playing pipe, lute and harp. Watercolour copy by Nina de Garis Davies of a wall-painting in the tomb chapel of Nakht. Ashmolean Museum, Oxford. Original *c.* 1400 BC.

185

138. (A) The temple of Horus at Edfu shows in its plan all the main characteristics of a typical cult temple. (B) The temple of Haroeris and Suchos at Kom Ombo has a double aisle and twin shrines for the two gods who share the dedication. (C) The cult temple of Seti I at Abydos has seven shrines, each with a corresponding aisle, dedicated to Horus, Isis, Osiris, Amen-Reʿ, Reʿ-Horakht, Ptah and the king himself. The Osiris chapel opens into an inner shrine dedicated to Osiris and his family Isis and Horus. (D) The cult temple of Amun at Luxor. The underlying basic form can still be detected in the earlier buildings at the southern end. The principal distinctive features of this temple are the courts and colonnades added at the front by successive rulers through the XVIIIth and XIXth dynasties. (E) The rock-cut temple of Ramesses II at Abu Simbel incorporates the essential features of a pylon, with the figures in three dimensions.

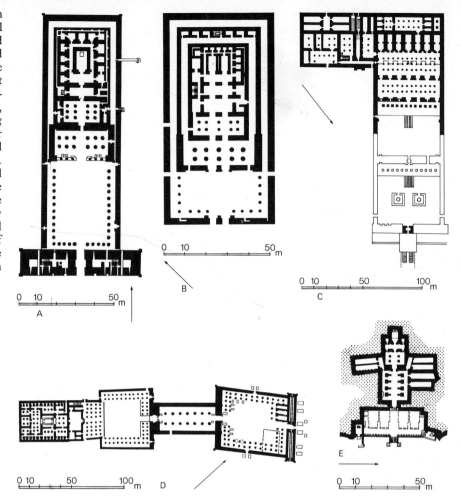

139, 140, 141. Three views of the north face of the pylon of the temple of Amun at Luxor: (139) view by Denon in 1799 shows the temple half-buried by debris from successive medieval occupants; (140) a recent view showing the sphinx-lined approach to the pylon; (141) a low relief carving from the wall of the first court showing a contemporary view of the pylon.

Pl 30. Above: unfinished relief from the royal tomb of Horemheb at Thebes, showing the underdrawing in red and the finished outline in black.

Pl 31. Left: glass head from Amarna. Now in the Louvre, Paris.

Pl 28. Opposite above: gold dish presented by Tuthmosis III to his general Djehuty in recognition of his military exploits. The centre of the dish represents a pond and is decorated with incised and embossed fish and papyrus umbels. Now in the Louvre, Paris.

Pl 29. Opposite below: calcite sarcophagus of Seti I. Now in Sir John Soane's Museum, London.

189

142. The roof chapel, site of the New Year ceremonies at the temple of Hathor, Dendera. A statuette of the goddess was carried here in procession and united with the sun in a rite that was kept invisible from the people below by the high wall surrounding this part of the roof. The Hathor-headed columns are peculiar to this temple.

Several of the Graeco–Roman temples, particularly Edfu, Dendera and Philae, have within the temple complex, but apart from the main building, a small shrine, usually surrounded by a peristyle with half-height inter-columnar walls. The reliefs illustrate the ritual of the divine marriage and birth of the child god associated with the temple, and for this reason these chapels are termed 'Mammisi', a Coptic term for a 'birthplace'.

Also within the temple complex, and sometimes at strategic positions along a processional way, small kiosks or peripteral temples were built, where the portable shrine of the god might rest [46].

Mortuary temples were arranged on the same basic plan as the cult temples, and the services conducted on similar lines. Theoretically the endowments allowed them to function indefinitely, but as succeeding generations of rulers diverted the product of the endowments to their own temples the older ones were gradually abandoned. However, some cults seem to have had a greater power of survival than others, depending perhaps on the popularity of the ruler, or on some less obvious feature, such as the stability of the endowment or a more conscientious priesthood.

RITUALS AND FESTIVALS

The daily cult for the Ptolemaic temple of Horus at Edfu has been reconstructed in detail, and this pattern was probably followed in all the major temples. It was based on the supposition that the god has the same needs and daily routine as his worshippers.

At dawn he was wakened by a choir and a priest removed the night attire from the cult image and washed and dressed it for the day, before making the first offering of food and drink. After the god had enjoyed the spiritual sustenance of the food, it was removed and presented to minor deities in the side chapels of the temple, and eventually to the priests. By the same ritual process, the so-called 'Reversion of Offerings', other material offerings to the god became available to the priesthood, and it was in this way that they received their maintenance and reward.

After his 'breakfast' the god might be called upon to receive visitors or deliver oracles, either by manipulation of an image or openly through his priests. At midday and in the evening he would partake of further meals, and eventually be put to bed for the night in his shrine.

This routine was frequently broken by festivals. Some lasted only a day and involved little more than a special meal or procession within the temple precincts, but others continued for several days while the god undertook a long boat journey to the shrine of a related deity.

Some of the feasts celebrated the anniversary of the king's accession, or one of his great victories, others were linked with a seasonal event like the New Year or Harvest. Events in the life of the god were also celebrated, such as the re-enactment of Osiris' suffering and resurrection at Abydos, or Hathor's journey from Dendera to unite with her husband Horus at Edfu. At Edfu the triumph of Horus over the evil god Seth was re-enacted, in a similar way to a medieval mystery play, on a stage built out in front of the temple pylon.* At Thebes, the procession of the god Min, the Valley festival (when the tombs and temples on the west bank were visited) and the Opet festival, which lasted for twenty-four days, while Amun left Karnak to visit his consort Mut at the temple of Luxor, were amongst the highlights of a year that comprised about 160 feast days.

Those festivals that involved processions outside the temple precincts were treated as holidays by the populace, who lined the route to glimpse the god's shrine or even travelled on long pilgrimages to attend the ceremonies. Herodotus talks of 700,000 pilgrims at the annual festival at Bubastis.

Myrrh and frankincense, imported in large quantities from Punt and probably from South Arabia, were used profusely in the ritual. Hatshepsut's attempts to transplant frankincense trees are illustrated at Deir el-Bahri, but they are unlikely to have been successful and the records show that trading expeditions continued to be sent out to obtain this valuable resin. Natron was also used in the ritual, its cleansing properties making it especially appropriate for purification ceremonies.

TEMPLE FURNITURE

The cult image was kept in a shrine at the innermost point of the temple. Existing examples in the Greek period temples are stone built and have the form of small independent buildings, even to the extent of having their own roof. Some are huge monolithic constructions weighing several tons, but most are built from smaller blocks, like the great granite shrine erected at Karnak by Philip Arrhidaeus. Apart from the nest of shrines around the coffin of Tutankhamun and a gold-covered shrine from the same burial, most of the large wooden shrines of earlier dynasties have all disappeared, although the side and one doorleaf of a shrine dedicated to Amun by Tuthmosis II was recovered from the debris of Deir el-Bahri. It was made in ebony and carved with scenes of Tuthmosis's offering to Amun inside, and repeated groups of lucky hieroglyphs outside. It was about 2 m. high, corresponding to an ebony shrine described in a text from Dendera, which was 3 cubits (about 1·70 m.) high.

Several small wooden shrines (about 30–40 cm. high) have survived, including a number from Sakkara, of Late Period or Greek date. They reproduced traditional features from the full-scale shrines, such as the double doors with a fastening bolt and the cavetto cornice.

At festival processions the cult image was paraded, suitably shrouded from profane eyes, usually in a large model boat carried on the shoulders of bearers or on a sledge. These boats were carefully built to incorporate traditional features and symbols of the appropriate god. They were usually of wood, overlaid with gold and inlaid with coloured faience. When not in use, they were kept in a special room, equipped with a stone pedestal, in the temple. In some instances

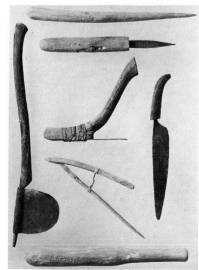

143. Items from foundation deposits at the funerary temple of Queen Hatshepsut, Deir el-Bahri: (top) inscribed calcite pebble and wooden magical emblems; (bottom) model-tools: axe, wooden 'hammer', mattock, adze, chisel, spike, and knife. Now in the Metropolitan Museum of Art, New York.

---

* The text of the play is recorded on one of the walls of the temple, along with scenes in relief.

the image was kept permanently on the boat, which was then the central shrine of the cult.

Larger boats were also constructed in which the gods actually travelled on the river from one temple to another. These magnificently equipped vessels were designed as huge reed boats with a large shrine amidships and high prows and stern posts ending in imitation papyrus umbels. Those who supervised their construction proudly recorded the fact on their funeral stelai. Symbols or fetishes of the gods were also carried in processions on standards shaped rather like the traditional idea of a gallows.

The actual cult images of the gods are never illustrated and none have been found, but we may fairly assume that they were made in the form usually given to the god when he is depicted in ritual scenes and in figurines and amulets. They were probably made in fine metal richly adorned with precious stones.

Apart from a few isolated items and the Late Period hoard from Bubastis, little has survived of the tremendous wealth of vessels and other objects used in

144. Items of temple equipment including (left) a large offering stand, (centre) censer, and (below) a large situla, the design picked out in white. Late Period. Now in the British Museum, London. Length of censer 48 cm.

Pl 32. Vignette from the *Book of the Dead* of Ankhefenkhonsu showing the dead man before Osiris and Isis. Now in the Cairo Museum. XXth to XXIst–dynasty.

the temple ritual. They were often of precious metal, easily portable, and therefore quickly looted, and most of them were doubtless carried off by the victorious Persian, Assyrian and Roman armies. Some idea of the wealth of this equipment can be gained from reliefs such as the one at Karnak, where Tuthmosis III is shown dedicating some 200 items of gold, silver, bronze and stone to the god Amun Re' [144]. The list includes a large number of gold, silver and stone vessels, some plain with various handles and pedestals, some very ornate, based on lotus, cartouche and fan shapes, large kraters with raised lotus plants round the rim, and vases in the form of hieroglyphs such as ♀ and 🍶, and with animal-shaped lids and spouts. Besides these there are items of furniture, including shrines, screens, tables and stands, clothes-chests in wood ornamented with goldwork, sceptres, staves and maces, stone altars, wood or metal offering-tables, each with a set of vessels, necklaces and bangles, gold models of butterfly clamps, brick moulds and hoes for foundation deposits, large quantities of lapis lazuli, malachite, carnelian, nearly 14,000 kg. of unworked lumps of gold and gold rings, and over 9,000 kg. of silver rings. A number of bronze doors were included, along with two granite obelisks with their pyramidions covered in electrum, and finally two great flag-poles, probably of cedar wood from Lebanon.

As well as small offering-tables from tombs there are some surviving altars, usually in calcite or a harder stone like granite. They are usually rectangular and commonly carved in relief with representations of offerings and the appropriate ritual text so that it might be effective even if the cult was not actually celebrated. The top was sometimes carved with the hieroglyph for an altar or offering ⬭ in relief, and in the sun temple of Niuserre' the great central altar was built up with four slabs of this shape arranged around a square, in which stood a large circular block. In the slaughter-yard of the Sun Temple was a row of ten circular stone basins, with small cups ranged round the rim, perhaps intended to receive the blood of slaughtered animals, although in normal cult temples the slaughtering took place in the butchery in the temple enclosure, not in the main temple building.

In many offering scenes the king is shown offering incense to the god in a censer whose shape was traditional from the Middle Kingdom onwards. It consists of a rod about 40 cm. long, terminating in a hawk's head by which it is held and, at the other end, in a hand holding an open bowl containing a small charcoal (?) fire. Half-way along the stem is an oval container from which small balls of incense are taken and fed to the fire in the bowl. Several examples of these censers exist in bronze.

Many of the gods carried sceptres or staves, some similar to the sceptre of the king, others of distinctive form for individual gods. Min, for instance, carries a flail, Osiris a flail and crook, while Ptah has an elaborate staff incorporating a forked foot and a *djed* pillar surmounted by the Seth-animal head of the *was* sceptre (see p. 182), and the *'nkh* hieroglyph, these together forming the traditional blessing of Life, Prosperity and Health.

From the Late Period and Hellenistic times large numbers of figurines survive that were used as votive offerings by visitors to the temples. In the excavations at Sakkara caches of these have been found, apparently buried as part of a 'spring clean', when so many votives had been amassed in the shrines that they had to be cleared out to make room for more. Since they had been offered to the god they could not be unceremoniously dumped but were buried within the temple precinct [159].

The commonest subjects for these figurines are the gods themselves. Isis and Horus, Osiris, Min and Ptah, are amongst the most popular, and the Apis bull was a local favourite at Sakkara. Other subjects include secular figures bearing offerings, and small models of offering-tables. The bodies of hawks, ichneumon, lizards and some other small animals were mummified and preserved in bronze caskets surmounted by a figure of the animal. Wooden figurines sometimes have a small mummified fragment concealed in a hollow pillar behind the figure.

The figurines are usually in bronze, although gold, silver and even iron were occasionally used, and cheaper examples are found in painted and plastered wood. Some are gilded and many have gold inlay work. The average height is about 15 cm., but many elements survive—headdresses, plumes, sceptres, etc.—that are obviously from considerably larger figures cast in several pieces. Most of the figures either have rings by which they could be suspended or tangs by which they could be fitted in bases which occasionally survive. They may be of bronze or wood, rectangular or in the shape of a sledge or throne.

PERSONAL RELIGION

As befitted a religious people, the Egyptians had a large number of charms or amulets, which would protect them from evil influence or enhance their own powers. They are commonly found in mummy wrappings but many also provided important protection for the living, who wore them as religiously as motorists today carry their St Christopher key-rings. When found on an undisturbed corpse they often appear to be in certain prescribed positions related to their specific function, and they are often made of a particular stone although most are made in faience. Small baked clay moulds in which the faience form was pressed are common: they usually have a groove in which a thin stick or straw could lie, passing through the middle of the lump of moulded faience. During firing it would burn away, leaving a small perforation by which the amulet could be suspended.

145. A group of common amulets: (left to right, top) Anubis, Isis and Horus, Thoueris, Djed pillar; all in faience. From Sakkara. Late Period. All now in the City Museum and Art Gallery, Birmingham. Height of Djed pillar 78 cm.

146. Left: small limestone bust similar to many found in the villages of Deir el-Medinah: the provenance of this piece is not known. New Kingdom. Height 11 cm. Right: limestone tablet crudely inscribed with the name of Isis and two ears. The inscription at the bottom reads: 'Made by Ta-wahy'. The tablet was probably presented as a votive to encourage Isis to give heed to Ta-wahy's prayer. New Kingdom. Height 9 cm. Now in the City Museum and Art Gallery, Birmingham.

All kinds of objects are used as amulets and only a very small selection is illustrated here [145]. It is often difficult to know where ornament stops and amulets start, for some are purely natural objects, like pretty sea-shells that may well have been only worn as ornament, but animal tusks were probably worn for their protective powers and were copied in stone. Even a cord tied with a particular knot had its own magical significance.

The most popular amulets were small figures of the gods and their attributes. The figure of Bes, a small bandy-legged dwarf of hideous countenance with plumed headdress and no other clothing, was a very popular figure who protected women and children. Masks of Bes were also common. Of the deities Thoeris was very popular, along with Sekhmet, Anubis, Min, Nefertun, and Isis with the infant Horus. By far the most common of all Egyptian amulets must be the Eye of Horus, the symbol of the eye that Seth destroyed in a fight with Horus and which was made whole (*wedjat*) by Thoth. Also popular are the telegraph-pole-like *djed* pillar of Osiris and the knotted girdle of Isis. Sceptres, uraei and various headdresses and crowns also occur frequently.

Many animals were closely associated with different deities and even such unlikely subjects as flies and locusts were used as amulets. Parts of the body, both human and animal, parts of plants and models of objects from everyday life all had their amuletic significance.

A number of small busts were found at Deir el-Medinah, usually in a niche in the first room of the house [146]. They are often associated with a stone headrest and almost all are anonymous, although they may have borne a name on a wooden ticket around the neck. They seem to carry on the tradition of the reserve heads of the IVth dynasty from Giza and were linked by the excavator with spells from the *Book of the Dead* which emphasize the importance of the head as a base for the spirit. Their presence in the home rather than the tomb seems to indicate a form of ancestor worship paralleled in our own time by the display of paintings and photographs.

14

The World of the Dead

FUNERARY BELIEFS AND RITUALS

Pride, if nothing else, leads Man to suppose that life will continue after death in some form or other and the Egyptians had their own ideas about the shape it would take. In so far as it is possible to distinguish them there are three major ideas that were in favour most of the time.

The oldest and most straightforward is met first in the predynastic period. From the nature of the equipment found with the Badarian and Naqada burials it seems likely that they believed in a future existence not much different from life on earth. In dynastic Egypt this belief gives rise to tomb reliefs and paintings which are, simultaneously, a record of the owner's life on earth and, more importantly, magical provision for a similar but better existence beyond the grave. There the hunting would be always successful, the harvests better, the banquet tables always overloaded and the serving girls even more attractive. The elaborate preparation made for this existence was not undertaken in hopeful anticipation of death, nor from any morbid preoccupation with it, but rather from love of this life and a determination to prolong its pleasures beyond the grave.

The pyramid texts and later vignettes in the royal tombs indicate a different afterlife for the king. As a god it was his privilege to join the company of other gods, whose main occupation was accompanying the sun god Re' in his daily boat journey across the sky. This idea was most powerful in the Old Kingdom and even with the gradual decline in the influence of Re' the concept was never completely abandoned, for it became inextricably mixed with the Osiris cult.

This cult was based on the myth of Osiris known throughout the dynastic period but not recorded in full until Plutarch. According to this, Osiris was a beneficent ruler in the Delta who was murdered by his jealous brother Seth by being tricked into entering a box that was thrown into the river. The body was washed up at Byblos and recovered by Osiris's wife Isis, but Seth stole it and dismembered it, scattering the parts throughout Egypt. Isis diligently recovered them, and reconstituted the body with the help of Thoth, the completely bandaged body being quoted later as an explanation for the practice of mummification. She then conceived a child by him and the young Horus grew up to avenge his father's murder in a heroic struggle with Seth. He succeeded to his father's throne, while his father became ruler of the Afterworld and a symbol of resurrection. There are several varieties of this myth, arising often from attempts to harmonize similar localized legends. Some, for instance, explain the site of a temple as the burial place of one of Osiris's limbs and the spot where it was found by Isis, but the Egyptian willingness to compromise meant that all variations were equally acceptable.

The king was early identified with Osiris and the increasing debasement of the monarchy in the latter part of the Old Kingdom meant that first the nobility and later all classes of Egyptians claimed the same rights; so a dead man was commonly given the epithet 'Osiris', and, as it were, referred to as Osiris John Smith.

It is interesting that the Egyptians did not personify the idea of death itself. There is no dark figure who taps men on the shoulder. The Egyptian attitude to death was mixed. The confident pictures of life in the next world are sometimes obviously conjectural; and the underlying doubts are well conveyed by two poems, which provide a contrasting set of thoughts, rather like Milton's *L'Allegro* and *Il Penseroso*.

> There is no one who has come back from there
> Who can tell their state
> Who can tell their needs
> Or who can still our hearts
> Until we travel to the place where they have gone
> Follow your desire as long as you live
> Put myrrh on your head and dress in fine linen.
> Make holiday and do not tire of it.
> A man cannot take his property with him.
> No one who has departed ever comes back.

> I have heard the songs in the ancient tombs
> And how they magnify life on earth
> And disparage the Afterworld.
> Why do they do so to the land of eternity
> The right and true, free from terror?
> Quarrelling is forbidden there
> And no one sets himself against his fellow,
> In this land where is no opponent.
> All our kinsfolk rest there since the first day of time
> And those yet to be, for millions of millions
> Will all come to it.
> There is none who can stay in the land of Egypt
> And none who will not reach that place.
> The passage of one's activities on Earth is like a dream.
> But they say 'Welcome, safe and sound' to the one who reaches the West.

The centre of the Osiris cult was Abydos where, during the Old Kingdom, he was linked with and largely replaced the local deity Khentamenty, whose name means 'The Foremost of the Westerners' (i.e. the chief of the dead who are buried in the western desert). An annual mystery play portrayed the myth and his image was carried in its portable shrine, the Neshmet boat, from his temple to his tomb, in the New Kingdom identified with the tomb of Djer. There was a popular pilgrimage to Abydos to take part in the procession, and model boats in which the dead might make the journey are provided in some tombs. In order to associate themselves with Osiris and share in his resurrection, many Egyptians chose to be buried at Abydos in the great cemeteries that cover the site; many more, especially in the Middle Kingdom, built small mud-brick chapels in which stelai were erected to commemorate their visit to Abydos and to act as a memorial of them in the sacred city.

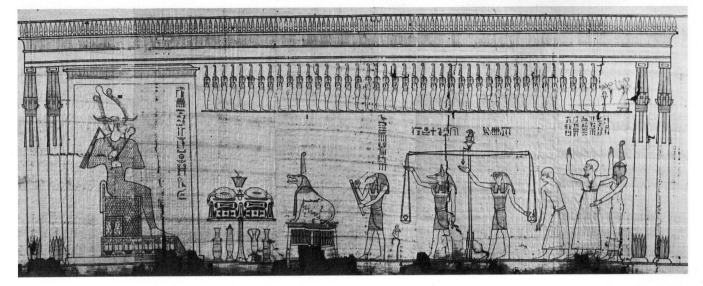

147. Vignette from the *Book of the Dead* showing the dead man watching the weighing of his heart against a feather, representing justice or truth, in the presence of Osiris. XXth to XXIst-dynasty.

One source of concern about the Afterworld was the judgement that a dead man faced. He was obliged to deny a whole series of possible sins (misnamed the Negative Confession) and his heart, the seat of intelligence, was weighed by Anubis against a feather, representing Truth. The result was observed by the scribe Thoth and if he were accounted blameless he was declared 'True of Voice', implying that his denial had been proven [147]. The epithet, usually translated as 'Justified', was consistently applied in every reference to him so the dead man's full title became, as it were, Osiris John Smith Justified. The same epithet was also applied, in circumstances that are not entirely clear, to some persons during their lifetime.

In his tomb the dead man is shown as he appeared at the peak of his success in this life, but it was plain that his mummified body lay buried and that it was a spiritual aspect which passed to the next world. This the Egyptians spoke of as his *Ka*, a kind of shadowy double that was born with him and lived through life with him, and it was for this *Ka* that the funerary equipment was provided in the tomb, the 'house of the *Ka*'. A man also had a *Ba*, shown as a human-headed bird, conveniently translated as 'soul', although that is misleading if considered too strictly in the modern sense. The *Ba* left the body at death and returned to it after the funeral, then used the body or substitute statue or picture as a base from which it could travel to the outer world, returning to the tomb at night. Theoretically the offerings were provided by the eldest son, but the duty could be entrusted to mortuary priests provided for by contracted endowments. Some cults, especially the royal ones, were kept up by faithful priests over many years, but the contracts often lapsed within a couple of generations and the tombs fell into ruin.

The wise Egyptian prepared for death in his later middle age. The climax of a great career was to be given the services of the royal necropolis workers with whom one might plan and supervise the construction and decoration of one's tomb. Even though there are detailed scenes of the funeral ceremonies and grieving relatives, it seems likely that the work was all carried out before death. For some reason, perhaps superstition, the tombs are not completely finished; sometimes quite large areas remain undecorated, occasionally it is clearly only a token area that is left untouched.

Apart from royal favour, a man seems to have been entirely responsible for his own funeral arrangements, and there is therefore great variation in the nature of provisions and appointments, depending on the dead man's resources. The father of Hatshepsut's favourite, Senmut, had a very poor burial in spite of his son's position and the comparatively wealthy burial of his wife. However, it is difficult to generalize about differences in burials, so much may depend on all manner of unrecorded family foibles. Certainly there was as much class distinction in death as in life, and very few could afford the full funeral arrangements. For the poor at all times a shallow grave and coffin of basketwork or pottery would have to suffice, and there are many instances of tombs being re-used.

The best documented funerals are those of the Theban nobles of the New Kingdom. They are recorded in detail in their tomb-paintings and are probably valid, given a few changes of details, for the upper classes at all times. They show, forming up from the home of the deceased, a procession of groups of servants bearing flowers, boxes of cakes, fruit and other food, tomb furniture such as stools, beds and chests, boxes of ushabtis and canopic jars, all carefully displayed to show the splendour and wealth of the dead man. The coffin, beneath a catafalque, mounted on a sledge, was drawn by a pair of oxen or by several men. Statues of the two goddesses Isis and Nephthys flanked the coffin as mourners. The procession was accompanied by a band of professional women mourners, dishevelled and dramatically weeping, the distraught widow and family and rather more composed friends and colleagues.

From the east bank the cortège went across the river in a procession of boats. The one containing the coffin carried a small group of mourners and a priest and was towed by another boat carrying the professional mourners and followed by other craft with the rest of the people. On the west bank the procession re-formed and was led by the priest to the tomb. The records depict the mourners reflecting on the good qualities of the dead man and making pious observations about the brevity of life.

The scene in the tomb courtyard seems often to have been a harrowing one as the grieving widow flung herself at the feet of the coffin which, at this stage, stood upright. While in this position the coffin was censed by the priest and the funeral ritual of the 'Opening of the Mouth' performed over it [149, 150]. The purpose of this was to reopen not only the mouth but other openings of the body such as the eyes, nose and ears so that the senses were revived. The same ceremony was performed over statues, reliefs and paintings to endow them with a form of life in the Afterworld.

The coffin, with a wreath of fresh flowers, was then interred and the funeral gifts positioned around it. There was often a degree of haste evident in these arrangements. Objects are sometimes broken or piled up in apparent confusion, but this would not affect the magical efficacy of the equipment for the dead man; it was, after all, intended for his benefit not that of some latter-day visitor. The reminder of death removed, the guests settled down to a funeral feast in the almost universal tradition. When that was over the remains of the meal, together with the guests' wreaths and symbolic remains from the mummification equipment, were buried nearby.

The continued well-being of the departed in the Afterworld depended on the efficacy of the offering formula, which was commonly inscribed on funerary stelai, on tomb doors and walls, and on pieces of funerary equipment. It consisted of a statement that the king will give to the gods, usually Osiris or some

148. The burial chamber of Queen Hetepheres, wife of Snofru, at Giza, soon after it was discovered in 1925. On top of the calcite sarcophagus and at the side may be seen the gold sheet which covered the wooden members of her bed, carrying-chair and tent. Other funeral offerings lie beside the sarcophagus. Meticulous recording of the position of these objects has made possible their reconstruction and they are now to be seen in the Cairo Museum [cf. *Pl 23*].

other funeral deity like Anubis, an offering for them to pass on to the dead man. The gifts most often specified are bread, beer, oxen and fowl, alabaster and linen, but over three hundred possible variations are known, usually compounded in the standard phrase 'every good and pure thing on which a god lives'. The formula begins with a characteristic group of signs ⨪ meaning 'An offering which the king gives' (*sc.* to Osiris etc.). With the help of an 'Opening of the Mouth' spell to make this effective, the dead man's *Ka* was well provided for and in theory at least the promise was backed up by an actual gift to the man's mortuary priest.

PREPARATION OF THE CORPSE

In the predynastic period, the body, buried in a shallow grave in dry sand, quickly dehydrated and was thus preserved. As the tombs became deeper and more elaborate these natural agencies no longer worked and steps were taken to preserve the body artificially. The practice became a fully developed craft with its own guild of practitioners, and in so far as it was considered a re-enactment of Isis bandaging the dismembered Osiris, it was also a ritual act accompanied by religious observances.

The first act in the process of mummification was to remove, through an incision on the left side, the contents of the abdomen, since these were the prime causes of decomposition. The heart was left *in situ*, but the other organs were removed and prepared separately for packing in four canopic jars [151]. The brain was also removed with a long instrument through a hole made behind the nostrils into the cranial cavity. The body was then packed with natron and slowly dried out over some forty days.

Once dried the body was washed clean of the salts, embalmed with oils and unguents and wrapped. The empty abdomen was stuffed with bandages or sometimes with sawdust or shavings, the incision sewn up and covered with a plate, sometimes of gold. In a rich burial the fingers and toes might be protected by gold stalls, and rings and necklaces were placed on the corpse. Then the body was wrapped more or less carefully, depending on the period. From the XVIIIth dynasty onwards there was an attempt to restore the natural appearance by use of pads under the cheeks or to indicate the muscles.

149. Painting of a funeral procession from the tomb chapel of the priest Pairi at Thebes. Top: the sarcophagus in a catafalque mounted on a sledge hauled by bedecked oxen, accompanied by the widow and followed by servants bearing a chair, model-boat, chests and other equipment. Middle: funeral rites over a statue and a priest performing the Opening of the Mouth ceremony over the mummy. Bottom: the pilgrimage to Abydos: Pairi and his wife sit under an awning on a barge shown twice, towed by a rowing boat and a sailing boat. XVIIIth-dynasty.

The wrappings usually bind the arms against the body and hold the legs together, although there are some mummies where the limbs are separately wrapped. Various amulets are distributed in the wrappings, usually in prescribed positions and in the Late Period the mummy was covered in a bead net.

Late Period mummies, in fact, present a deceptive appearance, for often the process of dehydration was not catered for. The corpse was simply painted with pitch and wrapped with bandages which, as the pitch hardened, made a stiff, airtight outer case, masking the putrefaction that continued inside. It was the use of pitch, for which the Arabic word is 'mumiya', which led to the modern word 'mummy'. The full process took some seventy days to complete but was often skimped for the sake of economy.

An important funerary amulet introduced in the Second Intermediate Period was the heart scarab, which was placed on the breast of the mummy. It was inscribed with a chapter of the *Book of the Dead*, instructing the man's heart

not to make trouble for him when weighed in the judgement before Osiris. The scarabs, about 5 cm. long, are usually in a hard stone, often in a gold mount and chain. Although the rubric specified that they should be of a green stone, probably serpentine, they are more commonly made of schist.

From the late Old Kingdom onwards the head of the mummy was often enclosed in a mask of cartonnage (layers of linen stuck together and covered with a thin coat of plaster), moulded to a fairly stereotyped set of features. The face was often gilded and a beard and uraeus added, these, being symbols of royalty, indicating the identification of the dead with the King Osiris. Details of the eyes and wig were either painted in or else the eyes were inlaid with alabaster and obsidian.

In the Middle Kingdom the mask was extended and covered the whole body. It was sometimes made in wood instead of cartonnage, resulting in the development of wooden anthropoid coffins. Painted bands and floral collars reproduced

150. A group of small calcite vessels and model knives possibly associated with the Opening of the Mouth ritual. The figure is also of calcite and the group lie on a pedestal shaped like an altar for libation. From Abydos; probably Middle Kingdom. Now in the Gulbenkian Museum of Oriental Art, University of Durham. Height 35·5 m.

151. Wooden canopic chest of the chief physician Gua, from el-Bersheh, containing four canopic jars in calcite, with heads made of wood. XIIth-dynasty. Now in the British Museum, London. Height 58 cm.

the ornaments on the actual mummy. In the New Kingdom the mask was used together with the anthropoid coffin, as in the burial of Tutankhamun.

At the end of the dynastic period the gilded mask was occasionally provided as part of a complete sheath or with separate bands and foot-pieces, sewn on to the mummy bandaging. The gilded face was set in a mask decorated, predominantly in pink, with figures of Osiris and usually with a winged scarab on the top of the head [152].

The masks are unlikely to have been portraits except perhaps in the case of royalty. They tended to follow the cast of features fashionable at the time, and it was not until the Roman period that an attempt at portraiture was made.

FUNERAL EQUIPMENT

The coffins and sarcophagi of the early dynastic period were regarded as miniature houses for the deceased and the decoration followed the *serekh* pattern of the early mastaba tombs. The Archaic Period coffins are short, intended for a contracted body rather than an extended corpse. Larger coffins with the same *serekh* design were used in the Old Kingdom and in the richer burials the coffins were placed in large stone sarcophagi which were sometimes plain, sometimes carved or painted with the *serekh*.

In the Middle Kingdom double wooden coffins were often provided [153]. The inner was usually anthropoid, the outer rectangular and elaborately painted with the *serekh* and a large pair of eyes in a panel by the left shoulder. The inside was decorated with pictures of personal objects and coffin texts. The royal sarcophagi are usually plain, but those of the royal princesses found at Deir el-Bahri were carved in sunk relief with scenes of daily life. The lids are slightly vaulted with projecting endboards.

After the Second Intermediate Period coffins were usually anthropoid in shape and elaborately painted. A feathered wing design completely covering the lid was popular in XVIIth dynasty and bands of inscribed funerary texts were painted on to represent the binding on the actual mummy. New Kingdom coffins have similar bands of inscription on a black, or in the XIXth dynasty white or yellow, background. A painted floral collar lies on the chest and the panels between the inscriptions are occupied by pictures of the funeral genii, such as the four sons of Horus (see p. 206) and Isis and Nephthys. Sometimes a painted and modelled board like a coffin lid was placed over the body inside the coffin, an economical way of suggesting a double coffin.

Few royal coffins survive but the evidence is that they were of gilded wood or even of gold inlaid with semi-precious stones and glass paste. Surviving intact examples are the three-nested coffins of Tutankhamun. They were enclosed in rectangular stone sarcophagi decorated inside and out with funeral deities in painted relief. In the XIXth dynasty the sarcophagi were mummiform, usually in granite or quartzite. Quite the finest is the white calcite sarcophagus of Seti I, which was inlaid with rows of funerary figures in blue paste.

The kings of the XXIst and XXIInd dynasties who were found at Tanis were buried in mummiform coffins of silver and gilded wood, two of them with silver hawks' heads. The sarcophagi were usually, but not exclusively, anthropoid. Psusennes, in fact, usurped a sarcophagus of Merenptah.

Of royal burials after the XXVth dynasty very little remains beyond a few of the queens' sarcophagi, which were usually rectangular with a rounded end, in granite or limestone. Several private sarcophagi have survived, either anthropoid or shaped like the royal ones. They are vast and very finely engraved, sometimes based on older examples like the XXVIth-dynasty Hepmen, who had a replica of Tuthmosis III's. Coffins rarely survive but if Petosiris's is an indication they were very fine. His was inlaid with hieroglyphs in polychrome glass.

There exist a few rare examples of catafalques or canopies that appear to have been used to cover the coffin in the funeral procession. This is illustrated in the XXIst dynasty as a big rectangular box on runners, but two Ptolemaic examples, one in Cairo, the other in Edinburgh [154], are built as long beds with a light framework over the coffin in the form of a shrine, brightly painted and decorated with carved figures of suitable protective deities. In the XXIst-dynasty tomb of Isitemkheb was a bundle of rolled-up leather sheets. The largest, 2·5 m. × 2·2 m., was painted sky-blue with a central panel of vulture goddesses flanked by rows of stars alternatively red and yellow. Four small pieces were decorated with a frieze of lotus and papyrus flowers, antelopes, and scarabs in appliqué work, using shapes of coloured leather. It seems likely that the sheets were stretched over a wooden frame, rather like the canopy of Queen Hetepheres, but the motifs and texts suggest a funeral use.

Although the viscera were removed from the body during mummification they were essential for well-being in the Afterworld and were separately preserved in so-called canopic jars [151]. The name arises by confusion with the figure of Osiris, who was worshipped at the Delta port of Canopus in the form of a jar, with a lid shaped like a human head.

The provision of these containers began in the Old Kingdom, when the jars

152. Painted and gilded cartonnage mask from a mummy of the Graeco-Roman period. The body was wrapped with an elaborate pattern of bandaging and the mask fitted over the head and chest. Now in the City Museum and Art Gallery, Birmingham. Height 50 cm.

153. A Middle Kingdom coffin as discovered in the burial chamber of a tomb at Beni Hasan.

154. A painted wood funeral canopy from the tomb of Mentusebauf, Archon of Thebes, *c.* 9 BC. Now in the Royal Scottish Museum, Edinburgh. Length 2·10 m.

were plain with bun-shaped lids. Strangely, they often show no sign of use. Variants include the rectangular alabaster chest of Hetepheres, which was divided into four compartments and had in fact been used. Canopic jars, usually in a wooden chest shaped like a small sarcophagus, are standard equipment in the Middle Kingdom, placed in a niche in the east wall of the burial chamber. Some of the royal boxes are in stone matching the sarcophagus. Jars of this period and of the XVIIIth dynasty have human heads, some of them very carefully modelled and having the appearance of being portraits. Tutankhamun had four small gold coffins inlaid with coloured glass like the full-size coffin and placed in a canopic chest. After the XVIIIth dynasty, the lids were based on the four sons of Horus. Human-headed Imsety guarded the liver; baboon-headed Hapi the lungs; dog-headed Duamutef protected the stomach, and the intestines were under the care of the falcon-headed Qebehsenuef. The jars themselves were identified with the goddesses Isis, Nephthys, Neith and Selkis. The perfunctory mummification in the Ptolemaic Period meant the viscera were often left in the body but the jars were still provided, sometimes as solid dummies made in one piece with the lid.

In the XVIIIth dynasty other sets of vases are occasionally found, all the dateable examples of which belong to the reign of Amenophis III. Their purpose is quite unknown and in each set the vases all have different shapes, some with and others without a handle, some with two; some have short, others long, necks. The lids of one set are carved with small figures in the round, a frog, calf, and an ox-head or Bes figure, and the vases themselves are often nearly solid with only a very small hollow at the top.

An important part of the tomb's appointment was the stele, so-named from the Greek word for pillar or monumental tablet. They are usually carved in limestone, but occasionally wooden examples survive. Archaic period stelai are roughly shaped tall blocks carved in relief with the name and title of the owner. The Old Kingdom type was a false door, ranging in height up to 3 m. or more, carved in an elaborate series of niches representing the doorway of a reed-work house. A narrow central slit represents the door itself with a rolled-up blind modelled at the top, and sometimes the figure of the owner striding through the door. The door is inscribed with the offering formula and a central panel at the top usually shows the owner sitting before a table. The First Intermediate Period stelai are often small rough slabs, crudely drawn and carved and garishly painted, but some elaborate examples are found, based on the Old Kingdom types.

The false door was largely replaced in the Middle Kingdom by a flat slab surrounded by a door-frame of torus moulding and cavetto cornice. The offering scene and formula were retained, often with a biography of the dead man. Many examples are found at Abydos, where they acted as memorials for those who could not afford actual burial in the cult centre of Osiris. Also found in the Middle Kingdom, but most common in the New Kingdom, is a type of stele with a rounded top in which are depicted a pair of *wedjat* eyes flanking the *shenu* sign. Below the lunette is a register showing the dead man with his family at a banquet or, in the later examples, making an offering to Osiris. Late Period stelai are often quite small, between 30 and 40 cm. high, usually consisting of a flat slab of limestone with red and cream figures and text painted on in black, or of a plastered slab of wood painted in red, green, black and cream. There is usually a winged disc in the lunette [155].

Before the stelai stood a small offering-table. This can range from a flat rectangular piece of limestone with a shallow depression in the top, to an inscribed slab with offerings carved in relief and a series of basins and channels to receive libations. Faience models of fruits and vegetables, jars and bowls, were also provided in some Middle Kingdom tombs at Lisht. Pottery offering-trays were used in poorer Old Kingdom burials but gradually became increasingly elaborate and were designed as the courtyards of model–houses—eventually in the Middle Kingdom the house was also depicted.

155. Group of three stelai showing development from the false-door type of the Old Kingdom to the similar architectural arrangement of the Coptic Period. Left: stele from the tomb of Inba at Sakkara, showing the dead man seated at a meal; his names and titles are inscribed on the door posts and lintel. Vth–dynasty. Centre: stele of Nebnehehabsu, probably from Thebes, carved in low relief, showing the owner making an offering before Osiris with Isis and Nephthys, and, in the lower registers, seated at a meal with members of his family. XIXth–dynasty. Right: figure of a boy thought to be an initiate into the cult of Isis standing in an apsidal niche, from Oxyrhynchus. IVth Century AD. Now in the City Museum and Art Gallery, Birmingham.

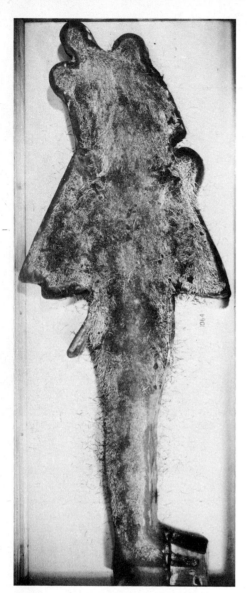

156. A wooden silhouette of Osiris filled with earth and corn which has been allowed to germinate as a symbol of the god's resurrection. From the tomb of Tutankhamun. XVIIIth-dynasty. Now in Cairo Museum.

The circular table mounted on a central column is the standard way of showing the offering-table in funeral scenes, but there are few actual examples dating later than the Old Kingdom. They are usually made in two parts, from limestone or calcite.

In the antechamber of Tutankhamun's tomb were three large beds covered in stucco and gilded, in the form of a pair of cows, lions and composite animals, part-hippopotamus, part-leopard, part-crocodile. These seem to have had a magical purpose as a means of transporting the king to the heavens as described in an ancient myth. No other intact examples are known but similar beds are illustrated in the tomb scenes of Ramesses III, and Osiris lies on a lion-headed bed in the reliefs recounting his death and resurrection at Abydos and Dendera.

Two other strange items of equipment are worth noting. The emblem of Anubis, which is illustrated frequently in funerary contexts, was a headless animal attached by the tail to a pole surmounted by a lotus bud and standing in a calcite base. A stuffed animal skin, wrapped in bandages, was found on such a stand in the pyramid of Sesostris I, and a gilded wood model was amongst the equipment in Tutankhamun's tomb.

In the XVIIIth dynasty a board, cut in the silhouette shape of Osiris and covered with earth, was placed in the tomb. Barley was sown in the earth on this 'Osiris bed' and germinated to form a green figure of the god of resurrection and hopefully to symbolize the new life of the tomb's owner [156].

Perhaps the commonest type of antiquity from Egypt is the *shabti* figure, whose purpose was to act as a substitute for the dead man if he were called upon to work in the Afterworld. These figures have a long history of development from at least the Middle Kingdom, and the Egyptians seem to have changed their minds about their precise function from time to time.

The name itself varies from the early form *shabti*, derived from the word for 'persea tree', from which early examples were made, to the form *ushabti*, common from the end of the New Kingdom onwards, probably by then mistakenly derived from the word 'to answer'. The *shabti* appears to be a development from the servant models of the Old Kingdom, which were designed to minister to the tomb's occupier. Small pottery mummiform figures in miniature coffins occur in the First Intermediate Period and in the Middle Kingdom there are mummiform figures in wood or stone, inscribed with the standard offering formula and their owner's name, serving the purpose of the Old Kingdom reserve heads. At this time the idea of a substitute worker was beginning to form and some coffins carry the magical text by which this substitution was achieved. In the Second Intermediate Period crude wooden figures, occasionally in coffins, are found sometimes inscribed with the offering formula, but at other times with a form of the magical text which, in its standard New Kingdom form, reads: 'O shabti, if [the deceased] is required for any tasks to be done [in the Afterworld] as a man is bound, to cultivate the fields, to water the banks and to carry sand to the east or west then you shall say "Here am I".' It is often abbreviated to little more than the names and titles of the owner.

In the New Kingdom and later the concept of substitution is complete. A variety of carefully worked materials were used in many colours. In the XXIst and XXIInd dynasties they are usually in blue faience, not too carefully fashioned, with details in black paint, and in succeeding dynasties workmanship declines even further and scruffy little clay figures are the norm. Royal shabtis of the XXVth dynasty mark the beginning of an improvement which is clear in the XXVIth dynasty, but the quality soon falls off again. One of the latest is in dark blue faience with details in pale green relief, made for a sailor called Soter in the Roman period and now in the British Museum.

Almost all the shabtis are in the shape of a mummy carrying a mattock and hoe, and a basket over the shoulder. From the beginning of the XXVIth dynasty they were fashioned with a pillar at the back. The number provided for each person varies: Tutankhamun had at least 400 and Horwadja 399. They are usually in boxes packed with sand and, between the XIXth and XXIInd dynasties, an overseer figure, dressed in a kilt and carrying a whip, was provided for each gang of ten.

Shabtis, like other pieces of funeral equipment, were mass-produced and are sometimes found with the name left blank. Two texts in the British Museum relate to the purchase of sets of shabtis in the XXIst or XXIInd dynasties; on the other hand, some of Tutankhamun's shabtis appear to have been presented as gifts [157].

The shabti text is one of many magical texts that go together under the description of funerary texts. They begin with the Vth-dynasty pyramid texts that describe the journey of the king to the Afterworld, and contain magical incantations to assist him. Some of the references in them suggest that they originated in predynastic times and were preserved by oral tradition. Their magic power was so strong that any hieroglyph that represented a potentially dangerous animal or object was replaced by an innocuous alternative or mutilated in such a way as to render it harmless. Knives, for instance, were shown in two pieces, and scorpions without their stings: fish were taboo as offerings for the dead and never appear.

In the Middle Kingdom these texts were no longer reserved for the king but were inscribed on the inside surface of the coffins of any who could afford them, and in the New Kingdom they were written on linen, leather or papyrus rolls to be buried with the dead owner. Often they are beautifully decorated with coloured vignettes or, in later examples, with line drawings. The arrangement of the different spells or chapters was not rigid, although most of the manuscripts follow a similar pattern and went under the title of *The Book of the Dead* or, more properly, *Incantations for Going Forth by Day*. In the New Kingdom other compilations were made of similar incantations. *The Book of What is in the Afterworld*, *The Book of Gates*, *The Book of Caverns* and others describe the journeys of the dead in the Afterworld and form the basis of many of the illustrations in the tombs in the Valley of the Kings [*Pl 32*].

In the Ramesside period wood figures of Osiris were provided as funerary equipment, some painted black all over, others with gilded face and brightly coloured body. Some are hollow and contain a copy of the *Book of the Dead*. In the XXIInd dynasty and later they were also linked with Ptah, by then associated with the funerary god Sokar, who was represented by a small model of a mummified falcon that sat on the pedestal of the figure. The pedestal is often hollow and decorated like a coffin and frequently contained a small fragment of the corpse. The figures usually carry an offering formula.

Discs of stiff linen or occasionally bronze are found below the heads of mummies from the XXVIth dynasty and later. They carry pictures of various deities and a spell from the *Book of the Dead* that it was hoped would keep the body warm.

From the XIth dynasty onwards the façades of the Theban tomb chapels were decorated with cones of pottery sunk into the wall, so that only the circular base remained to be seen, giving the effect, perhaps intentional, of the ends of

157. Group of three shabtis, showing front and back views, right to left: XVIIIth-dynasty, stone; XIX–XXth-dynasty, blue faience with details in black; XXVIth-dynasty, green faience. Now in the City Museum and Art Gallery, Birmingham. Height (right) 10·5 cm.

158. A Middle Kingdom coffin as discovered in the burial chamber of a tomb at Beni Hasan, showing tomb models ranged along the top and the *wedjat* eye motif.

roof beams. From the XVIIIth dynasty onwards the bases were stamped with impressions giving the owner's names and titles.

New Kingdom burials were sometimes equipped with unbaked mud-bricks set in niches in each of the four walls of the burial chamber. To ward off evil, which might approach from any direction, they were inscribed with a magical text and carried an amulet, a wooden mummy in the northern one, a torch of reed with a wick in the southern one, an unbaked clay jackal on the east and a faience *djed*-pillar on the west.

For his day-to-day existence in the bigger and better Egypt beyond the grave, the dead man also needed the paraphernalia that surrounded him in this life. Although it may be sufficient to have an object pictured on the wall or even named in a list, obviously the magic was stronger if it could actually be provided and a wealthy man would take any number of objects into his tomb; food and food dishes, furniture, cosmetic sets and clothing, weapons and tools. Some of them might be tools of his trade or his insignia of office, an heirloom or souvenir, any favourite personal item. A number of items were also clearly made especially for the burial. They were inscribed with the funerary formulae and often made of non-utilitarian materials, for example the gold dagger and ivory boomerang of Tutankhamun. The same king took a number of items from his childhood—a small nursery chair and a battered model boat that might well have been a beloved toy. He even took his ceremonial fly whisks, although one would think they were not necessary unless the flies of paradise are also bigger and better!

The elaborate preparations which the Ancient Egyptians made for the burial has resulted in their gaining a reputation for an obsession with death. Nothing could be further from the truth, for they were a lively people with many interests; but it is from these funeral arrangements that we come to know much of their true nature and their way of life.

Their tombs were intended to house the dead and to perpetuate their memory; in this they have succeeded better than they could ever have imagined possible.

159. A pit below the stone-paved floor of a shrine at Sakkara, partially excavated, showing a wooden statue of Osiris, a wooden shrine and several bronze statuettes. Two more wooden shrines and over a hundred bronzes were eventually recovered from this cache. *c.* 350 BC.

Further reading

GENERAL

Aldred, C., *The Egyptians*, London, 1961: *Guide to the Egyptian Collections in the British Museum*, London 1964.

Baikie, J., *Egyptian Antiquities in the Nile Valley*, London 1932.

Breasted, J. H., *Ancient Records of Egypt*, Chicago 1906.

Drioton, E., and Vandier, E., *L'Egypte*, Series Clio, Paris 1952.

Edwards, I. E. S., Gadd, C. J., Hammond, N. G. L. and Sollberger, E., *Cambridge Ancient History*, Revised Edition, Vols I and II.

Emery, W. B., *Egypt and Nubia*, London 1965.

Englebach, R., *Introduction to Egyptian Archaeology*, Cairo 1946.

Gardiner, A. H., *Egypt of the Pharaohs*, Oxford 1961.

Glanville, S. R. K., *The Legacy of Egypt*, 1st ed., London 1942.

Harris, J. R., *The Legacy of Egypt*, 2nd ed., London 1971.

Hayes, W. C., *The Scepter of Egypt*, Vols I and II, New York 1953 and 1959.

Lange, K. and Hirmer, M., *Egypt*, London 1968.

Montet, P., *Eternal Egypt*, London 1965.

Nims, C., *Thebes of the Pharaohs*, London 1965.

Posener, G., *et al*, *A Dictionary of Egyptian Civilization*, London 1962.

Smith, W. S., *The Art and Architecture of Ancient Egypt*, London 1958.

Vandier, J., *Manuel d'archéologie Egyptienne*, Vol I, Paris 1952.

Weigall, A. E. P., *Guide to the Antiquities of Upper Egypt*, London 1910.

Wilson, J. A., *The Burden of Egypt*, Chicago 1951; paperback version: *The Culture of Ancient Egypt*, Chicago 1951.

The principal journal in English dealing with all aspects of Egyptology is the *Journal of Egyptian Archaeology* published annually by the Egypt Exploration Society, 3 Doughty Mews, London WC1N 2PG.

CHAPTER 1

Dawson, W. R. and Uphill, E. P., *Who was Who in Egyptology*, 2nd ed., London 1972.

Disher, M. W., *Pharaoh's Fool*, London 1957.

Edwards, A., *A Thousand Miles up the Nile*, London 1877.

Egypt (Nagel's Encyclopedia-Guide), Geneva 1972.

Godley, D. (Ed.), *Herodotus*, Bk. II, London 1921.

Greener, L., *The Discovery of Egypt*, London 1966.

Herold, J. C., *Napoleon in Egypt*, London 1964.

James, T. G. H., *The Archaeology of Ancient Egypt*, London 1972.

Kees, H., *Ancient Egypt, a Cultural Topography*, London 1961.

Kaiser, W., 'Zur inneren Chronologie der Naqadakultur', in *Archaeologia Geographica*, III, Jahrgang 5–6 (1956–7), pp. 69–77 & pls. 15–26.

Long, R. D., 'Ancient Egyptian Chronology, Radiocarbon Dating and Calibration', in *Zeitschrift für Aegyptische Sprache*, Band 103 (1973), pp. 30–45.

Petrie, W. M. F., *Ten Years Digging in Egypt* 1881–91, London 1892. *Seventy Years in Archaeology*, London 1931.

Trigger, B., *Nubia under the Pharaohs*, London 1976.

Waddell, W. G. (Ed.), *Manetho*, Cambridge, Mass. 1940.

Wilson, J. A., *Signs and Wonders upon Pharaoh*, Chicago 1964.

CHAPTER 2

Arkell, A. J., and Ucko, P. J., 'Review of Predynastic Development in the Nile Valley', in *Current Anthropology* 6 (1965), pp. 145–67.

Baumgartel, E., *Cultures of Predynastic Egypt*, London 1947.

Brunton, G. and Caton-Thompson, G., *The Badarian Civilization*, London 1928.

Caton-Thompson, G. and Gardner, E. W., *The Desert Fayyum*, London 1934.
Hayes, W. C., *Most Ancient Egypt*, Chicago 1965.
Petrie, W. M. F., *Diospolis Parva*, London 1901.
Trigger, B., *Beyond History: The Methods of Prehistory*, New York 1968.

CHAPTER 3
Aldred, C., *Egypt to the End of the Old Kingdom*, London 1965.
Emery, W. B., *Archaic Egypt*, Harmondsworth 1961; *The Tomb of Hemaka*, Cairo
    1938; *Hor-Aha*, Cairo 1939; *Great Tombs of the First Dynasty*, Vols. I–III,
    Cairo 1949, 1954 and 1958.
Petrie, W. M. F., *Royal Tombs of the First Dynasty*, London 1900;
    Royal Tombs of the Earliest Dynasties, London 1901.
Saad, Z. Y., *Royal Excavations at Saqqara and Helwan*, Cairo 1948;
    Royal Excavations at Helwan, Cairo 1951.

CHAPTER 4
Davies, N. de G., *The Mastabah of Ptahhetep and Akhethetep at Saqqarah*,
    London 1900–1901.
Duell, P., *The Mastaba of Mereruka*, Chicago 1938.
Edwards, I. E. S., *The Pyramids of Egypt*, Harmondsworth 1947.
Fakhry, A., *The Pyramids*, Chicago 1969.
Firth, C. M., Quibell, J. E. and Lauer, J. P., *The Step Pyramid*, Cairo 1935 and 1936.
Goneim, M. Z., *The Buried Pyramid*, English edition, London 1956.
Lauer, J. P., *Saqqara*, London 1976; *La Pyramid à Degres*, Cairo 1936–39.
Reisner, G. A., *History of the Giza Necropolis*, Cambridge, Mass. 1942, 1955;
    Development of the Egyptian Tomb, Cambridge, Mass. 1936.
Smith, W. S., *A History of Egyptian Sculpture and Painting in the Old Kingdom*,
    Cambridge, Mass. 1946.
Steindorff, G., *Das Grab des Ti*, Leipzig 1913.

CHAPTER 5
Newberry, P. E., *Beni Hasan*, Vols. I and II, London 1890–3; *El Bersheh*, Vols. I
    and II, London 1892–3.
Pendlebury, J. D. S., *Aegyptiaca, A Catalogue of Egyptian Objects in the Aegean Area*,
    Cambridge 1930.
Reisner, G. A., *Excavations at Kerma*, Cambridge, Mass. 1923.
Wainright, G. A., *Balabish*, London 1920.
Winlock, H. E., *The Rise and Fall of the Middle Kingdom in Thebes*, New York 1947;
    Excavations at Deir el-Bahri 1911–31, New York 1942.

CHAPTER 6
Aldred, C., *Akhenaten*, London 1968.
Davies, N. de G., *The Rock Tombs of El Amarna*, Vols. I–VI, London 1903–8.
Desroches-Noblecourt, C., *Tutankhamen*, Harmondsworth 1965.
Peet, T. E., Frankfort, H., and Pendlebury, J. D. S., *City of Akhenaten*, Vols. I–III,
    London 1923–51.
Riefstahl, E., *Thebes in the Time of Amenhotep III*, Oklahoma 1964.
Steindorff, G. and Seele, K. C., *When Egypt Ruled the East*, Chicago 1963.

CHAPTER 7
Bothmer, B. V., *Egyptian Sculpture in the Late Period*, Brooklyn, 1972.
Emery, W. B., *Nubian Treasure*, London 1948.
Kitchen, K. A., *The Third Intermediate Period in Egypt*, Warminster 1972.
Montet, P., *Les Enigmes de Tanis*, Paris 1952.
Shinnie, P. L., *Meroe*, London 1967.

CHAPTER 8

Bell, H. I., *Egypt from Alexander the Great to the Arab Conquest*, Oxford 1948;
  Cults and Creeds in Graeco–Roman Egypt, Liverpool 1957.
Bevan, B., *History of Egypt under the Ptolemaic Dynasty*, London 1927.
Bourquet, P. M. du, *Coptic Art*, London 1971.
Smith, H. S., *A Visit to Ancient Egypt*, Warminster 1974.
Turner, E., *Greek Papyri*, Oxford 1968.
Walters, C. C., *Monastic Archaeology in Egypt*, Warminster 1970.
Wessel, K., *Coptic Art*, London 1965.

CHAPTER 9

Landström, B., *Ships of the Pharaohs*, London 1970.
Newberry, P. E., *Scarabs*, London 1908.
Parker, R. A., *Calendars of Ancient Egypt*, Chicago 1950.
Yadin, Y., *The Art of Warfare in Biblical Lands*, London 1963.

CHAPTER 10

Baker, H. S., *Furniture in the Ancient World*, London 1966.
Bruyère, B., *Rapport sur les fouilles de Deir el-Médinah, IIIeme partie*, Cairo 1939.
Montet, P., *Everyday Life in Egypt*, London 1958.
Winlock, H. E., *Models of Daily Life in Ancient Egypt*, New York 1955.

CHAPTER 11

Aldred, C., *The Development of Ancient Egyptian Art*, 3200–1315 BC, London 1961.
Davies, Nina M. de Garis, and Gardiner, A. H., *Ancient Egyptian Paintings*,
  Chicago 1936; *The Tomb of Huy, Viceroy of Nubia in the Reign of Tutankhamun*,
  London 1926.
Davies, Nina de Garis, *Picture Writing in Ancient Egypt*, Oxford 1958;
  The Tomb of the Vizier Ramose, London 1941.
  Norman and Nina de Garis Davies have published many of the Theban tombs
  of the New Kingdom nobles, in partnership or in collaboration with A. H.
  Gardiner.
Gardiner, A. H., *Egyptian Grammar*, Oxford 1957.
Lichtheim, M., *Ancient Egyptian Literature*, London 1975.
Mekhitarian, A., *Egyptian Painting*, Geneva 1954.
Petrie, W. M. F., *Objects of Daily Use*, London 1927.
Schäfer, H., *Principles of Egyptian Art* [trans. J. Baines], Oxford 1974.
Simpson, W. K., Faulkner, R. O. and Wente, E., *The Literature of Ancient Egypt*,
  Yale 1923.

CHAPTER 12

Aldred, C., *Jewels of the Pharaohs*, London 1971.
Badawy, A., *History of Egyptian Architecture*, Giza 1954.
Černý, J., *A Community of Workmen at Thebes in the Ramesside Period*, Cairo 1973.
Clarke, S., and Engelbach, R., *Ancient Egyptian Masonry: The Building Craft*,
  London 1930.
Davies, N. de G., *The Tomb of Rekhmire' at Thebes*, New York 1943.
Forbes, R. J., *Studies in Ancient Technology*, Leiden 1955.
Hodges, H., *Technology in the Ancient World*, Harmondsworth 1971.
Lucas, A., *Ancient Egyptian Materials and Industries*, 4th ed., London 1962,
  edited by J. R. Harris.
Riefstahl, E., *Ancient Egyptian Glass and Glazes in the Brooklyn Museum*,
  New York 1968.
Singer, C., Holmyard, E. J. and Hall, A. R., *History of Technology*, Oxford 1954.
Smith, E. B., *Egyptian Architecture as Cultural Expression*, New York 1938.
Wilkinson, A., *Ancient Egyptian Jewellery*, London 1971.

CHAPTER 13

Cerny, J., *Ancient Egyptian Religion*, London 1952.
David, A. R., *Religious Ritual at Abydos, c. 1300 BC*, Warminster 1973.
Frankfort, H., *Ancient Egyptian Religion*, New York 1948.
Morenz, S., *Egyptian Religion*, London 1973.

CHAPTER 14

Budge, E. A. Wallis, *The Mummy*, Cambridge 1925.
Carter, H. and Mace, A. C., *The Tomb of Tut-Ankh-Anun*, London 1923–33.
Edwards, I. E. S., *Treasures of Tutankhamun*, London 1972.
Elliot-Smith, C. and Dawson, W., *Egyptian Mummies*, London 1924.
Gardiner, A. H., *The Attitude of the Ancient Egyptians to Death and the Dead*,
    Cambridge 1935.
Garstang, J., *The Burial Customs of Ancient Egypt*, London 1907.
Petrie, W. M. F., *Shabtis*, London 1935.

List of Illustrations

Colour Plates

of Menna, Thebes. Reproduced by courtesy of the University of Chicago Press. Photo: Gordon Roberton.

17 The great eastern gate of Medinet Habu. Photo: Martin Davies.

18 The hypostyle hall of the temple of Seti I at Karnak. Photo: Martin Davies.

19 The temple of Ramesses II at Abu Simbel. Photo: John Ruffle.

20 The monastery of Anba Hadra. Photo: Martin Davies.

21 A sequence of harvest activities. Watercolour copy by Nina de Garis Davies of a wall-painting in the tomb of Menna. Thebes. Reproduced by courtesy of the University of Chicago Press. Photo: Gordon Roberton.

22 Menna watching agricultural workers. Watercolour copy by Nina de Garis Davies of a wall-painting in the tomb of Menna, Thebes. Reproduced by courtesy of the University of Chicago Press. Photo: Gordon Roberton.

23 The reconstructed chair of Queen Hetepheres. Photo: John Ross.

24 Headdress of a queen of Tuthmosis II. Photo: Werner Forman Archive.

25 The main hall of the tomb chapel of Nefertari. Photo: Hirmer Fotoarchiv, Munich.

26 Musicians playing pipe, lute and harp. Watercolour copy by Nina de Garis Davies of a wall-painting in the tomb of Nakht. Reproduced by courtesy of the Metropolitan Museum of Art, New York. Photo: Gordon Roberton.

27 Menna and his family fishing and fowling. Watercolour copy by Nina de Garis Davies of a wall-painting in the tomb of Menna. Reproduced by courtesy of the University of Chicago Press. Photo: Gordon Roberton.

28 The gold dish of Djehuty. Musée du Louvre, Paris. Photo: Service de Documentation Photographique de la Réunion des Musées Nationaux.

29 The calcite sarcophagus of Seti I. Sir John Soane's Museum, London. Photo: Gordon Roberton.

30 Unfinished relief from the tomb of Horemheb. Photo: John Ruffle.

31 Glass head from Amarna. Photo: John Ruffle.

32 Detail from the *Book of the Dead* of Ankhefenkhonsu. Photo: Hirmer Fotoarchiv, Munich.